The maps in this book are made by GIS professionals and students. Their work is integrating geographic science into all aspects of life, changing how we see things and how we act. Included in *Esri Map Book Volume 31* are many examples of natural resources, demographics, and mapping other statistical data. Others describe the use of GIS for land use and city planning, marketing and business analysis. There are also maps about human health, supporting response to disasters, and humanitarian missions.

GIS technology is quickly evolving, taking advantage of the latest trends in cloud computing, big data, real-time measurement, smart devices, and distributed processing. All of this is transforming the role of GIS in society, helping us understand and embrace our global interconnectedness.

GIS is already helping us make better decisions, smarter communities, and a brighter future for our world. At the frontier is system development for citizen engagement with open data and open services. This will increasingly play a major part of government in the digital age.

Over time we will measure everything that moves or changes on the planet and increasingly make this data available over the Internet. GIS will become a system of systems, a kind of nervous system of the planet. Web-based maps will emerge as a fundamental language for understanding and storytelling.

I am proud to share these fine examples by GIS users who are transforming the world. Their work is contributing to an age of geographic enlightenment.

Warm regards,

Jack Dangermond

TABLE OF CONTENTS

World Consumer Styles

Michael Bauer Research GmbH
Nuremberg, Bavaria, Germany
By Michael Bauer Research GmbH

Contact

Sabine Petrasek
sabine.petrasek@mb-research.de

Software

ArcGIS 10.3.1 for Desktop

Data Source

Michael Bauer Research GmbH

The basis of World Consumer Styles is a global consumer survey for segmentation of the population ages 15 and older by lifestyle segments. First, official Household Budget Surveys of the National Statistical Offices, selected from the point of representativeness and data quality, were evaluated in terms of the consumption of all goods and services against those criteria for which small-scale geographic data was available or researchable.

From this, important findings have been incorporated in a questionnaire, which was conducted in a global survey from large and medium or representative countries of all continents and regions of the world. The survey results were validated in terms of consumption with the analyses of official Household Budget Surveys. The questions on values, attitudes, and behavior were asked to enable enrichment of the sociodemographic and geographic segmentation approach to psychographic and behavioral segmentation criteria.

Using a specific cluster analysis of the variables on the consumption in the product groups and services finally selected, significant demographic, socioeconomic, and geographic as well as the psychographic and behavioral data, ten consumer style segments were formed.

Courtesy of Michael Bauer Research GmbH.

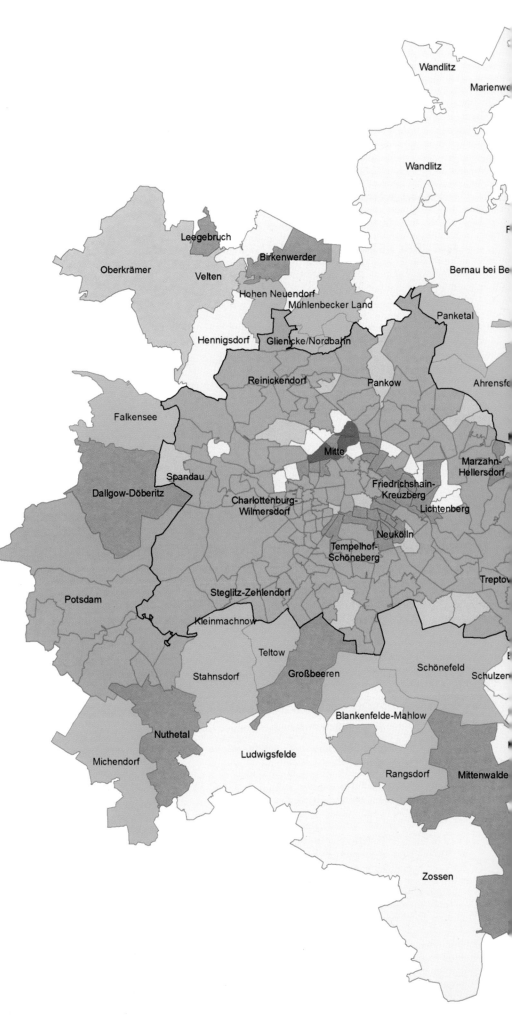

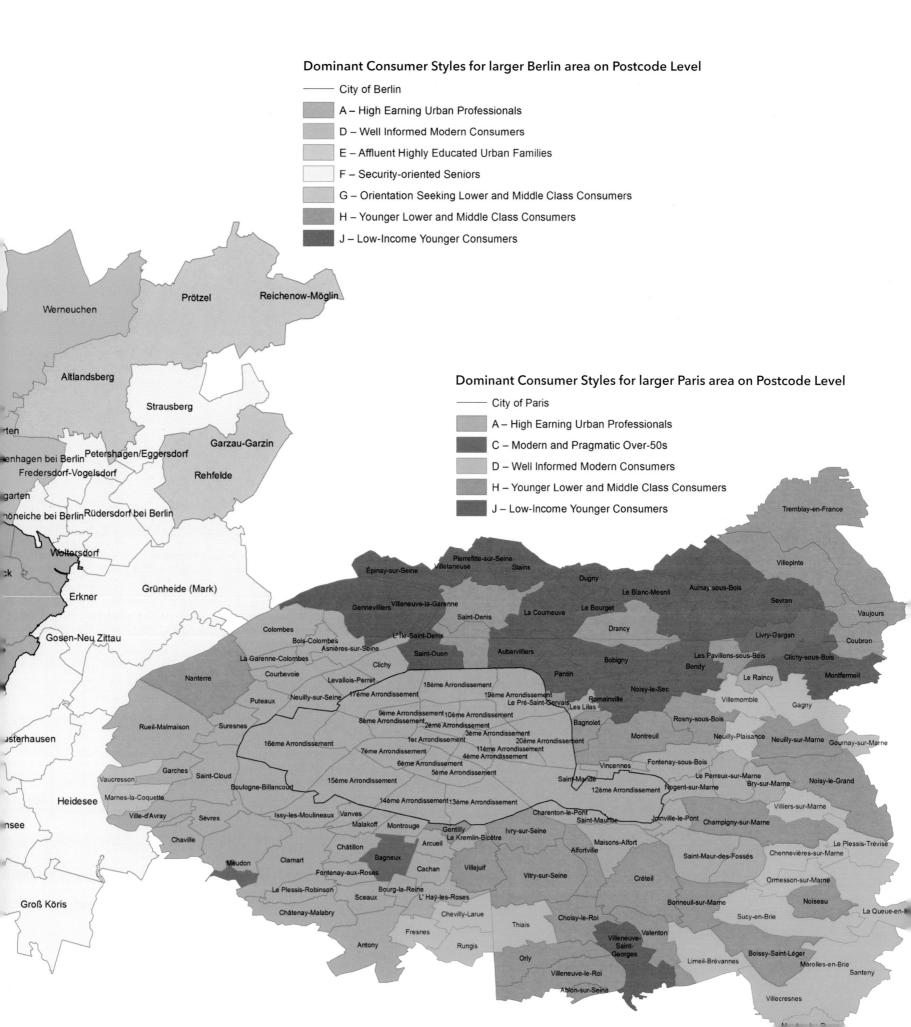

Dominant Consumer Styles for larger Berlin area on Postcode Level

— City of Berlin

A – High Earning Urban Professionals

D – Well Informed Modern Consumers

E – Affluent Highly Educated Urban Families

F – Security-oriented Seniors

G – Orientation Seeking Lower and Middle Class Consumers

H – Younger Lower and Middle Class Consumers

J – Low-Income Younger Consumers

Dominant Consumer Styles for larger Paris area on Postcode Level

— City of Paris

A – High Earning Urban Professionals

C – Modern and Pragmatic Over-50s

D – Well Informed Modern Consumers

H – Younger Lower and Middle Class Consumers

J – Low-Income Younger Consumers

Using Kriging Geostatistical Analysis in Property Valuation

Jefferson County Property Valuation Administrator (PVA)
Louisville, Kentucky, USA
By Amanda Fairfax Dirkes

Contact

Jefferson County Property Valuation Administrator
pvagis@jeffersonpva.ky.gov

Software

ArcGIS 10.0 for Desktop

Data Sources

Louisville/Jefferson County Information Consortium (LOJIC), Jefferson County Property Valuation Administrator (PVA)

This spatial study assessed the land value of parcels located in the central business district (CBD) of Louisville, Kentucky. Using the ArcGIS Geostatistical Analyst extension and data on sales of vacant land in the CBD over the last four decades, the Jefferson County Property Valuation Administrator (PVA) interpolated the base land values of properties and used these results in the reassessment process.

Comparing these results with a similar study in 2008 revealed trends in high-value properties moving eastward, a phenomenon backed by the revitalization efforts and remodeling of housing projects in the eastern downtown area. There has also been a northward trend, with the center of high value shifting from the city's tallest office building to the newly constructed arena on the Ohio River waterfront. By applying this same methodology in the future, the PVA can assess similar trends and use the statistical results to more accurately value land in the downtown area.

Ohio River

Sales Information

○ Adjusted Sale Price ($/sq.ft.)

☐ Sale Parcels

☐ Parcel Lines

Street Centerlines

Street Type

Interstate   Ramp   Arterial   Local

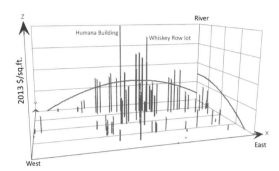

Trend Analysis

The 3D graph of the input data points describes trends in land values. The two highest stick points represent greatest land value in 2013 $/sq.ft. as well as the two methods used to resolve a lack of vacant land sales.

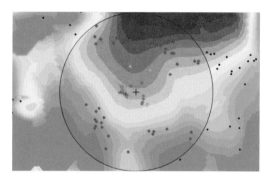

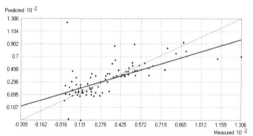

GA Wizard Steps 2-5

Step 2 designates Exploratory Trend Surface (scale of Kriging) and also defines the Function type of input data as exponential.

- Steps 3 and 4 deal with binning and nearest neighbors.

- Step 5 shows how well the model performs, with the goal being to minimize the Average Standard Error, in dollars.

- Window also shows the goodness-of-fit to regression line (in blue) and regression function.

cel Interpolation Classes

ue Ranges ($/sq. ft.)

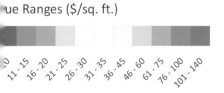

11 - 15   16 - 20   21 - 25   26 - 30   31 - 35   36 - 45   46 - 60   61 - 75   76 - 100   101 - 140

N

| 0 | 0.125 | 0.25 | 0.5 |
Miles

Residential Housing Analysis–Effective Year Built

Colliers International
Tampa, Florida, USA
By Mike Gordon

Contact
Mike Gordon
mike.gordon@colliers.com

Software
ArcGIS 10.3 for Desktop

Data Sources
Esri, Hillsborough County Property Appraiser

Colliers International is a global commercial real estate company that offers a full range of services to its clients. This map was created to help a client visualize the composition of home ages in a certain area of Tampa, Florida. By using the tax parcels for Hillsborough County, home ages were segmented into different time periods by the "effective year built," the year the structure had last undergone significant renovations. By displaying only residential zoned parcels, a visualization of the growth of Tampa starts to become apparent, revealing where the city's oldest neighborhoods are and how they grew. The analysis also shows which neighborhoods are gentrifying.

Courtesy of Colliers International Tampa Bay, Mike Gordon.

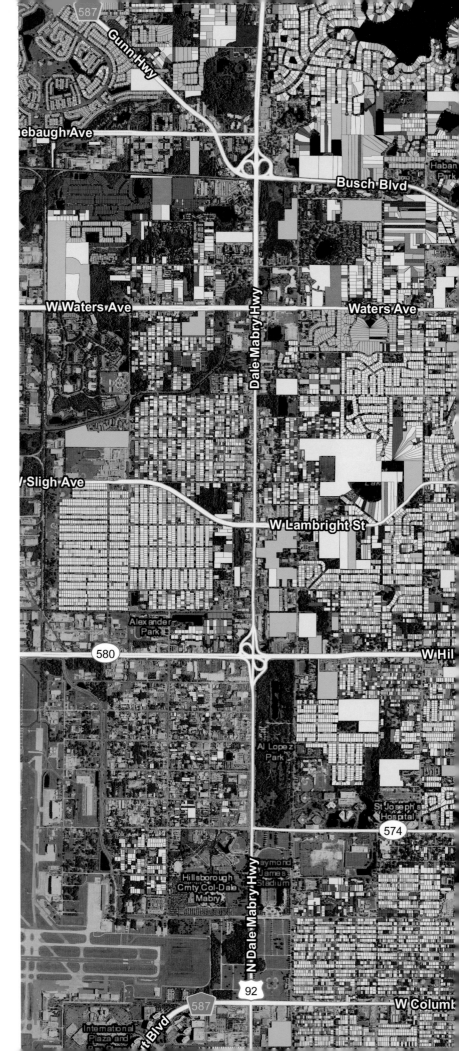

Effective Year Built

- 1900 - 1970
- 1971 - 1980
- 1981 - 1995
- 1996 - 2005
- 2006 - 2014

US 75 Corridor Retail Trade Analysis, 2002–2014

Collin County
McKinney, Texas, USA
By Bret Fenster, Mohamed Hassan, Kendall Holland, Ramona Luster, Tim Nolan, Gabriela Voicu, and Bill Bilyeu

Contact

Bret Fenster
bfenster@co.collin.tx.us

Software

ArcGIS 10.3.1 for Desktop

Data Sources

Texas Comptroller's Office, City of Allen, Town of Fairview, City of Richardson, City of Dallas, City of Plano, Texas Department of Transportation, North Central Texas Council of Governments, Collin County GIS

Rather than funding US 75 highway improvements through a tollway designation, Collin County is looking at innovative ways of funding improvements by capturing a portion of new sales tax revenues in the highway corridor. Revenue projections will be provided to the Texas Legislature in order to assess the viability of diverting future sales taxes toward corridor improvements.

The Texas State Comptroller retail trade data is represented in graphs which correlate to the highway corridor and retail zoning areas in the cities. The retail trade data was provided at the ZIP Code level due to current law, which restricts releasing sales data at the address or point level.

This study will be continued with point data that does not include the sales totals (ZIP drop data request). The point data will be geocoded and then selected with the highway corridor buffer. The selected records will then be sent back to the Texas State Comptroller so they can produce an area report, which will aggregate the sales for the businesses in the corridor buffer. Approximate sales tax revenues will then be projected for the proposed Sales Tax-Transportation Reinvestment Zone (ST-TRZ). The desired goal is keeping the lanes on a busy regional highway free from tolls and improving the mobility of the citizens in Collin County.

Courtesy of Collin County government.

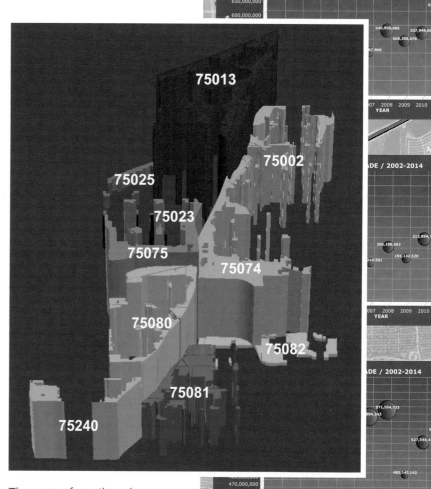

The sum of retail trade from 2002 to 2014 is shown above for each ZIP Code. The extrusion formula: (GROSS SALES/1,000,000)

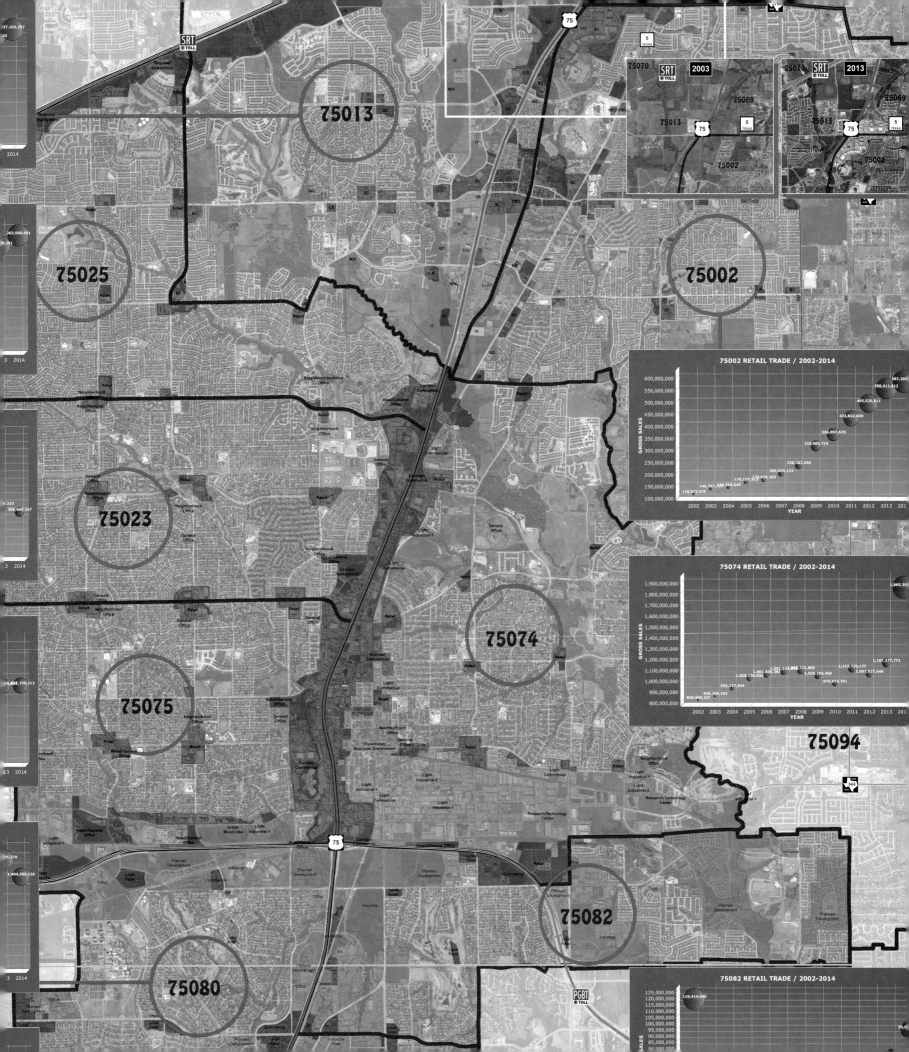

75013

75025

75023

75075

75080

75002

75074

75094

75082

75070 2003

75013

75069

75002

75020 2013

75013

75069

75002

75002 RETAIL TRADE / 2002-2014

GROSS SALES

600,000,000	
550,000,000	587,266
500,000,000	558,011,812
450,000,000	495,525,611
400,000,000	433,832,830
350,000,000	366,097,678
300,000,000	318,605,724
250,000,000	238,383,658
200,000,000	205,505,123
150,000,000	170,157,177 936,363
	140,767,7 569,640
100,000,000	118,572,578

2002 2003 2004 2005 2006 2007 2008 2009 2010 2011 2012 2013 201
YEAR

75074 RETAIL TRADE / 2002-2014

GROSS SALES

1,900,000,000	1,865,30
1,800,000,000	
1,700,000,000	
1,600,000,000	
1,500,000,000	
1,400,000,000	
1,300,000,000	
1,200,000,000	
1,100,000,000	1,091,513,8 721,800 1,113,735,177 1,167,277,772
1,000,000,000	1,028,154,82 605,383 1,050,206,469 1,067,927,646
900,000,000	935,127,646 975,973,791
800,000,000	826,900,227 865,369,153

2002 2003 2004 2005 2006 2007 2008 2009 2010 2011 2012 2013 201
YEAR

75082 RETAIL TRADE / 2002-2014

125,000,000	119,414,640
120,000,000	
115,000,000	
110,000,000	
105,000,000	
100,000,000	
95,000,000	
90,000,000	
85,000,000	

Grand Canyon National Park and Vicinity

US Department of Agriculture (USDA) Forest Service
Salt Lake City, Utah, USA
By Andrew Keske

Contact

Andrew Keske
akeske@fs.fed.us

Software

ArcGIS 10.1 for Desktop, Terrain Texture Shader

Data Sources

Digital Elevation Models from the US Geological Survey National Map Viewer and processed in portion using Terrain Texture Shader software tool developed by Leland Brown and Natural Graphics

Grand Canyon National Park, located in Northern Arizona, is known throughout the world for its striking expanse and colorful landscapes. The canyon is rich in flora and fauna, and has a cultural history dating back thousands of years. With the park's place as a national treasure, management of the canyon and most adjoining lands is today a shared responsibility of the US Forest Service and the US Park Service.

Using a variety of techniques, this map helps to view Grand Canyon National Park and immediate surroundings in a unique way. Cartographic realism is a term/technique in cartography used to describe a map that depicts a landscape not in a realistic state but as it might be expected or desired to look. Here, cartographic realism shows the park as visitors expect it to be. New visual insights on terrain, geology, forest cover, and some of the current human interactions can be seen clearly.

Courtesy of USDA Forest Service.

Flaming Gorge Reservoir Illuminated with an Overcast Sky

Long Island University
Brookville, New York, USA
By Patrick Kennelly, Long Island University,
and James Stewart, Queens University

Contact

Patrick Kennelly
Patrick.Kennelly@liu.edu

Software

ArcGIS 10.2 for Desktop

Data Source

US Geological Survey National Map Viewer and
Download Platform

Flaming Gorge Reservoir is a popular recreational attraction straddling the Utah-Wyoming border. This map was created as an academic research project to demonstrate how an advanced hillshading technique the authors developed could be used in ArcGIS to visualize terrain on a map. The map shows shading and shadowing effects available in the ArcGIS Sky Models tool, as both rims of the canyon cast shadows into the gorge.

The map was rendered with 250 hillshaded grids. The direction and relative brightness of each grid correspond to the distribution of luminance in an overcast sky using standards defined by the International Commission of Illumination, the worldwide authority on light, illumination, color, and color spaces.

Courtesy of Long Island University.

New National Map for Switzerland: Map Sheet Grindelwald

Federal Office of Topography (swisstopo)
Wabern, Switzerland
By Cartography Division

Contact

Christoph Streit

christoph.streit@swisstopo.ch

Software

ArcGIS 10.2.2 for Desktop

Data Source

Federal Office of Topography (swisstopo)

In 2013, the Federal Office of Topography, also known as swisstopo, began a comprehensive upgrade of the largest official map document for Switzerland—the national map at 1:25,000 scale—with 247 sheets. It is the most accurate and detailed topographic map of Switzerland for hikers, alpinists, vacationers, and adventurers. The sheets feature complete and differentiated rail, road, and route networks plus detailed representations of settled areas, hydrography, vegetation, and terrain; shown here is part of a map sheet 1229 Grindelwald, published in spring 2015.

Copyright © 2015, Federal Office of Topography (swisstopo), CH-3084 Wabern.

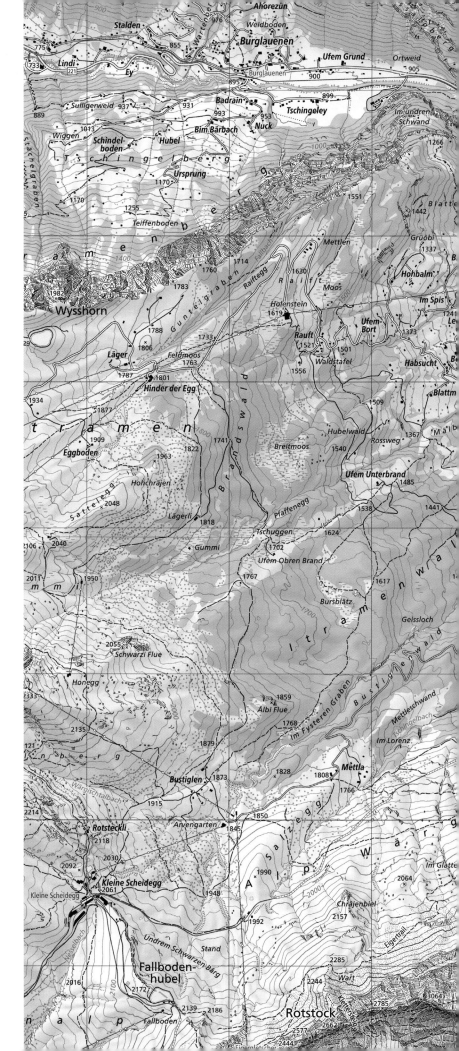

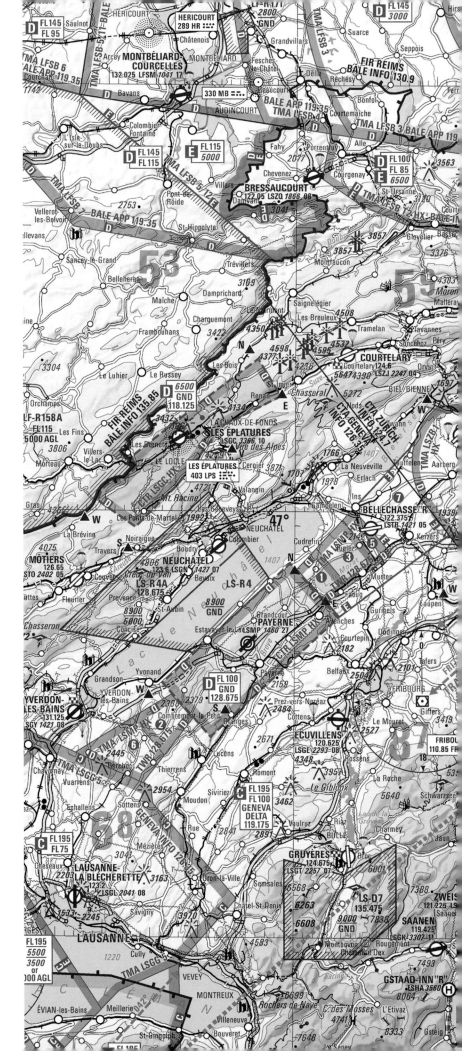

Swiss Aeronautical Chart ICAO
1:500,000

Federal Office of Topography (swisstopo)
Wabern, Switzerland
By Federal Office of Topography (swisstopo)
Cartography Division, and Swiss Air Navigation
Services Ltd. (skyguide)

Contact

Christoph Streit
christoph.streit@swisstopo.ch

Software

ArcGIS 10.2.2 for Desktop, Adobe Illustrator

Data Sources

Federal Office of Topography (swisstopo), and
Swiss Air Navigation Services Ltd., (skyguide)

The official Aeronautical Chart ICAO 1:500,000 of Switzerland
is updated and published annually by Swiss Air Navigation
Services, Ltd., also known as skyguide, and the Federal Office
of Topography, also known as swisstopo, as prescribed in the
regulations of the international aeronautical conventions.

The chart includes airports and airfields, classified airspace,
restricted and hazardous areas, as well as air traffic control
information for Switzerland and the adjoining foreign territories. Further information about airspace in Switzerland and
airport radio frequencies, along with other useful information
for pilots, is included in this product.

*Copyright © 2015 skyguide CH-8602 Wangen bei Dübendorf / swiss-
topo CH-3084 Wabern.*

Rush Hour in Tokyo

Tokyo Map Research Inc.
Fuchu City, Tokyo, Japan
By Kei Sato

Contact

Kei Sato
k_sato@t-map.co.jp

Software

ArcGIS 10.2 for Desktop

Data Sources

Train Timetable, 2010 population Census of Japan

Tokyo is a global megacity and more than 30 million people live within 40 miles of Tokyo. Many people commute from suburbs to downtown every morning, so in the five wards of central Tokyo, the daytime population is about 3.6 million, while the nighttime population is about 0.9 million.

Commuters are supported by the railroad network. This map shows the location of the trains operated at 8:00 a.m. on weekdays by the train timetable. Cities and towns of Tokyo are classified into nine categories by the difference between daytime and nighttime population. The accuracy of the information of the location of trains on the station at 8:00 a.m. is high. On the other hand, that of the trains on the railroad between stations at 8:00 a.m. is relatively low.

Courtesy of Tokyo Map Research Inc.

Location of the Trains at 8:00 a.m. (Main Map)

Conservation Outcomes: Madagascar and the Indian Ocean Islands

Conservation International
Arlington, Virginia, USA
By Kellee Koenig

Contact

Kellee Koenig
kkoenig@conservation.org

Software

ArcGIS 10.3.1 for Desktop

Data Sources

Conservation International; (derived by author from) BD500, Foiben-Taosarinitanin'i Madagasikara; (derived by author from) Système des Aires Protégées de Madagascar; VMap0, National Geospatial-Intelligence Agency

The Madagascar and Indian Ocean Islands biodiversity hotspot includes the island of Madagascar, as well as the independent nations of Seychelles, the Comoros, and Mauritius, and French departments and territories of the Western Indian Ocean. The Critical Ecosystem Partnership Fund's (CEPF) Conservation Outcomes map shows the highest geographical priorities for biodiversity investments within the hotspot with distribution data for 1,655 globally threatened species and 379 other patrimonial species (site endemics or species not yet assessed but considered endangered by experts) used to identify 369 key biodiversity areas (KBAs).

For Madagascar, Conservation International's Moore Center for Science and Oceans analyzed the ecosystem services provided by the KBAs. This analysis was used to support the prioritization process that led to the identification of thirty-eight priority KBAs in Madagascar, and nineteen, nine, and twelve priority KBAs for the Comoros, Mauritius, and the Seychelles, respectively. The map will be in active use until at least 2020. CEPF uses the map to guide the award of $8.25 million in grants to civil society organizations working to protect and manage biodiversity in the priority KBAs.

Copyright 2014 Conservation International Maps.

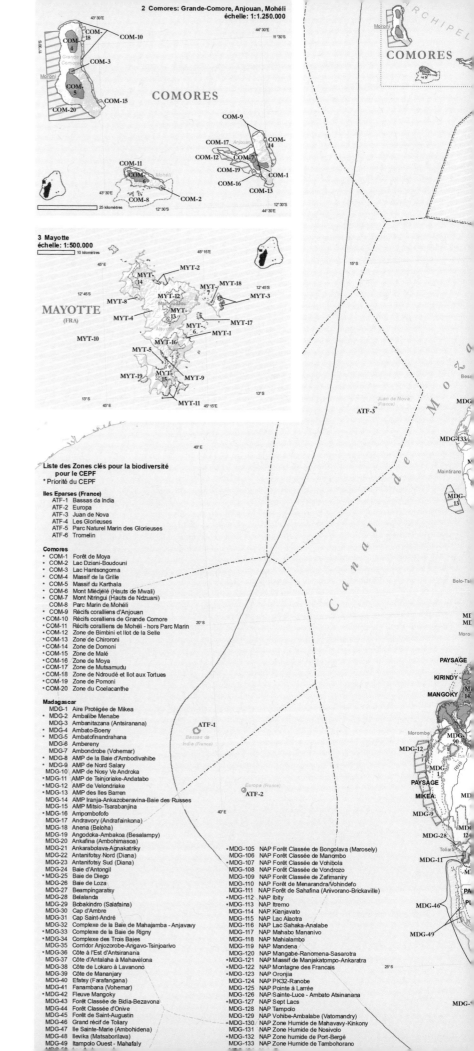

Tejon Ranch

Tejon Ranch Company
Tejon Ranch, California, USA
By Craig McClain

Contact
Tejon Ranch GIS Department
gisteam@tejonranch.com

Software
ArcGIS 10.3 for Desktop

Data Source
Tejon Ranch Company

Located an hour north of the Los Angeles metropolitan area, Tejon Ranch's remarkable landscape is a dramatic tapestry of rugged mountains, steep canyons, oak-covered rolling hills, and broad valleys. Oaks of almost every kind can be found on the land, along with conifer forests, Joshua trees, and spectacular spring displays of wildflowers. This map is used as an introduction to Tejon Ranch and the components that make up the business-related content of the ranch operations.

The rich natural resources of Tejon Ranch, along with its location along Interstate 5, the major north-south transportation corridor in California, provide a variety of other opportunities beyond the traditional ranching and farming operations. The principles of conservation and good stewardship are historic core values of the Tejon Ranch Company, which has established huge conservation areas and enacted a habitat conservation plan to protect a wide variety of plant and animal species. The company also uses the latest environmentally sensitive practices in ranching, farming, and real estate operations.

Courtesy of Tejon Ranch GIS Department.

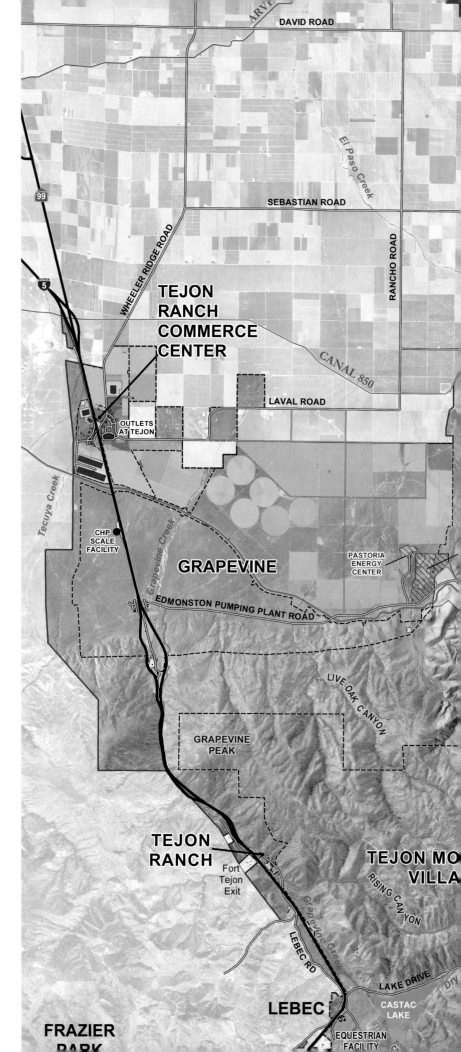

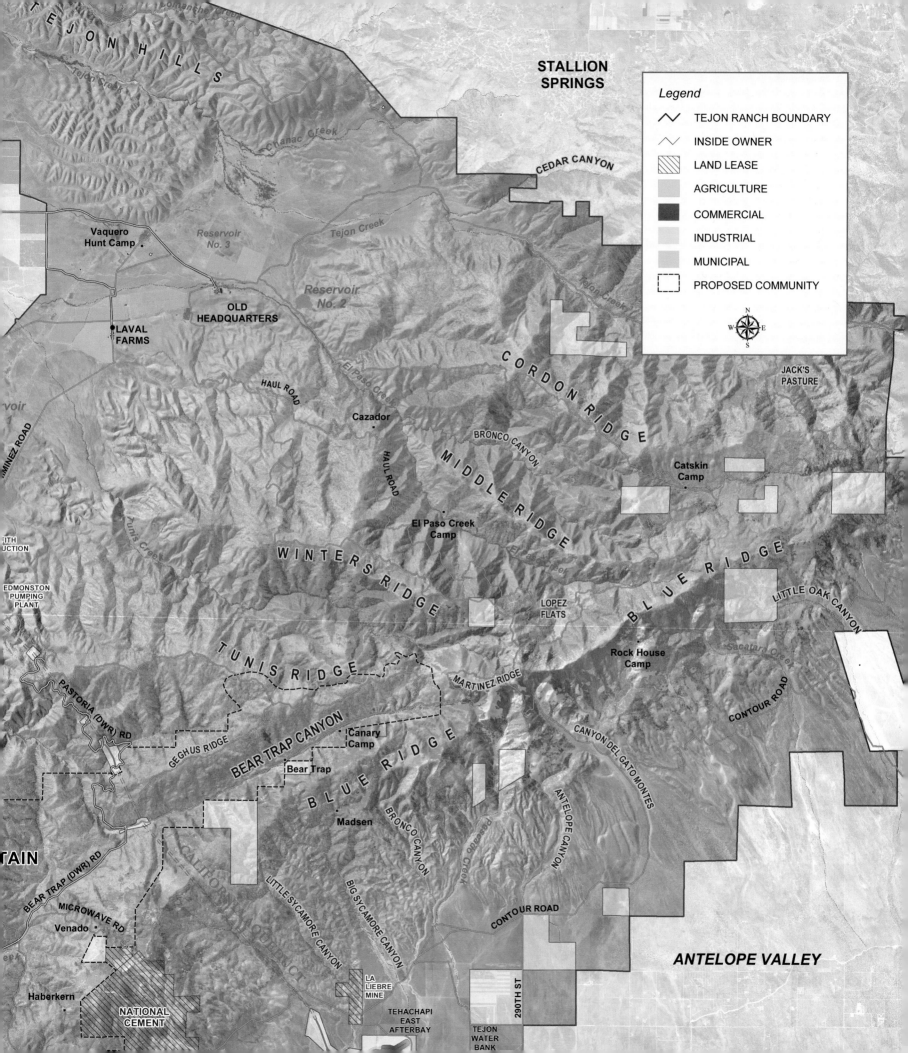

CONSERVATION AND SUSTAINABLE DEVELOPMENT

GIS Techniques Used for Stream Mapping and Restoration

Amec Foster Wheeler
Lakeland, Florida, USA
By Aziza Baan

Contact

Aziza Baan
aziza.baan@amecfw.com

Software

ArcGIS 10.2.1 for Desktop

Data Sources

Amec Foster Wheeler, Southwest Florida Water Management District, Florida Department of Transportation, National Agriculture Imagery Program

Headwater streams and small rivers have been understudied and undervalued, leading to their demise. Amec Foster Wheeler is changing that in Florida with its innovative GIS-based stream assessments and natural channel restoration designs. The four techniques outlined here have been used to help classify, plan, design, build, monitor, and map streams.

GIS has become an integral part of the company's stream research to help determine how a stream fits and functions within the landscape. The technical expertise and knowledge gathered with the help of GIS are applied to significant water conservation, water supply, and water quality issues such as minimum flow and levels and the numeric nutrient criteria. GIS has helped Amec Foster Wheeler become more cost-effective by directly applying science, engineering, and fluvial geomorphology expertise into the software for stream analysis.

Courtesy of Amec Foster Wheeler, Water Resources Department, Lakeland, Florida.

26

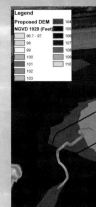

APPLICATIONS: Restoration & Reclamation De

GIS DESIGN & MECHANICAL CONS

2009

Legend
Proposed DEM
NGVD 1929 (Feet)
96.7 - 97
98
99
100
101
102
103

Existing Ditch with planned Stream Planform derived from our Regressions and GIS Analysis

Proposed Stream

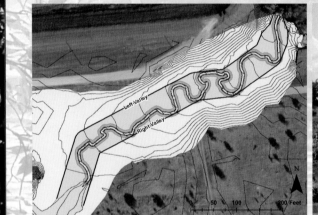

Proposed Stream and Planting Plan

Cons

2010

Constructed Man-Made Natural Stream (2010 Imagery)

Construc

The purpose of this project was to seamlessly convert a ditch into a na connecting a reclaimed depressional swamp to a forested wet

GIS was used as the main tool for the analysis, plannin Using a developed regression and GIS analysis we were able

GIS has become a fundamental tool in our innovative natural stream to place the design of a natural stream that will fit and function fully

UCTION

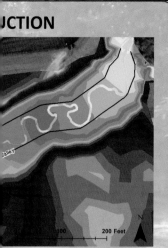

Valley Digital Elevation Model (DEM)

n (9 Weeks)

2014

n-Made Natural Stream 14 Imagery)

flatwoods alluvial channel preservation area.

designing.
sign the stream.

el restoration techniques en wetlands once built.

GIS HISTORIC STREAM DETERMINATION

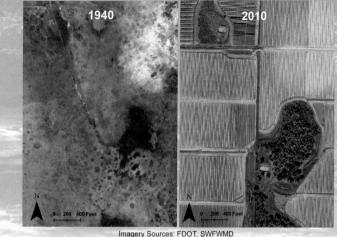

Imagery Sources: FDOT, SWFWMD

By using GIS, we can determine if there was a stream existing historically by aerial interpretation as well as using regressions that relate drainage area to valley slope.

GIS STREAM MAPPING AND INVENTORY

Imagery & LiDar Sources: SWFWMD

Aerial and LIDAR derived DEM interpretation were used to digitize streams for a property that was over 7000 Acres.

GIS Desktop Analysis proved to be quicker and cost effective method than sending out field technicians.

STREAM VEGETATION MAPPING

Legend

Habitat

◊ Sand Patches

⊛ Submerged Aquatic Vegetation (SAV)

⊚ Aquatic Vegetation

◆ Large Woody Debris (LWD)

TINS were generated in GIS from survey data.

Stream vegetation points were added as a layer and placed over the stream surface elevation model to determine any patterns from the different types of habitats.

Modeling Cougar Corridors in Owens Valley

Cal Poly University, Pomona
Pomona, California, USA
By Elliott Popel, Jeremy Munns, Fei Xie, and Lin Wu

Contact
Lin Wu
lwu@cpp.edu

Software
ArcGIS 10.2 for Desktop, Adobe Illustrator, Adobe InDesign

Data Sources
US Geological Survey, Inyo County

Cougars are the most significant apex predator of the Owens Valley in California, but they are at risk of population decline due to the shifting conditions of the valley and impending climate change. Populations of cougars in the Sierra Nevada and Inyo-White Mountains are also at risk of being cut off from each other as these conditions become a barrier to gene flow.

Student researchers used ArcGIS to create a fuzzy suitability model of existing suitable conditions in the valley and then connected points of suitability together with a least-cost path model. Using this data, environmental planners can designate corridors between mountain ranges where they can most effectively focus conservation efforts.

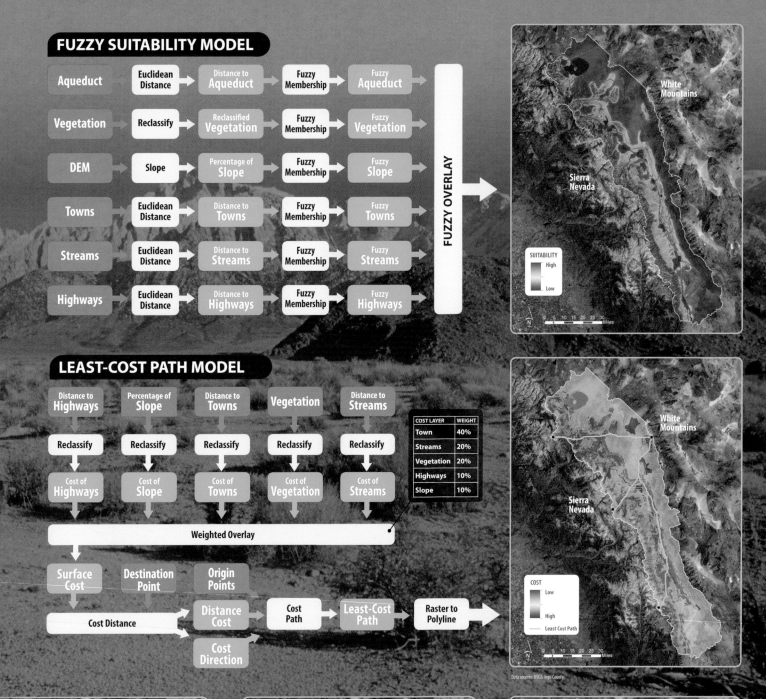

FUZZY SUITABILITY MODEL

Aqueduct → Euclidean Distance → Distance to **Aqueduct** → Fuzzy Membership → Fuzzy **Aqueduct** →

Vegetation → Reclassify → Reclassified **Vegetation** → Fuzzy Membership → Fuzzy **Vegetation** →

DEM → Slope → Percentage of **Slope** → Fuzzy Membership → Fuzzy **Slope** →

Towns → Euclidean Distance → Distance to **Towns** → Fuzzy Membership → Fuzzy **Towns** →

Streams → Euclidean Distance → Distance to **Streams** → Fuzzy Membership → Fuzzy **Streams** →

Highways → Euclidean Distance → Distance to **Highways** → Fuzzy Membership → Fuzzy **Highways** →

FUZZY OVERLAY →

SUITABILITY
High
Low

White Mountains
Sierra Nevada

N
0 5 10 15 20 25 30 Miles

LEAST-COST PATH MODEL

Distance to **Highways** → Reclassify → Cost of **Highways** →

Percentage of **Slope** → Reclassify → Cost of **Slope** →

Distance to **Towns** → Reclassify → Cost of **Towns** →

Vegetation → Reclassify → Cost of **Vegetation** →

Distance to **Streams** → Reclassify → Cost of **Streams** →

COST LAYER	WEIGHT
Town	40%
Streams	20%
Vegetation	20%
Highways	10%
Slope	10%

Weighted Overlay

Surface Cost   **Destination Point**   **Origin Points**

Cost Distance → **Distance Cost** → **Cost Path** → **Least-Cost Path** → **Raster to Polyline** →

Cost Direction

COST
Low
High
Least Cost Path

White Mountains
Sierra Nevada

N
0 5 10 15 20 25 30 Miles

Data sources: USGS, Inyo County

SLOPE COST
Low
High

N
0 5 10 15 20 25 30 Miles

DISTANCE COST
Low
High

N
0 5 10 15 20 25 30 Miles

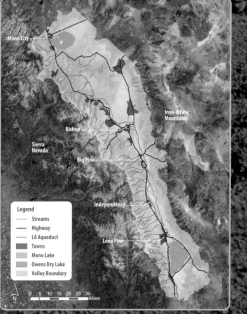

Mono City
Bishop
Big Pine
Independence
Lone Pine
Inyo-White Mountains
Sierra Nevada

Legend
Streams
Highway
LA Aqueduct
Towns
Mono Lake
Owens Dry Lake
Valley Boundary

N
0 5 10 15 20 25 30 Miles

Spatial Priorities for Habitat Connectivity in the Berkshire Wildlife Linkage

The Nature Conservancy (TNC)
Boston, Massachusetts, USA
By Jessica Dyson, Laura Marx, and Andy Finton

Contact

Jessica Dyson
jdyson@tnc.org

Software

ArcGIS 10.2.2 for Desktop

Data Sources

University of Massachusetts, Amherst; The Nature Conservancy

The Berkshire Wildlife Linkage is one of nine important habitat linkages in the Staying Connected Initiative, a public-private partnership seeking to enhance landscape connections across the Northern Appalachian/Acadian region of the eastern United States and Canada.

In western Massachusetts, The Nature Conservancy (TNC) envisions a landscape stretching from the Green Mountains in Vermont to the Hudson Highlands in New York and beyond, where core habitats are protected as well as corridors between them. This map shows where focusing TNC's primary strategies to achieve that vision—land protection, road barrier mitigation, and outreach to landowners and towns—will have the most impact on regional habitat connectivity, ensuring the ability of wildlife to move across large distances and across multiple generations.

Fine-scale landscape features and field-collected data are used to further understand where individual animals are moving, and identify landholdings for targeted outreach and land protection. Improving habitat connectivity across the Berkshire Wildlife Linkage will enhance the ability of wildlife to adapt to a changing climate and contribute to a resilient landscape that helps prevent and prepare for climate change.

Courtesy of The Nature Conservancy.

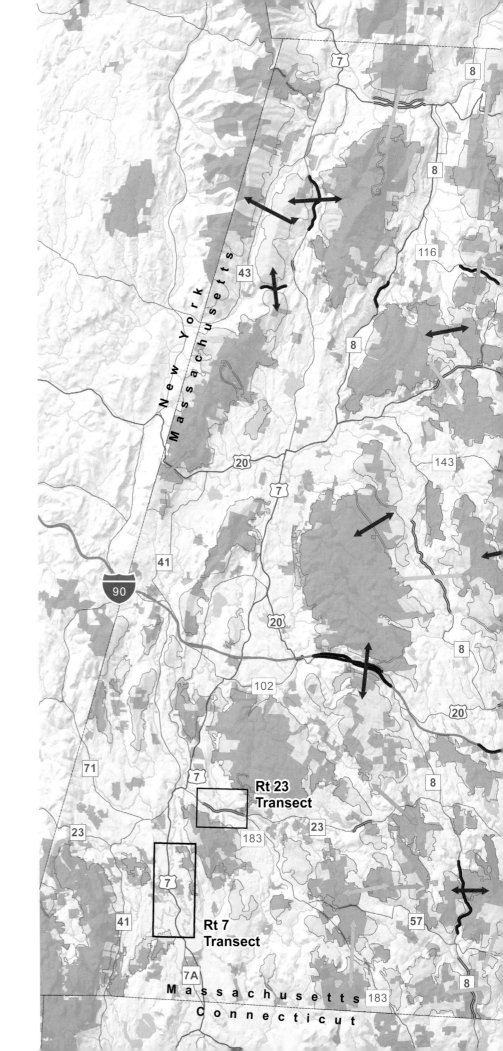

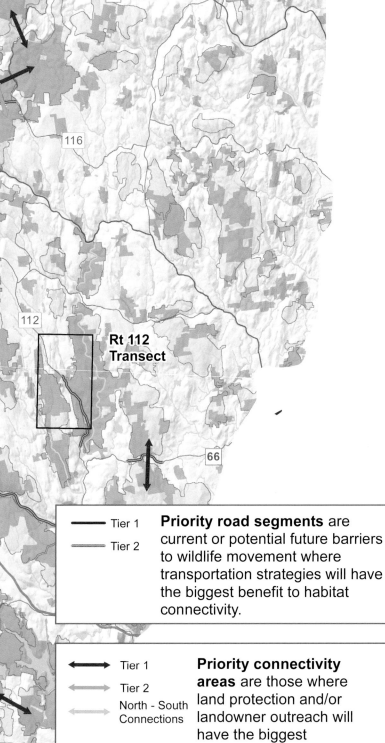

Vermont

Massachusetts

8A

2

116

9

112

Rt 112
Transect

66

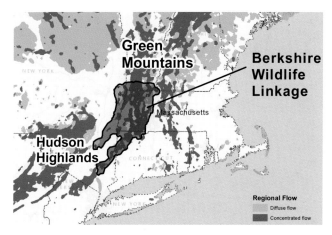

Green
Mountains

Berkshire
Wildlife
Linkage

Hudson
Highlands

Massachusetts

NEW YORK

CONNECTICUT

NEW YORK

Regional Flow
Diffuse flow
Concentrated flow

**Winter Tracking
Results**

Tracks

- ◐ Bobcat
- ○ Canid
- ◑ Coyote
- ● Deer
- ◔ Red fox
- ● Turkey
- ○ Weasels

— Road Transects

Crossings

- ✦ Bobcat
- ✧ Canid
- ✦ Coyote
- ✚ Deer
- ✦ Red fox
- ✚ Turkey

Route 23, Great Barrington MA

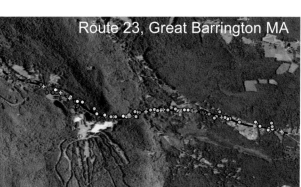

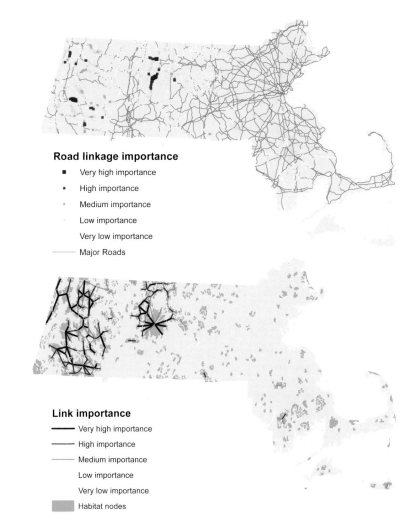

Road linkage importance

- ■ Very high importance
- ▪ High importance
- · Medium importance
- Low importance
- Very low importance
- — Major Roads

Link importance

- — Very high importance
- — High importance
- — Medium importance
- Low importance
- Very low importance
- Habitat nodes

— Tier 1
— Tier 2

Priority road segments are current or potential future barriers to wildlife movement where transportation strategies will have the biggest benefit to habitat connectivity.

◀▶ Tier 1
◀▶ Tier 2
◀▶ North - South Connections

Priority connectivity areas are those where land protection and/or landowner outreach will have the biggest benefit to maintaining habitat connectivity.

31

Greater Sage-Grouse Habitat Depiction for Environmental Impact Statements

US Department of Agriculture (USDA) Forest Service
Salt Lake City, Utah, USA
By Timothy Love, Tony Korologos, and Dalinda Damm

Contact
Timothy Love
tblove@fs.fed.us

Software
ArcGIS 10.2.2 for Desktop

Data Source
USDA Forest Service

The USDA Forest Service has partnered with the Bureau of Land Management to develop six greater sage-grouse environmental impact statements and associated records of decision. This map shows greater sage-grouse habitat within seven western states where the Forest Service has developed specific forest plan language in an attempt to preserve the species in lands it manages.

A large proportion of habitat shown was derived from greater sage-grouse breeding centers using geoanalysis functionality such as buffering, spatial analysis, and layer intersection. A significant difficulty encountered when developing these layers was finding agreement between both organizations along with other federal organizations, states, conservation groups, and corporate entities. The subsequent datasets have easily been the most shared during development of environmental impact documents, and are the most requested information now that formal decisions have been made. Providing the layers in a standard geodatabase format has eased sharing difficulties and facilitated further analysis of this data.

Courtesy of USDA Forest Service.

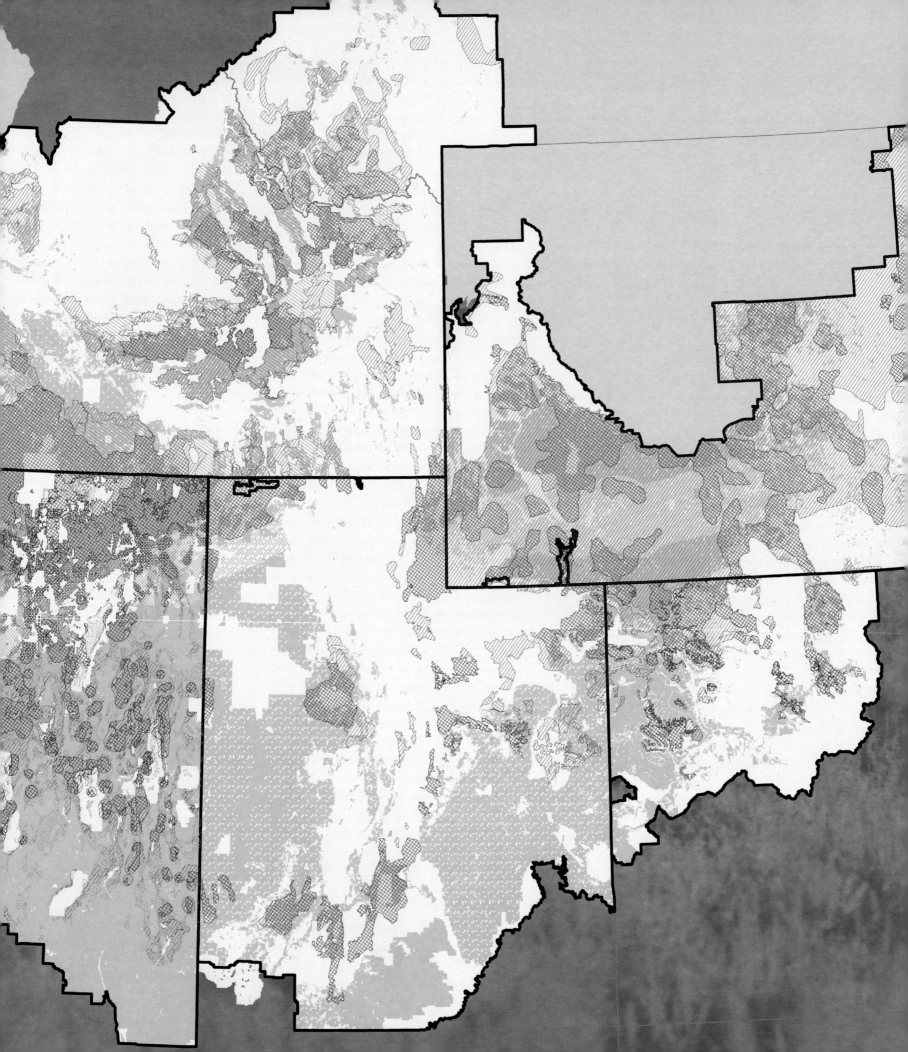

Predicting Swamp Rabbit Habitat in Southeast Missouri

Missouri Department of Conservation
Columbia, Missouri, USA
By Philip Marley, Debby Fantz, and Vicki Jackson

Contact
Philip Marley
Philip_Marley@fws.gov

Software
ArcGIS 10.3.1 for Desktop, DIVA, GARP, and MAXENT

Data Source
Missouri Natural Heritage Database

Swamp rabbits (Sylvilagus aquaticus) are a Missouri mammal of conservation concern due to habitat loss and fragmentation. This fragmentation has resulted in small, isolated habitats which may not be able to support viable populations, but they may function to increase connectivity of larger blocks of habitat. Determining the current distribution of swamp rabbits in southeast Missouri is essential for conservation purposes but locating new habitat and populations has proven difficult.

The ability to use computer processing to determine preferred animal habitats based on a predetermined set of criteria is very beneficial with swamp rabbits. Predictive modeling helps to leverage geospatial data with known location data from the Missouri Natural Heritage database to identify suitable swamp rabbit habitat. These sites can then be surveyed to determine if any previously unknown populations exist. This data is used to determine locations for swamp rabbit surveys and drive conservation efforts.

Courtesy of Missouri Department of Conservation.

Extant

Extirpated

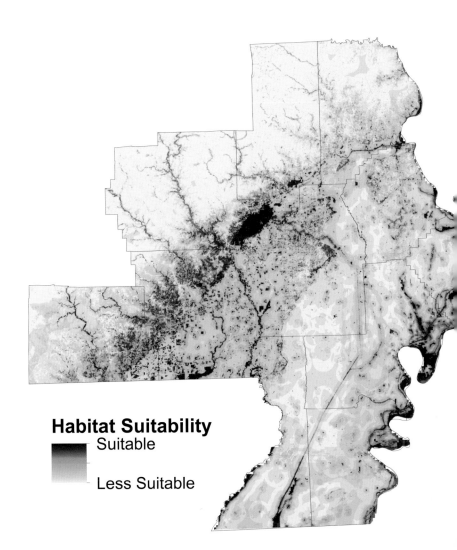

Habitat Suitability
Suitable

Less Suitable

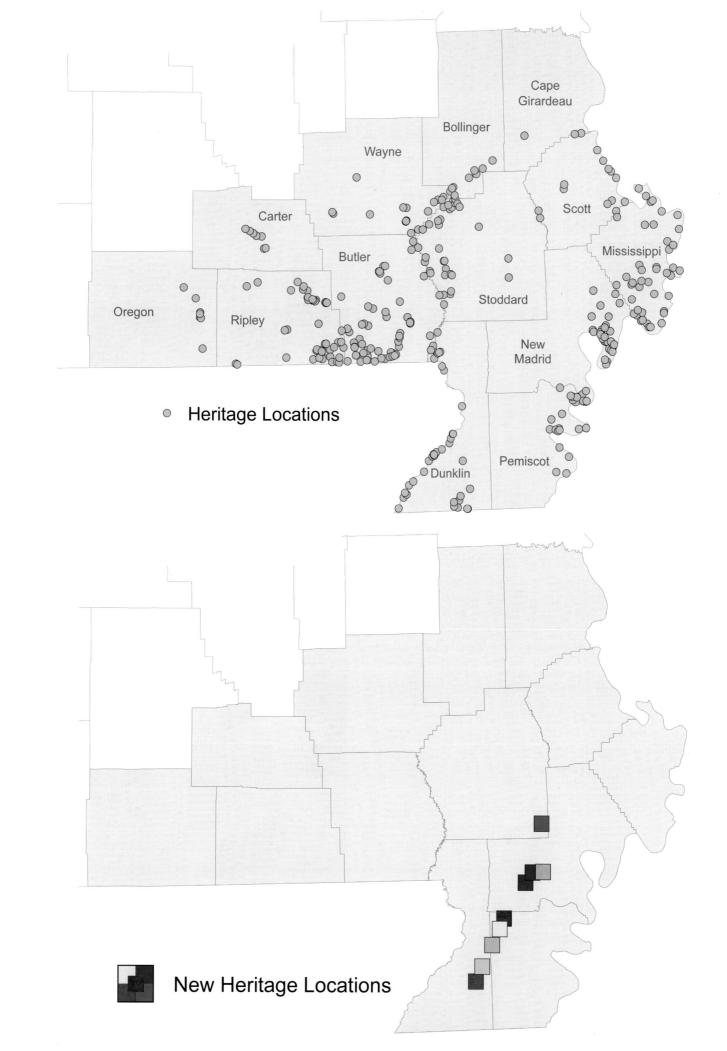

Heritage Locations

New Heritage Locations

Ice-Associated Seal Surveys in the Eastern Bering Sea

National Marine Mammal Laboratory, Alaska
Fisheries Science Center
Seattle, Washington, USA
By Erin Richmond

Contact

Erin Richmond
erin.richmond@noaa.gov

Software

ArcGIS 10.3.1 for Desktop

Data Sources

Alaska Fisheries Science Center, National Oceanic
and Atmospheric Administration Fisheries

Ice-associated seals are key components of Arctic marine
ecosystems and are of conservation concern due to global
climate change and diminishing sea ice habitat. Monitoring
these species is a fundamental goal for the National Oceanic
and Atmospheric Administration's National Marine Fisheries
Service to meet management and regulatory mandates.

Biologists at the Alaska Fisheries Science Center in Seattle,
WA, conducted aerial surveys in the eastern Bering Sea
during spring months to collect baseline data on the distribution and abundance of four species of ice-associated seals
(bearded, ribbon, ringed, and spotted). Surveys were flown
using a fixed-wing aircraft with a paired system of digital
cameras and thermal imagers mounted in the belly port.

The maps and data products presented here shed light on
the dynamics of Arctic marine ecosystems by providing data
crucial for developing sound plans for management, conservation, and responses to potential environmental impacts.

*Courtesy of Erin Richmond, National Marine Mammal Laboratory,
Alaska Fisheries Science Center.*

RIBBON SEAL (*Histriophoca fasciata*)

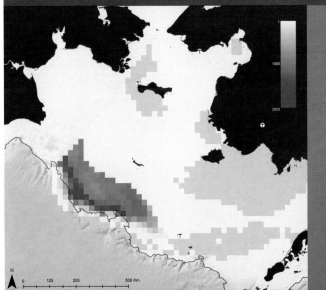

▲ **Seal Sightings**

Thermal imagery collected during
compared to the surrounding env
Georeferencing of seal sightings w

▲ **Species Distribution Model**

M
k
s

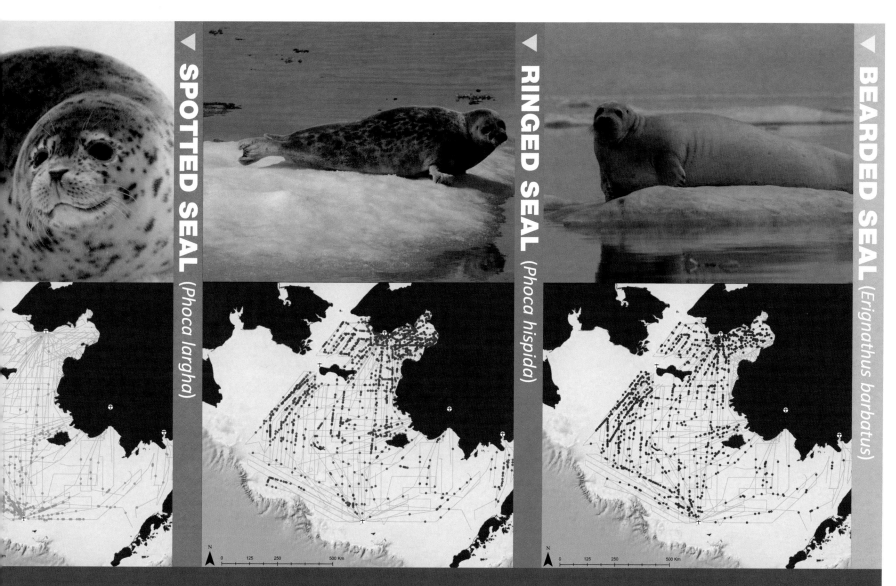

SPOTTED SEAL (*Phoca largha*)

RINGED SEAL (*Phoca hispida*)

BEARDED SEAL (*Erignathus barbatus*)

...veys was analyzed to detect seals or "hotspots" on the ice that showed extreme heat signatures when ...nt. High resolution digital imagery with matched timestamps was then used for species identification. ...omplished by matching photo timestamps with GPS data and linearly interpolating where needed.

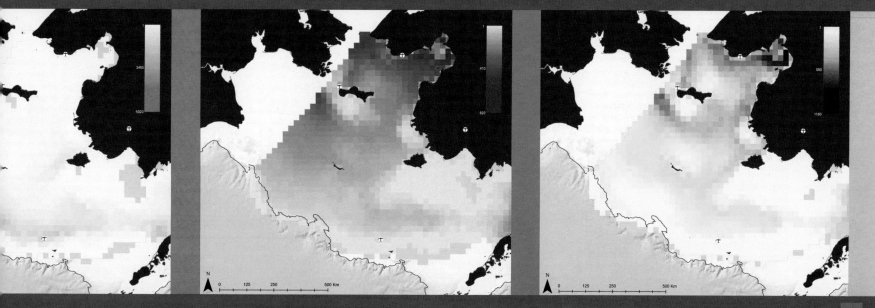

...cies abundance estimates were calculated for the eastern Bering Sea study area using mean posterior predictions based on a 25 x 25 ... grid. Patterns in seal abundance adhere to historic and expected species distributions in the eastern Bering Sea, in addition to observed seal ...based on analyzed imagery collected from the field. Grey grid cells indicate where the abundance was estimated to be zero.

Fort Hunter Liggett Net Zero

US Army Reserve
Fort Hunter Liggett, California, USA
By Spencer Larson

Contact
Spencer Larson
spencer.b.larson.ctr@mail.mil

Software
ArcGIS 10.2 for Desktop

Data Sources
Urban Collaborative, Fort Hunter Liggett
Directorate of Public Works, Department of Fish
and Wildlife

This map highlights US Army Garrison Fort Hunter Liggett (USAG FHL), located in Monterey County, California, and its Net Zero energy, waste, and water initiatives. Net Zero initiatives help the Army manage its resources in a sustainable manner. Actions have already been implemented and more are planned to help USAG FHL reach this goal.

At Fort Hunter Liggett, completion of a two-megawatt photovoltaic solar array; a battery system to save surplus power produced by the solar array; and planned solar water heaters, geothermal heat pumps, and additional rooftop solar help the base move closer to energy security and not rely on outside electrical utility providers. As part of the net zero waste initiative, FHL has recycled nearly 200 tons of material in the first half of the 2015 fiscal year. At the current rates, that's over a half ton of recyclables per person per year based on the total base population. Additionally, a waste gasification system is being constructed to burn the remaining nonrecyclable waste into usable energy. This will help FHL meet its Net Zero waste installation goal. With these energy and waste initiatives USAG FHL is poised to become the first US Army installation to be Net Zero in both waste and energy.

Courtesy of Spencer Larson, Army Reserve Installation Management Directorate/Fort Hunter Liggett Directorate of Public Works.

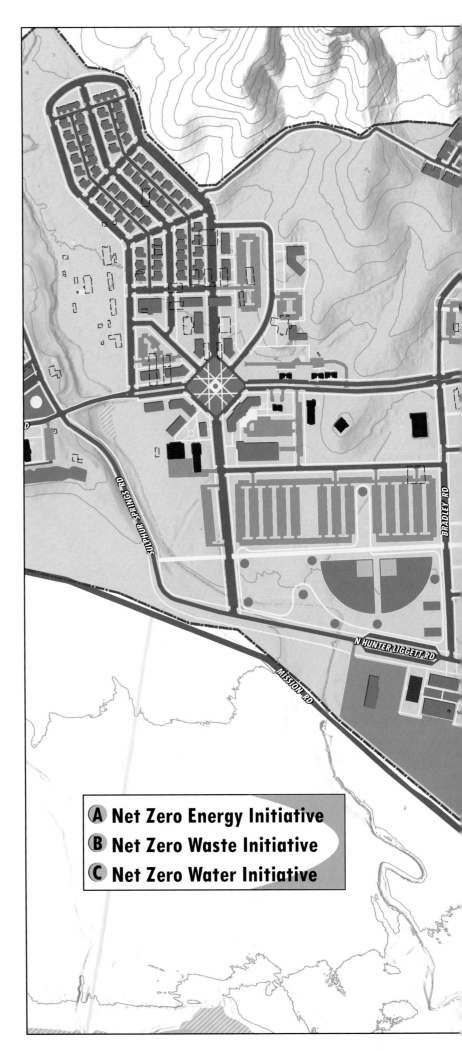

Ⓐ **Net Zero Energy Initiative**
Ⓑ **Net Zero Waste Initiative**
Ⓒ **Net Zero Water Initiative**

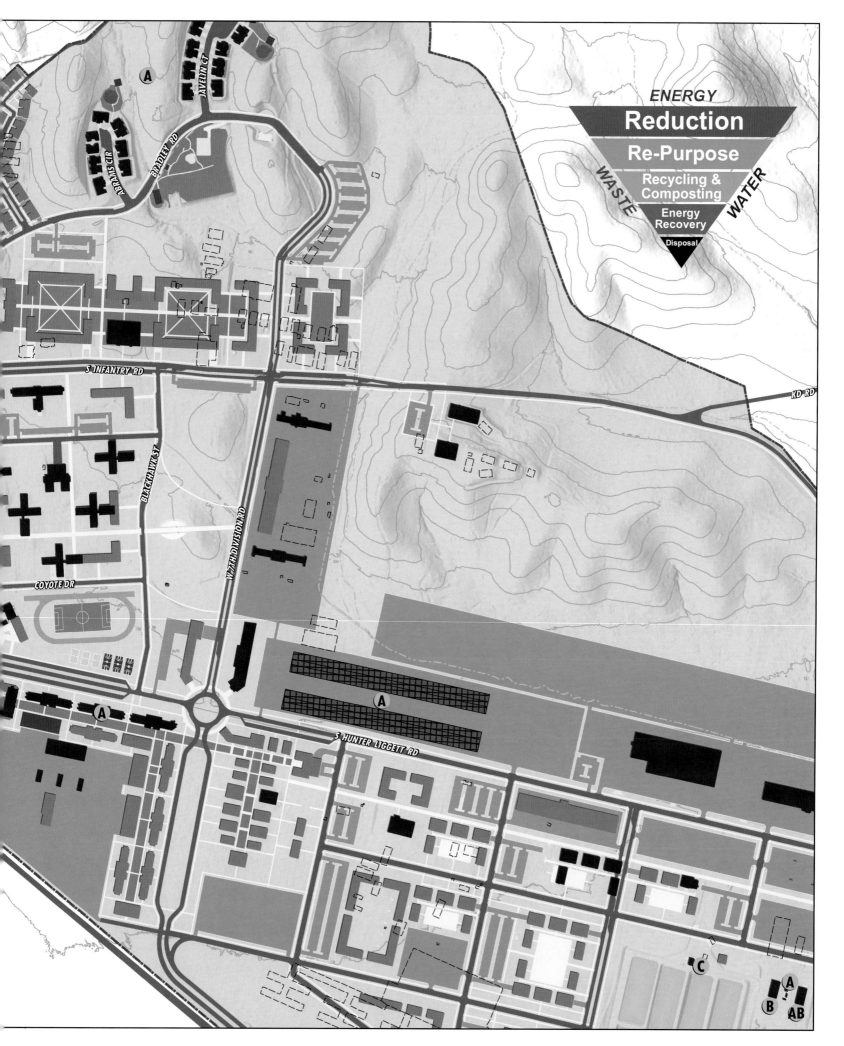

ENERGY

Reduction

Re-Purpose

Recycling & Composting

Energy Recovery

Disposal

WASTE

WATER

Impact of Snow Depth on Truck Mobility in Afghanistan: February 2013

US Army Corps of Engineers (USACE)
Washington, DC, USA
By Jennifer S. Macpherson

Contact

Jennifer S. Macpherson
jmacmedia8@aol.com

Software

ArcGIS 10.1 for Desktop

Data Sources

Affleck, Rosa T., S. Gaughan, J. Macpherson. "An Assessment of Winter Weather on Military Vehicles." Winter 2012-2013. Prepared for Headquarters International Security Assistance Force, Special Forces Photos: Department of Defense; BAE Systems Land & Armaments

From 2010 to 2013, researchers at the US Army Corps of Engineers' (USACE) Cold Regions Research and Engineering Laboratory applied the NATO Reference Mobility Model to assess the impact of winter weather on cross-country wheeled vehicle mobility in Afghanistan for the International Security Assistance Force's Special Forces. This map represents the speed prediction assessments for four of these vehicles during February 2013: the Stryker Armored Personnel Carrier, the Medium Tactical Vehicle M1084, the High Mobility Multipurpose Wheeled Vehicle, and the Heavy Expanded Mobility Tactical Truck.

These assessments were based on a variety of terrain conditions, including slope, snow cover, snow depth, and soil. The monthly expected snow conditions were determined for the entire country based on the Special Sensor Microwave/Imager and the passive microwave estimates of snow/water equivalent (SWE). Weekly historical SWE data was used to determine historical mean, normal ranges, and extremes for each month of the winter season. The resulting information was then used to produce monthly speed maps for each vehicle class based on GIS analysis of topography, and the snow and soil distribution.

Courtesy of Jennifer Macpherson, USACE Cold Regions Research and Engineering Laboratory.

STRYKER ARMORED PERSONEL CARRIER
Type: 8x8 Amored Fighting Vehicle
Weight: 19 tons
Length: 22 ft
Width: 8.11 ft
Height: 8.8 ft
Top Speed: 62 mph

HIGH MOBILITY MULTIPURPOSE WHEELED VEHICLE (HMMWV)
Type: 4x4 Light Utility Vehicle
Weight: 5,900 pounds
Length: 15 ft
Width: 7 ft
Height: 6 ft
Top Speed: 70 mph

From 2010-2013, researchers at the US Army Corps of Engineers Cold Regions Research and Engineering Laboratory (CRREL) applied the NATO Reference Mobility Model (NRMM) to assess the impact of winter weather on cross-country wheeled vehicle mobility in Afghanistan for ISAF Special Forces. The NRMM is a computer model developed in the early 1970s that combines many mobility-related technologies into one comprehensive package designed to predict the mobility of vehicles in on-and-off road terrain. These assesments were based on terrain conditions including slope, snow cover, and snow depth.

This map represents the speed prediction assessments for four vehicles, the HMMWV, MTV M1084, HEMTT and Stryker for the month of February 2013. Results illustrate the lighter, faster HMMWV has greater range at higher speeds than the heavily armored HEMTT or Stryker. The monthly expected snow conditions were determined for the entire country based on the SSM/I (Special Sensor Microwave/Imager) and the passive microwave estimates of snow/water equivelent (SWE). Weekly historical SWE data were used to determine historical mean,

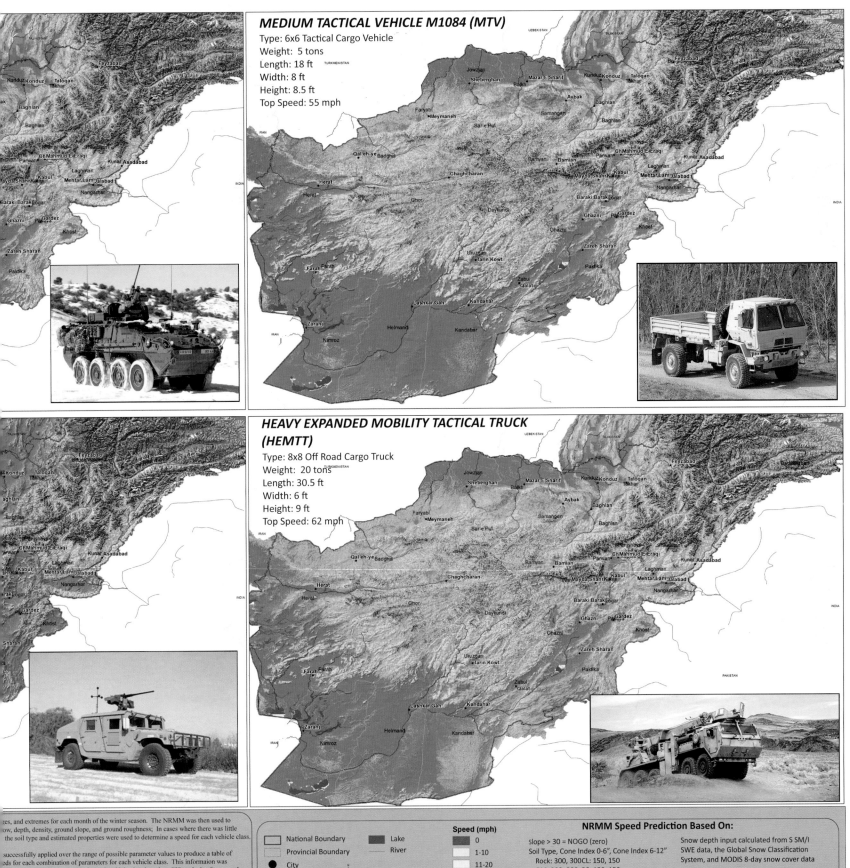

MEDIUM TACTICAL VEHICLE M1084 (MTV)

Type: 6x6 Tactical Cargo Vehicle
Weight: 5 tons
Length: 18 ft
Width: 8 ft
Height: 8.5 ft
Top Speed: 55 mph

HEAVY EXPANDED MOBILITY TACTICAL TRUCK (HEMTT)

Type: 8x8 Off Road Cargo Truck
Weight: 20 tons
Length: 30.5 ft
Width: 6 ft
Height: 9 ft
Top Speed: 62 mph

es, and extremes for each month of the winter season. The NRMM was then used to
ow, depth, density, ground slope, and ground roughness; In cases where there was little
the soil type and estimated properties were used to determine a speed for each vehicle class.

successfully applied over the range of possible parameter values to produce a table of
ds for each combination of parameters for each vehicle class. This informaion was
o produce monthly speed maps for each vehicle class based on GIS analysis of topography,
w and soil distribution.

National Boundary
Provincial Boundary
● City

Lake
River

Speed (mph)
0
1-10
11-20
21-30
31-40
No Data

NRMM Speed Prediction Based On:

Slope > 30 = NOGO (zero)
Soil Type, Cone Index 0-6", Cone Index 6-12"
Rock: 300, 300CL: 150, 150
GM: 300, 300 SC: 150, 150
ML: 150, 150 SP: 150, 150
SM: 150, 150 OH: 150, 150
SW: 150, 150

Snow depth input calculated from S SM/I
SWE data, the Global Snow Classification
System, and MODIS 8-day snow cover data

Obstacles (mounds and trenches) not accounted
for.

Surface Roughness = 0.1 Root Mean Square

ed in ESRI ARCMAP 10.1 (Desktop, Model Builder, Spatial Analyst), ARC CATALOG 10.1, ADOBE ILLUSTRATOR
by Jennifer Macpherson (Remote Sensing & GIS Center of Expertise, USACE)
2015

Sources: Affleck, Rosa T., S. Gaughan, J. Macpherson, *An Assessment of Winter Weather on Military Vehicles* (Winter 2012-2013). Prepared for Headquarters ISAF, Special Forces
Photos: Department of Defense; BAE Systems Land & Armaments

GIS Education at Work

Yale University
New Haven, Connecticut, USA
By Henry B. Glick and Lindsi Seegmiller with support from students of S. D. Maples

Contact
Henry Glick
henry.glick@gmail.com

Software
ArcGIS 10.1 for Desktop, Inkscape 0.48.4, GIMP 2.8.10

Data Sources
Crowd-sourced coordinates, Esri World Ocean Basemap, Global Multi-resolution Terrain Elevation Data 2010; Natural Earth administrative boundaries

Geospatial education provides countless opportunities to not only reach a multitude of students but also to impact research and humanitarian efforts globally. Based on thousands of coordinates crowd-sourced from more than a decade of student-driven GIS research, this map illustrates the probability of a single geospatial educator, S. D. Maples, having influenced research of effected change.

Through a broad lens, this analysis speaks to the role that higher education plays in geographic information sciences and helps to highlight the relative impact the global GIS community has on understanding, organizing, and improving the world. Through the eyes of Maples' students, friends, and colleagues, this map also illustrates the geographic breadth of gratitude for his support.

Courtesy of Henry Glick and Lindsi Seegmiller.

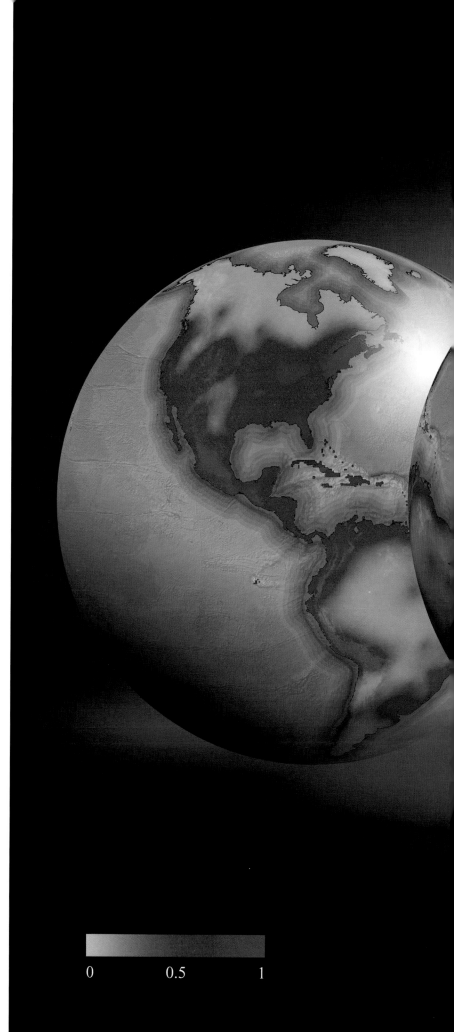

0   0.5   1

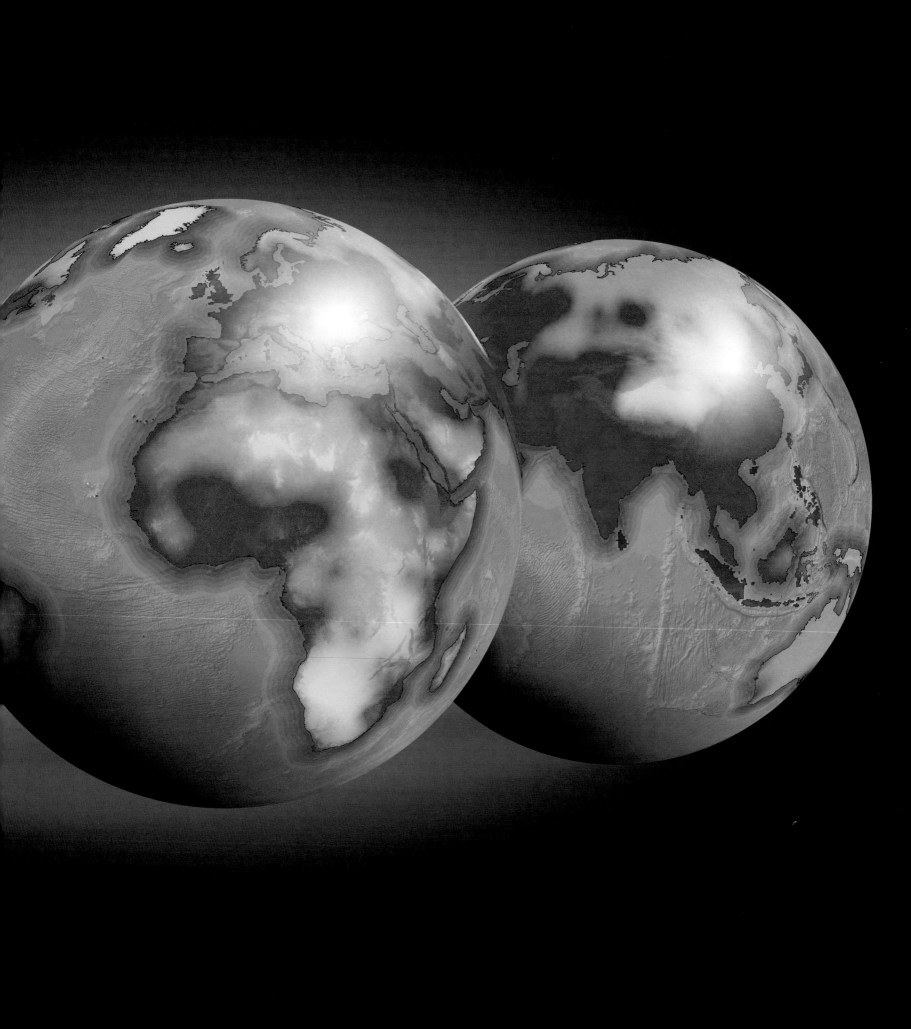

Location-Based Predictive Analytics in K–12 Facility Planning

Parkhill, Smith & Cooper, Inc.
Salt Lake City, Utah, USA
By Michael Howard and Monte Hunter

Contact
Michael Howard
mhoward@team-psc.com

Software
ArcGIS 10.3 for Desktop

Data Source
Texas Comptroller of Public Accounts

This study used location-based predictive analytics to model and estimate the cost per square foot for new school construction. The model included data on over 500 elementary schools built between 2007 and 2013 in Texas, including the cost per square foot as reported by school districts.

While there is undoubtedly a strong relationship between cost and square footage, there are more variables at play influencing construction costs than school size alone. Unfortunately, statewide comparison of construction costs is not apples to apples. A limitation of linear regression over a large geographic study area is that a one-size-fits-all model can be biased by locally significant variables. The model was strengthened by analyzing the data using GIS and geographically weighted regression, which only considers neighboring schools when calculating the regression trend.

Visualizing how far each school deviates from the regression line gives a clearer picture for comparison. The maps illustrate the residual values as a percentage over or under the predicted cost values on the geographically weighted regression line.

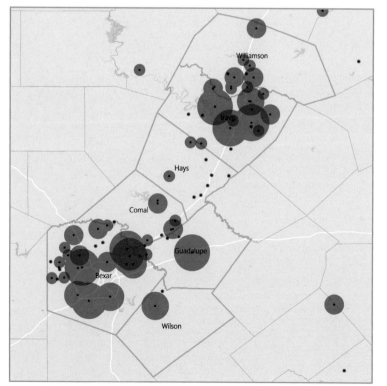

Analyzing the relationship between Cons
Square Feet using Linear Regression (Glo

Percent Over- or Under- Cost Prediction Line using G

Austin-San Antonio   Dalla

tion Cost and
Model)

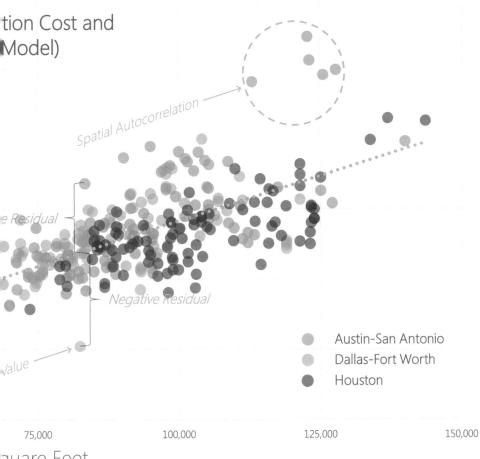

Spatial Autocorrelation

e Residual

Negative Residual

Value

- Austin-San Antonio
- Dallas-Fort Worth
- Houston

75,000   100,000   125,000   150,000

quare Feet

graphically Weighted Regression (Local Model)

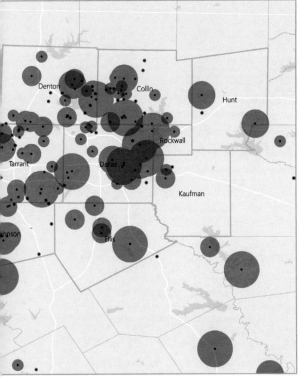

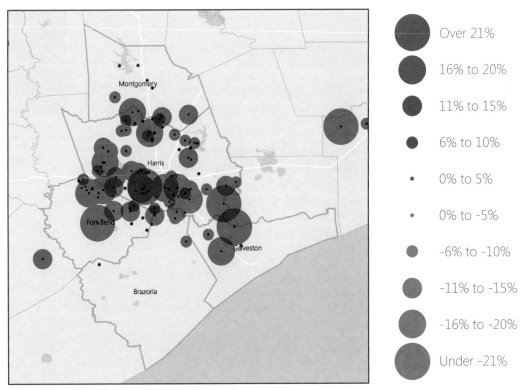

- Over 21%
- 16% to 20%
- 11% to 15%
- 6% to 10%
- 0% to 5%
- 0% to -5%
- -6% to -10%
- -11% to -15%
- -16% to -20%
- Under -21%

ort Worth   Houston

High Temporal Frequency Unmanned Aerial Systems Imagery in GIS

University of Wisconsin-Eau Claire
Eau Claire, Wisconsin, USA
By Brendan Miracle, Michael Bomber, and Dr. Joseph P. Hupy

Contact

Joseph Hupy
hupyjp@uwec.edu

Software

ArcGIS 10.3 for Desktop, Pix4Dmapper, GEMS Software Tool, Mission Planner, Adobe Illustrator

Data Sources

Imagery collected with the GEMS Sensor Payload at 60 meters above ground, flown with the 3DR Iris+, RPFS Spectre, and TurboACE Matrix platforms

Unmanned aerial systems are revolutionary to the world of GIS for their abilities to not only provide high spatial resolution imagery, but also for providing data at high temporal resolution. This series of images demonstrates how unmanned aerial systems can be used to frequently analyze different types of vegetation growth in contrasting environments.

RGB (red, green, blue) and near-infrared (NIR) imagery were simultaneously collected using the GEMS Sensor Payload each week. The finished RGB and NIR orthomosaics were imported to ArcMap to create a composite image. When the composite images were completed, false infrared images were then used to calculate a normalized difference vegetation index to visualize the varying vegetation health between each week.

Courtesy of Brendan Miracle, Michael Bomber, and Dr. Joseph P. Hupy of the University of Wisconsin-Eau Claire Department of Geography and Anthropology.

Community Garden

Week 1 - 6/4/2015

Pond

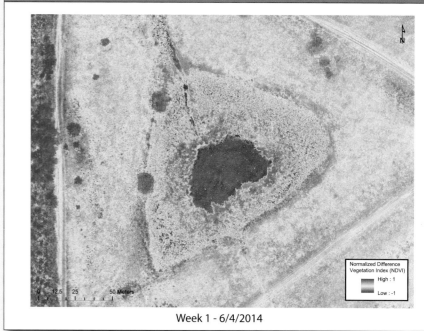

Week 1 - 6/4/2014

Normalized Difference Vegetation Index (NDVI)
High : 1
Low : -1

0 2.5 5   10 Meters

k 2 - 6/12/2015

Week 3 - 6/18/2015

Week 4 - 6/26/2015

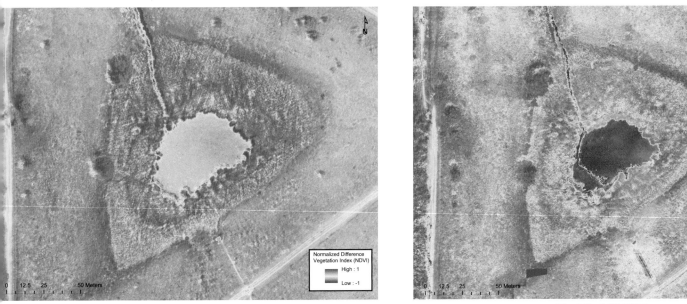

Normalized Difference Vegetation Index (NDVI)
High : 1
Low : -1

0 12.5 25   50 Meters

Week 2 - 6/12/2014

Week 3 - 6/18/2015

Mission Planning

Image Processing

Trivariate Sea Ice Presence

National Ice Center (NIC)
Washington, DC, USA
By Mark Denil

Contact
Mark Denil
mark.denil@noaa.gov

Software
ArcGIS 10.1 for Desktop, Adobe Illustrator

Data Sources
US National/Naval Ice Center

The goal of this project was to provide a comprehensive, easily understood evaluation of the history of documented sea ice presence for US National Ice Center (NIC) clients and analysts. The three-dimensional color gradient allows complex conditions to be quickly assessed visually. The NIC is a multiagency operational center run jointly by the US Navy, the National Oceanic and Atmospheric Administration, and the US Coast Guard.

Courtesy of US National/Naval Ice Center.

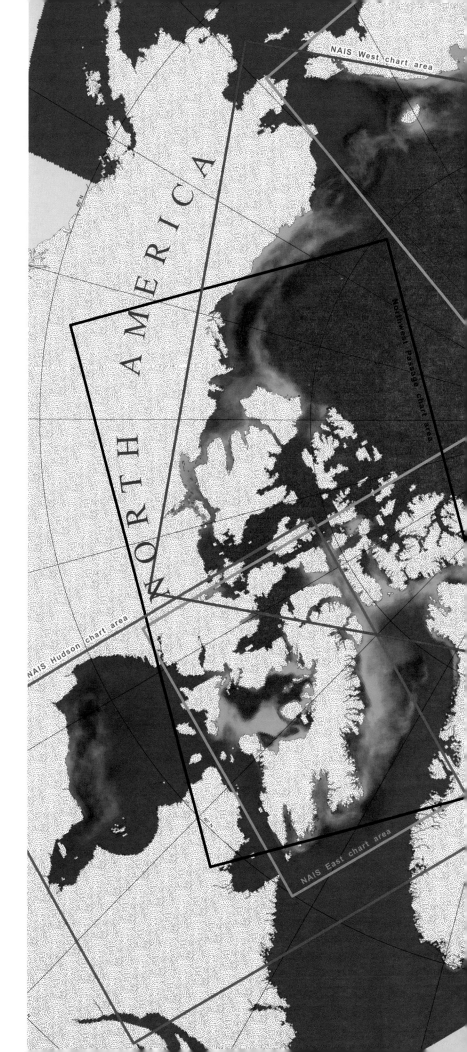

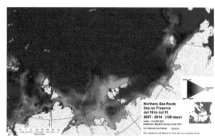

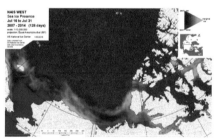

Dispalyed here is a full set of the six standard image maps for the Arctic that are output in PNG format for use on Power Point briefing slides. They differ from the PDF format printable maps by having all the map furniture located within the map rectangle. This leaves useful slide real estate for other briefing information, even when the image is used full frame.

A similar set of standard maps exists for the Antarctic.

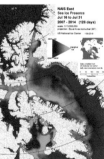

Standard data product outputs:

- geodatabase feature classes

- kml files

- pdf maps (for print at 8½ x 11)

- png images (for PowerPoint slides)

Two geodatabase feature classes are output for each pole and year:

- one covering a single year and one compendium: 2007 to date

- each feature class has 24 layers 1st of the month to the 15th 16th of the month to month's end

Other study periods can be built up from the half month data.

49

Polar Bear Population Status and Trends

Government of Canada
Gatineau, Quebec, Canada
By Mark Richardson, Environment and Climate
Change Canada

Contact

Mark Richardson
mark.richardson@canada.ca

Software

ArcGIS 10.1 for Desktop, ArcGIS Spatial Analyst

Data Sources

Canadian subpopulation status provided by the
PBTC 2015 and PBSG 2014

This map shows the recent trend in polar bear subpopulations across the circumpolar Arctic. Assessments are based on recent scientific information that is compared to previous population estimates over a 12-to-15-year time period. Subpopulation polygons are primarily based on movement patterns of female bears wearing satellite collars, but should be considered management units as they do not represent true biological subpopulations because they are not genetically distinct.

The trend assessments in the thirteen Canadian subpopulations are based on work by the Canadian Polar Bear Technical Committee (PBTC). Trend assessments for the remaining six subpopulations of polar bears are made by the International Union for Conservation of Nature/Species Survival Commission Polar Bear Specialist Group (PBSG). Estimated population sizes are determined via field research, such as mark-recapture methodologies employed over a period of three to four years, and modeling techniques. The most recent assessment was conducted in 2015 by PBTC.

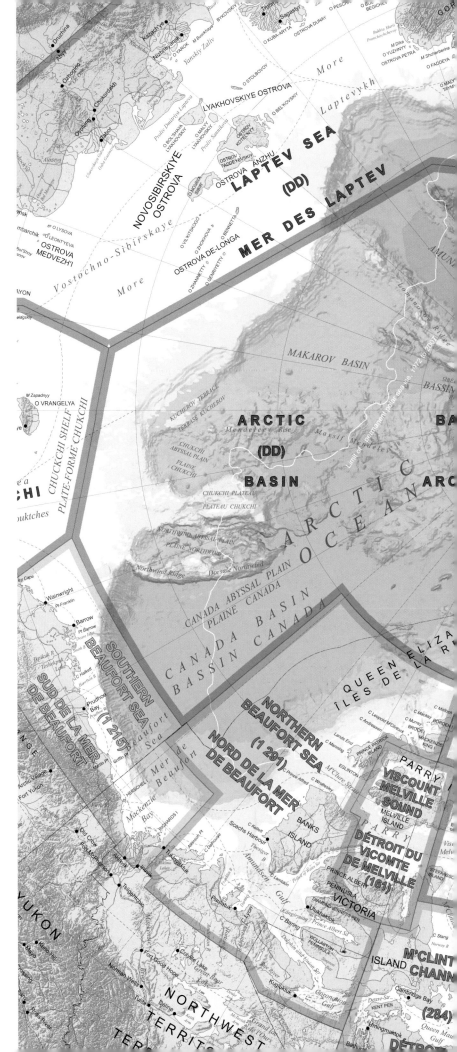

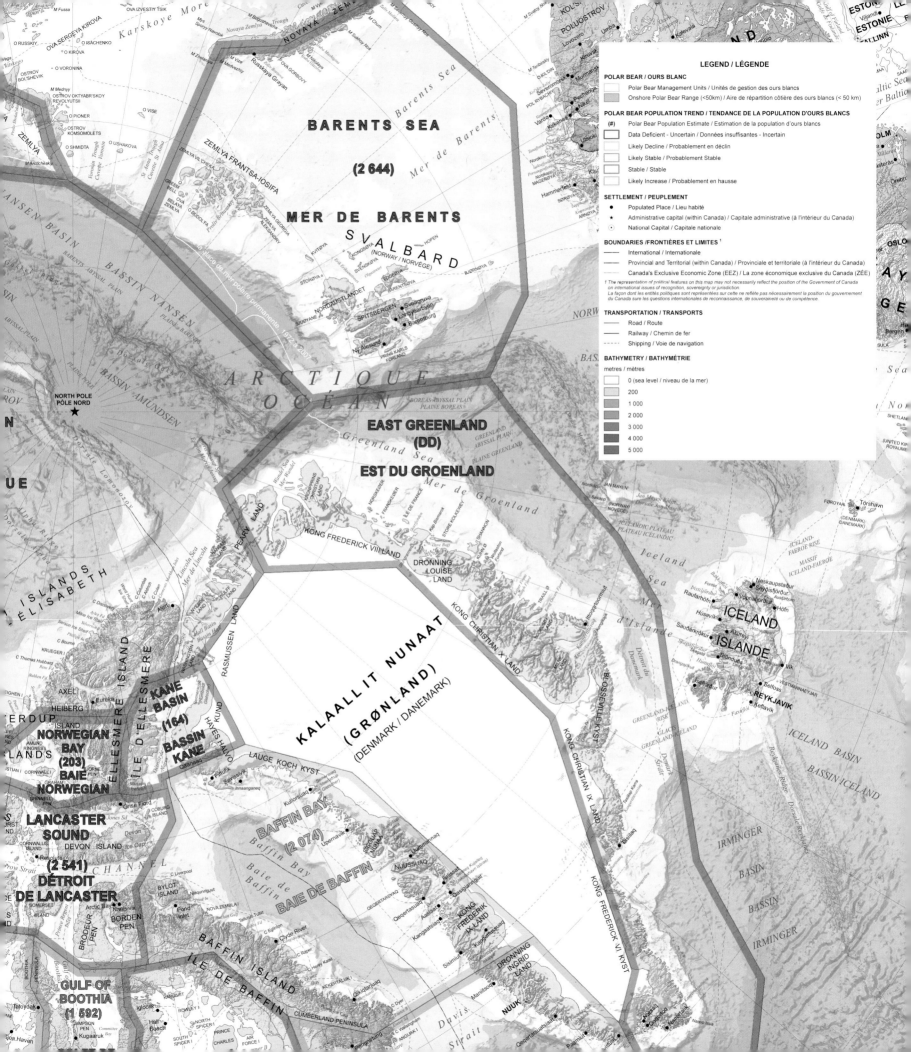

LEGEND / LÉGENDE

POLAR BEAR / OURS BLANC

Polar Bear Management Units / Unités de gestion des ours blancs
Onshore Polar Bear Range (<50km) / Aire de répartition côtière des ours blancs (< 50 km)

POLAR BEAR POPULATION TREND / TENDANCE DE LA POPULATION D'OURS BLANCS

(#) Polar Bear Population Estimate / Estimation de la population d'ours blancs
Data Deficient - Uncertain / Données insuffisantes - Incertain
Likely Decline / Probablement en déclin
Likely Stable / Probablement Stable
Stable / Stable
Likely Increase / Probablement en hausse

SETTLEMENT / PEUPLEMENT

• Populated Place / Lieu habité
★ Administrative capital (within Canada) / Capitale administrative (à l'intérieur du Canada)
⊙ National Capital / Capitale nationale

BOUNDARIES /FRONTIÈRES ET LIMITES [1]

International / Internationale
Provincial and Territorial (within Canada) / Provinciale et territoriale (à l'intérieur du Canada)
Canada's Exclusive Economic Zone (EEZ) / La zone économique exclusive du Canada (ZÉE)

[1] The representation of political features on this map may not necessarily reflect the position of the Government of Canada on international issues of recognition, sovereignty or jurisdiction.
La façon dont les entités politiques sont représentées sur cette ne reflète pas nécessairement la position du gouvernement du Canada sur les questions internationales de reconnaissance, de souveraineté ou de compétence.

TRANSPORTATION / TRANSPORTS

Road / Route
Railway / Chemin de fer
Shipping / Voie de navigation

BATHYMETRY / BATHYMÉTRIE
metres / mètres

0 (sea level / niveau de la mer)
200
1 000
2 000
3 000
4 000
5 000

Estimate of the Future Carbon Budget on the Korean Peninsula

Korea University
Seoul, Republic of South Korea
By Damin Kim and Woo-Kyun Lee

Contact
Damin Kim
daminkim14@gmail.com

Software
ArcGIS 10.2.1 for Desktop

Data Source
Global land cover 30 and RCP 8.5 scenario

A carbon budget is the amount of carbon dioxide that a country, company, or organization has agreed is the largest it will produce in a particular period of time. On the Korean peninsula, while South and North Korea are located at the same latitude zone (from 30 to 40 degrees), they have different environmental conditions, especially forests, which makes a difference in carbon sequestration ability.

To manage and reduce carbon dioxide emissions, it is necessary to quantify carbon emissions caused by humans and carbon uptake from the terrestrial ecosystem. The aim of the study was to show the difference between the two countries and to elucidate the variation in the future carbon budget due to climate change for preparing approaching vulnerability.

Copyright 2015 Environmental GIS/RS Center.

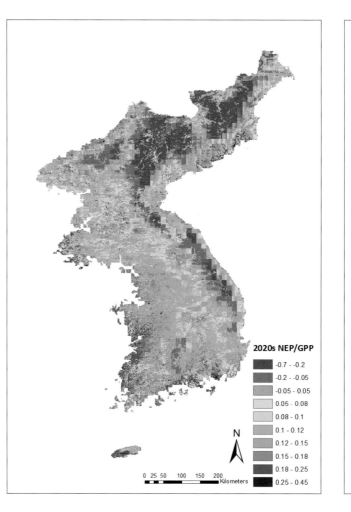

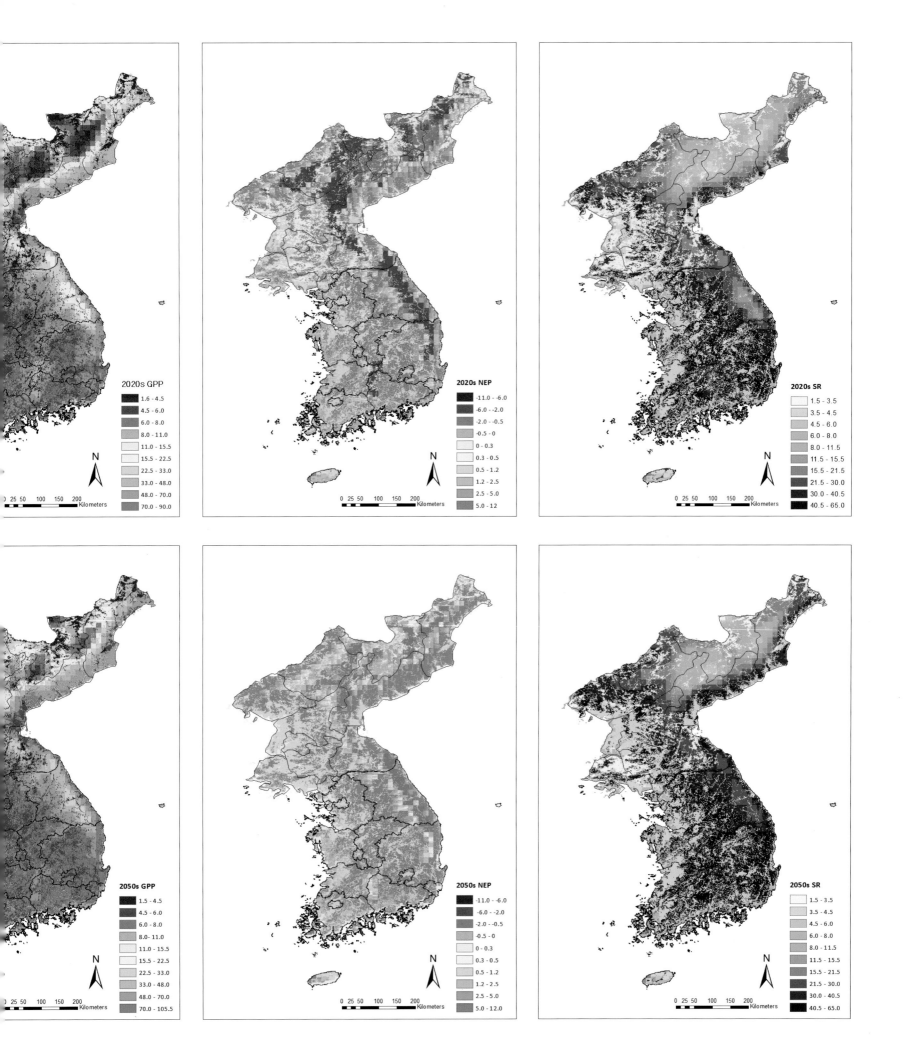

2020s GPP

- 1.6 - 4.5
- 4.5 - 6.0
- 6.0 - 8.0
- 8.0 - 11.0
- 11.0 - 15.5
- 15.5 - 22.5
- 22.5 - 33.0
- 33.0 - 48.0
- 48.0 - 70.0
- 70.0 - 90.0

N

0 25 50 100 150 200 Kilometers

2020s NEP

- -11.0 - -6.0
- -6.0 - -2.0
- -2.0 - -0.5
- -0.5 - 0
- 0 - 0.3
- 0.3 - 0.5
- 0.5 - 1.2
- 1.2 - 2.5
- 2.5 - 5.0
- 5.0 - 12

N

0 25 50 100 150 200 Kilometers

2020s SR

- 1.5 - 3.5
- 3.5 - 4.5
- 4.5 - 6.0
- 6.0 - 8.0
- 8.0 - 11.5
- 11.5 - 15.5
- 15.5 - 21.5
- 21.5 - 30.0
- 30.0 - 40.5
- 40.5 - 65.0

N

0 25 50 100 150 200 Kilometers

2050s GPP

- 1.5 - 4.5
- 4.5 - 6.0
- 6.0 - 8.0
- 8.0 - 11.0
- 11.0 - 15.5
- 15.5 - 22.5
- 22.5 - 33.0
- 33.0 - 48.0
- 48.0 - 70.0
- 70.0 - 105.5

N

0 25 50 100 150 200 Kilometers

2050s NEP

- -11.0 - -6.0
- -6.0 - -2.0
- -2.0 - -0.5
- -0.5 - 0
- 0 - 0.3
- 0.3 - 0.5
- 0.5 - 1.2
- 1.2 - 2.5
- 2.5 - 5.0
- 5.0 - 12.0

N

0 25 50 100 150 200 Kilometers

2050s SR

- 1.5 - 3.5
- 3.5 - 4.5
- 4.5 - 6.0
- 6.0 - 8.0
- 8.0 - 11.5
- 11.5 - 15.5
- 15.5 - 21.5
- 21.5 - 30.0
- 30.0 - 40.5
- 40.5 - 65.0

N

0 25 50 100 150 200 Kilometers

Fire Progressions—North Rim of Grand Canyon National Park

National Park Service, Grand Canyon National Park
Grand Canyon, Arizona, USA
By Eric Gdula

Contact

Eric Gdula
eric_gdula@nps.gov

Software

ArcGIS 10.2 for Desktop

Data Source

National Park Service

This map depicts individual fire perimeters from fourteen protracted fire events spanning fourteen years on the North Rim of Grand Canyon National Park. The dark colors represent early/initial fire perimeters while the redder colors indicate the most recent/final perimeters.

Data was acquired as needed based on fire activity. On active fires, two perimeters per day might be acquired, though several days might pass between perimeters due to slow growth. Initial perimeters are mapped by walking when fires are small. As fires grow and walking is no longer safe, perimeters are acquired from the park's helicopter.

Courtesy of Grand Canyon National Park, Division of Fire and Aviation.

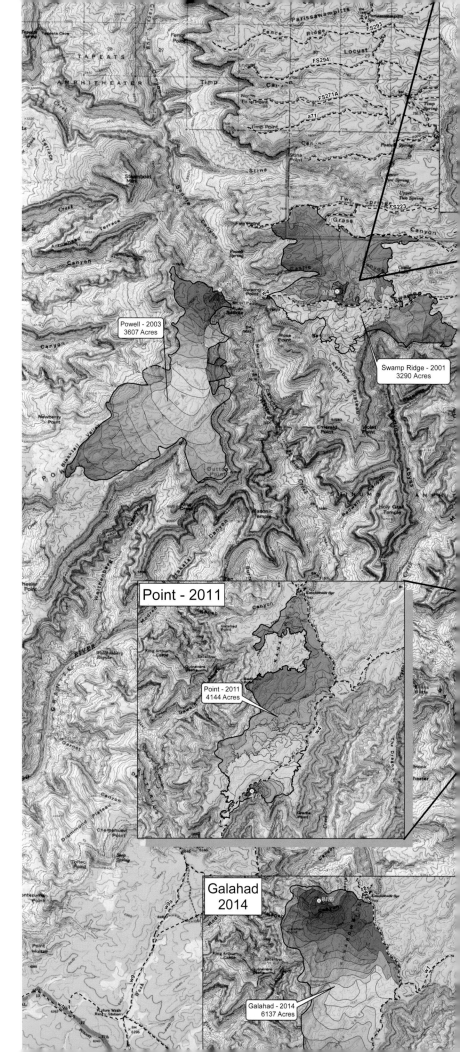

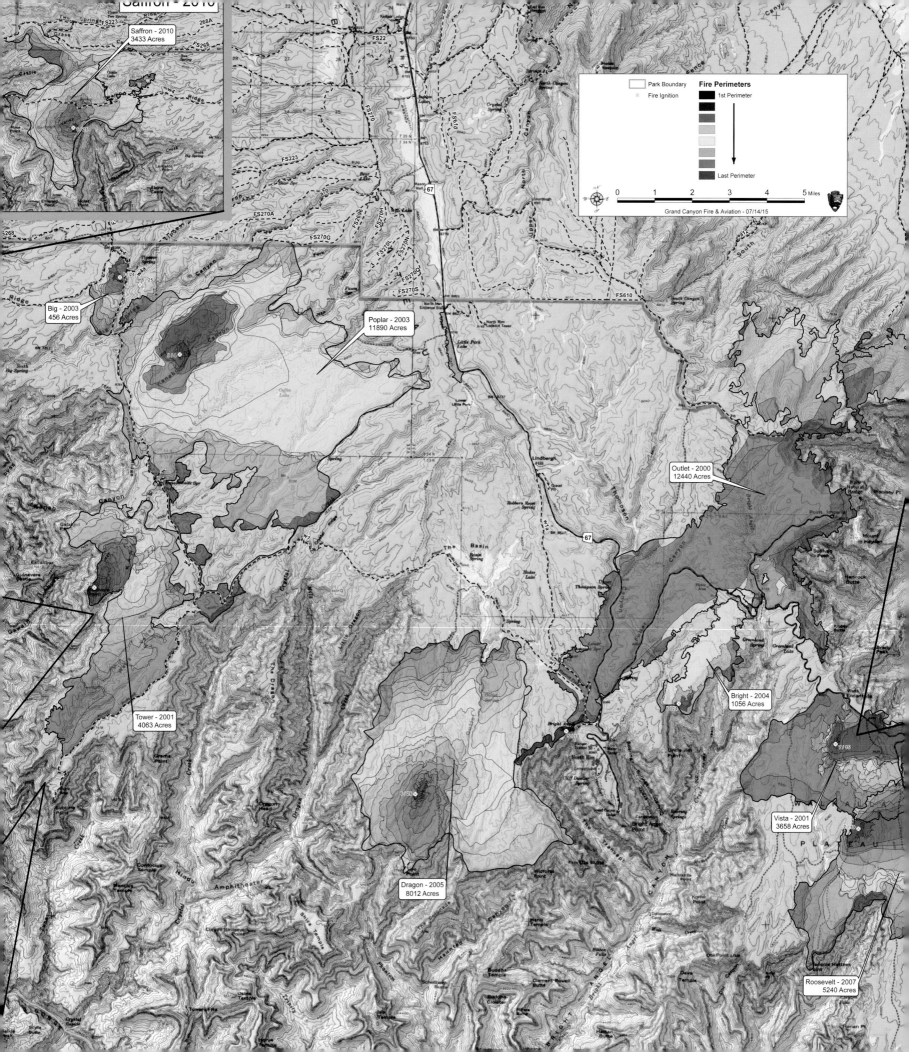

Saffron - 2010
3433 Acres

Big - 2003
456 Acres

Poplar - 2003
11890 Acres

Outlet - 2000
12440 Acres

Bright - 2004
1056 Acres

Tower - 2001
4063 Acres

Vista - 2001
3658 Acres

Dragon - 2005
8012 Acres

Roosevelt - 2007
5240 Acres

Park Boundary

Fire Ignition

Fire Perimeters

1st Perimeter

Last Perimeter

0   1   2   3   4   5 Miles

Grand Canyon Fire & Aviation - 07/14/15

A Three-Part Suitability Analysis for Cobb County, Georgia

Cobb County
Marietta, Georgia, USA
By James Fitzgerald and Jennifer Lana

Contact
Jennifer Lana
Jennifer.Lana@cobbcounty.org

Software
ArcGIS 10.2 for Desktop

Data Sources
Cobb County, Cobb County Base Data, Geospatial Data Gateway, and Georgia GIS Clearinghouse

Due to remarkable growth in Cobb County, Georgia, county officials set out to answer the common question of where to live. Cobb County is part of the Atlanta metro region, and the US Census estimates growth at 6.2 percent, which equates to about 11,000 new residents yearly.

Analysis determined the most and least desirable residential locations based on crime incidents, public facilities, schools, yearly income, residential property values, and cell tower positions. Real estate professionals, developers, citizens, and newcomers can benefit from the analysis by concentrating and dedicating efforts to the most desired locations based on those factors. Just as citizens focus on the most desirable locations, elected officials can focus their attention to improve the least desirable locations. This analysis sets a benchmark for understanding the county's needs moving forward. This will support putting into practice effective measures for improvement and allocating funds to assist desirability for the entire county.

Courtesy of Cobb County, Georgia.

Suitability Analysis

⊕ Airports

—— Major Road Buffer

☐ Interstate Noise Buffer

☐ CobbCounty

Desirability Range

Highest Desirability

Lowest Desirability

City of Scottsdale Fire Headquarters Maps

City of Scottsdale

Scottsdale, Arizona, USA

By Mele D. Koneya and Adam Shuckhart

Contact

Mele D. Koneya

mkoneya@scottsdaleaz.gov

Software

ArcGIS 10.2.2 for Desktop, ArcGIS Spatial Analyst, ArcGIS Network Analyst, Adobe Photoshop, Adobe Illustrator, Abobe InDesign

Data Source

City of Scottsdale

Developed by the City of Scottsdale GIS staff under the direction of the Scottsdale Fire Department, these maps display station locations, station apparatus, and city landmarks on a basemap. In addition, two separate maps show the calls for service density and four-minute response areas.

An interactive display allows users to change the map display by sliding the transparent overlays, which show incidents and four-minute response polygons over the basemap. Additionally, the basemap was coated with a special material so that markers can be used to sketch on the maps.

The interactive display allows Fire Department staff to show elected officials and the public where the greatest density of calls for service is, the coverage provided by the four-minute response areas, and how the locations of stations impact the level of service the Fire Department provides.

Courtesy of City of Scottsdale GIS.

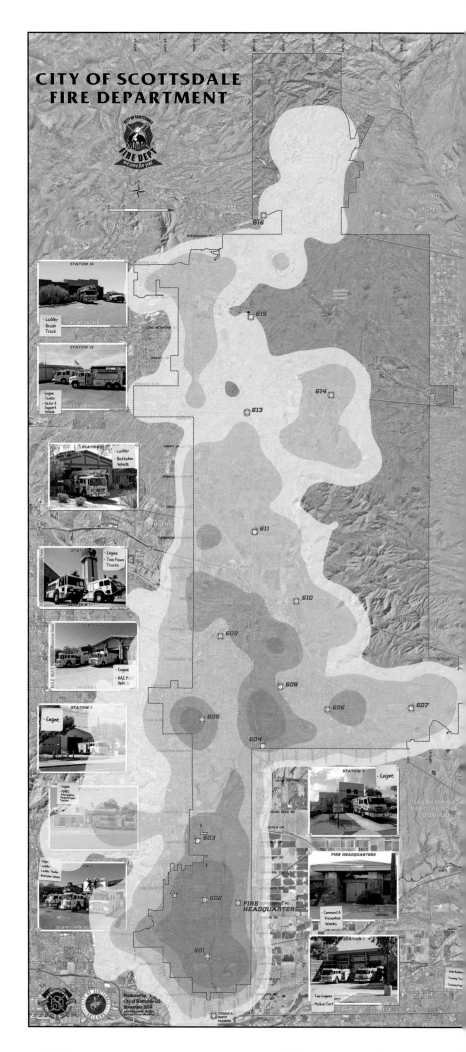

CITY OF SCOTTSDALE
FIRE DEPARTMENT

STATION 16
- Engine
- Brush Truck

STATION 15
- Ladder
- Brush Truck

STATION 13
- Engine
- Tender
- Gator & Support Vehicle

STATION 14
- Engine
- Tender

STATION 16
- Engine
- Brush Truck

STATION 14
- Engine
- Tender

SFD by the numbers

Total Stations 15
Number of Apparatus 33
Sworn Personnel 245
Civilian Personnel 15
City Area .... 184.5 sq. miles
City Extent .... 31 miles - North to South
City Population 226,918

Four Minute Polygons

SFD Response time goal: within 4 minutes, 80% of the time

Average Travel Time (min:sec) 4:29

STATION
- Ladder
- Battalion Vehicle

STATION
- Engine
- Two Foam Trucks

STATION 10
- Engine
- 50RT Truck

STATION 9
- Engine
- HAZ MAT Vehicle

STATION 5
- Engine

STATION 7
- Engine
- Brush Truck

STATION 4
- Engine

STATION 3
- Engine
- PPRS (Pre-positioned Patient Response System)

FIRE HEADQUARTERS
- Command & Prevention Vehicles

STATION 6
- Ladder
- Ladder Tender

STATION 2
- Engine
- Ladder Tender
- Battalion Vehicle

STATION 1
- Two Engines
- Medical Cart

THOMAS A. HONTZ TRAINING FACILITY

Produced by:
City of Scottsdale GIS
November 2016

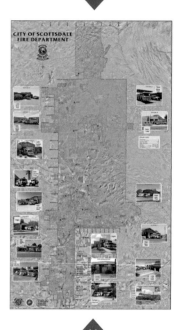

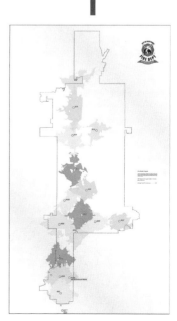

Coal Creek Floodplain Mapping and Flood Hazard Management Zones

Northwest Hydraulic Consultants (NHC)
North Vancouver, British Columbia, Canada
By Joe Drechsler and Sarah North

Contact
Joe Drechsler
jdrechsler@nhcweb.com

Software
ArcGIS 10.1 for Desktop

Data Sources
The BC Freshwater Atlas, City of Fernie, Focus Engineering

The flood inundation map was created using numerical modeling results that were converted to water surfaces, from which a digital elevation model was subtracted. This resulted in a depth grid, indicating the inundation extent of the simulated flood scenario. Maps such as these are used to assist city planners in determining flood construction levels.

The flood hazard zones were determined by combining the numerical modeling water depth data with water velocity data to determine high-risk areas. These zones are used to indicate areas that pose different threat levels during a flood event.

Courtesy of NHC, the City of Fernie, British Columbia.

Mount Morris Dam Failure Hazus Simulation within Monroe County, New York

Monroe County, New York
Rochester, New York, USA
By Justin D. Cole, GISP

Contact
Justin Cole
justin.cole.GIS@gmail.com

Software
ArcGIS 10.2.2 for Desktop, Hazus 2.2

Data Sources
Monroe County lidar, parcels, town boundaries, Hazus inundation models, and critical infrastructure; City of Rochester building models

Mount Morris Dam is located on the Genesee River in Mount Morris, New York, and is roughly 62 miles from the next control structure in the city of Rochester; upstream of the dam is 97 miles of river. The dam at full capacity would be about 17 river miles of water and 180 feet high.

For this analysis, Monroe County officials used only the straight volume of water being discharged down the river and that would take an hour to reach the city, which was an overestimation but good for discussion. This data was plugged into Hazus risk-assessment software loaded with the county's lidar digital elevation model. The processing took eleven days and the results mirrored older paper copies of a break estimate.

This model illustrates that any real flooding of the Genesee River would split the county in half before High Falls. Many of the county facilities are in this zone, so the analysis resulted in discussion on backups to maintain services. Even with the inundation model, the 3D models of downtown illustrate the amount of damage possible. Many of the areas have water above the first floors of the buildings, and all underground areas would be flooded out.

Courtesy of Justin D. Cole, GISP.

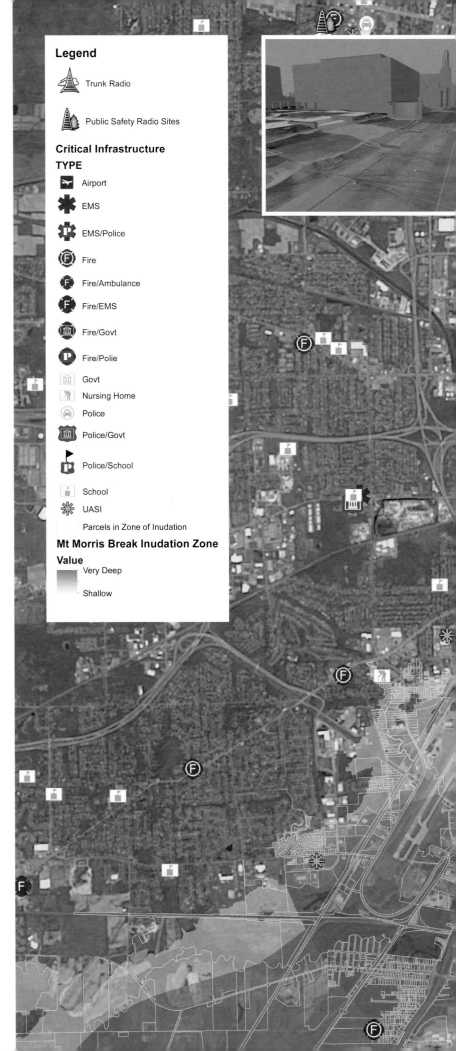

Legend

⛺ Trunk Radio

🗼 Public Safety Radio Sites

Critical Infrastructure
TYPE
✈ Airport
✳ EMS
✚ EMS/Police
Ⓕ Fire
F Fire/Ambulance
Ⓕ Fire/EMS
Ⓕ Fire/Govt
Ⓟ Fire/Polie
🏛 Govt
Nursing Home
Police
Police/Govt
⚑ Police/School
School
❋ UASI
Parcels in Zone of Inudation

Mt Morris Break Inudation Zone
Value
Very Deep
Shallow

City of Boston Hurricane Evacuation Zone Development

City of Boston
Boston, Massachusetts, USA
By Stacey Schwartz

Contact

Stacey Schwartz
stacey.schwartz@boston.gov

Software

ArcGIS 10.0.2 for Desktop

Data Sources

US Army Corps of Engineers, City of Boston

The City of Boston Office of Emergency Management (OEM) produced the city's *Hurricane Evacuation Zones* map by adapting, refining, and further developing the US Army Corps of Engineers' (USACE) proposed evacuation zones for Boston.

This undertaking began after the USACE's 2013 release of the Massachusetts Hurricane Surge Inundation Mapping products. OEM wanted to achieve the highest fidelity possible with regard to threatened areas and, based on that information, develop evacuation zones that effectively and efficiently addressed at-risk sections of the city. Eight storm scenarios were used, with each one accounting for a variation in direction and storm intensity. OEM also wanted to assess the impact of each of these with regard to population density of the threatened areas.

These maps illustrate the end result of this yearlong project. They depict the layered analytical aggregation of census blocks into hurricane evacuation zones based on modeled inundation impacts for different tropical storm scenarios. The evacuation zones continue to be updated as population, landscape, and storm surge variables change.

Courtesy of Boston Office of Emergency Management.

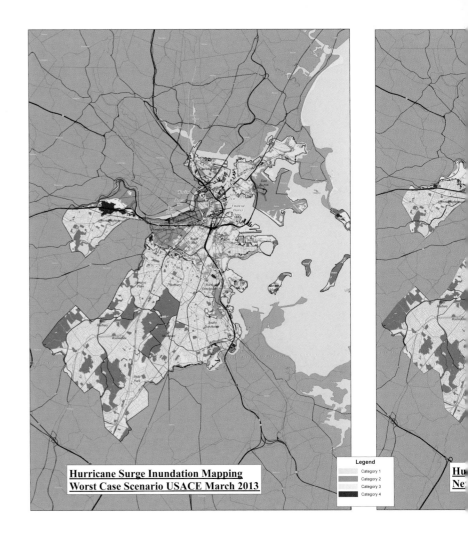

Hurricane Surge Inundation Mapping
Worst Case Scenario USACE March 2013

Legend
Category 1
Category 2
Category 3
Category 4

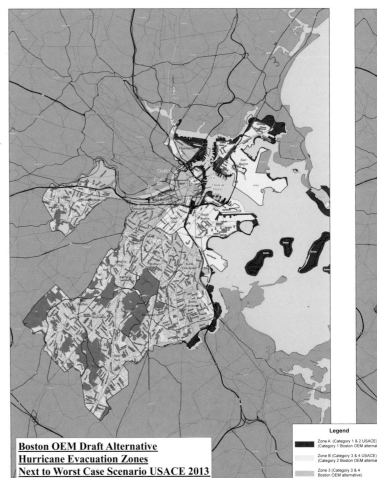

Boston OEM Draft Alternative
Hurricane Evacuation Zones
Next to Worst Case Scenario USACE 2013

Legend
Zone A (Category 1 & 2 USACE)
(Category 1 Boston OEM alternative)
Zone B (Category 3 & 4 USACE)
(Category 2 Boston OEM alternative)
Zone 3 (Category 3 & 4
Boston OEM alternative)

Surge Inundation Mapping
rst Case Scenario USACE March 2013

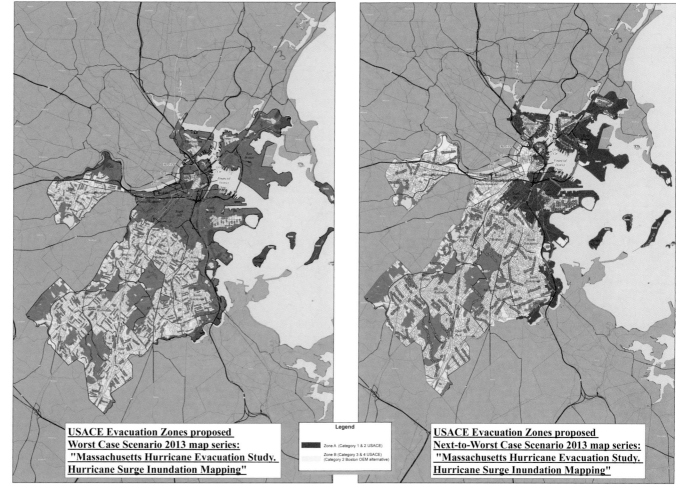

USACE Evacuation Zones proposed
Worst Case Scenario 2013 map series:
"Massachusetts Hurricane Evacuation Study.
Hurricane Surge Inundation Mapping"

Legend

Zone A (Category 1 & 2 USACE)

Zone B (Category 3 & 4 USACE)
(Category 2 Boston OEM alternative)

USACE Evacuation Zones proposed
Next-to-Worst Case Scenario 2013 map series:
"Massachusetts Hurricane Evacuation Study.
Hurricane Surge Inundation Mapping"

Boston OEM Draft Alternative
Hurricane Evacuation Zones
Worst Case Scenario USACE 2013

WCS (Worst Case Scenario) and NWC (Next-Worst Case Scenario) Hurricane Evacuation Zones

Legend

Zone A NWC Category 1
Population 33,255

Zone B WCS Category 1 and
NWC Category 2
(Popoulation 135,089)

Zone C WCS Category 2 and
both WCS and NWC Categories 3 & 4
Population 139,375

0   0.5   1   2
Miles

N

Traffic, Accidents, and Safety—A Historical Analysis of Collision Patterns in Southern California

Southern California Association of Governments (SCAG)
Los Angeles, California, USA
By Jung Seo, Tom Vo, and Jonathan Rivas

Contact
Jung Seo
seo@scag.ca.gov

Software
ArcGIS 10.3 for Desktop

Data Source
California Highway Patrol's Statewide Integrated Traffic Records System

The Southern California Association of Governments (SCAG) is the nation's largest metropolitan planning organization, representing six counties, 191 cities, and more than 18 million residents. SCAG undertakes a variety of planning and policy initiatives to encourage a more sustainable Southern California now and in the future.

These maps depict the collision patterns from 2003 to 2012 in Southern California to better understand the changes in car, bicycle, pedestrian, and truck collision patterns and also to examine the spatial relationship between high collisions and disadvantaged communities. It uses data from the Statewide Integrated Traffic Records System maintained by the California Highway Patrol.

Courtesy of Southern California Association of Governments.

Pedestrian Collisions

2003

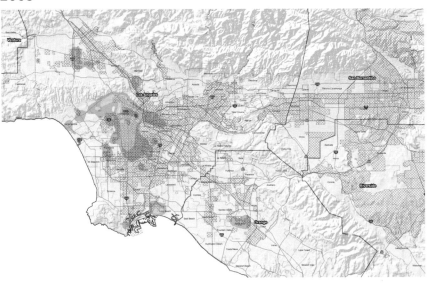

2008

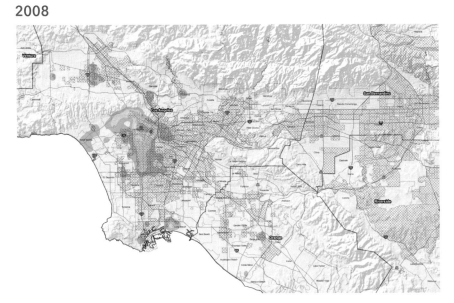

2012

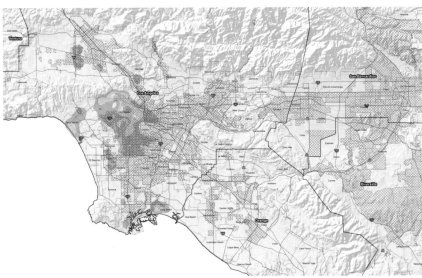

Truck Collisions

2003

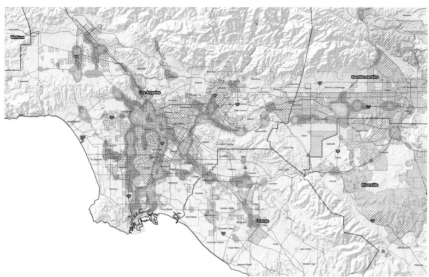

2008

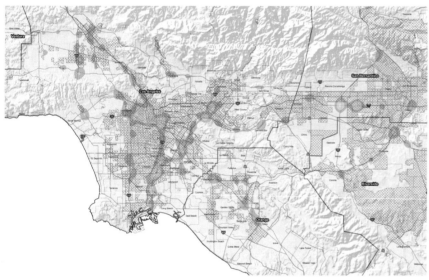

2012

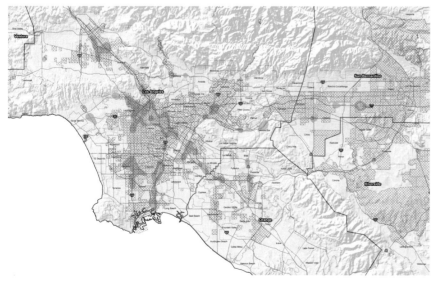

Bike Collisions

2003

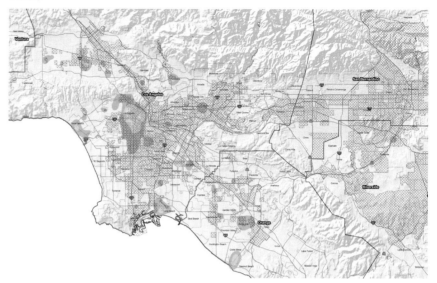

2008

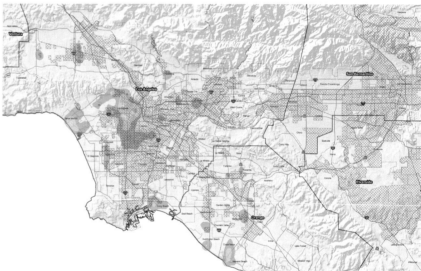

2012

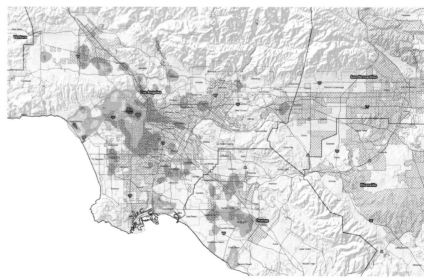

Sea-Level Rise Vulnerability Mapping of South Florida

Florida Atlantic University
Boca Raton, Florida, USA
By Hannah Cooper

Contact
Hannah Cooper
hcooper2013@fau.edu

Software
ArcGIS 10.2.2 for Desktop

Data Source
Florida Division of Emergency Management lidar

South Florida is known as ground zero for sea-level rise (SLR) due to its low elevations and gentle slopes characterizing coastal areas that support human populations and natural ecosystems. Decision makers are faced with the problem of adapting to SLR.

High-resolution and better vertical accuracy SLR vulnerability maps are critical because they illustrate potential assets at risk in their local communities. An existing lidar digital elevation model from the Florida Division of Emergency Management was used to identify areas vulnerable to long-term flooding. Overall, this SLR vulnerability map serves as a valuable tool in raising local decision makers' awareness of the potential impacts in their municipality as they are beginning to consider adaptation strategies.

Courtesy of Hannah Cooper.

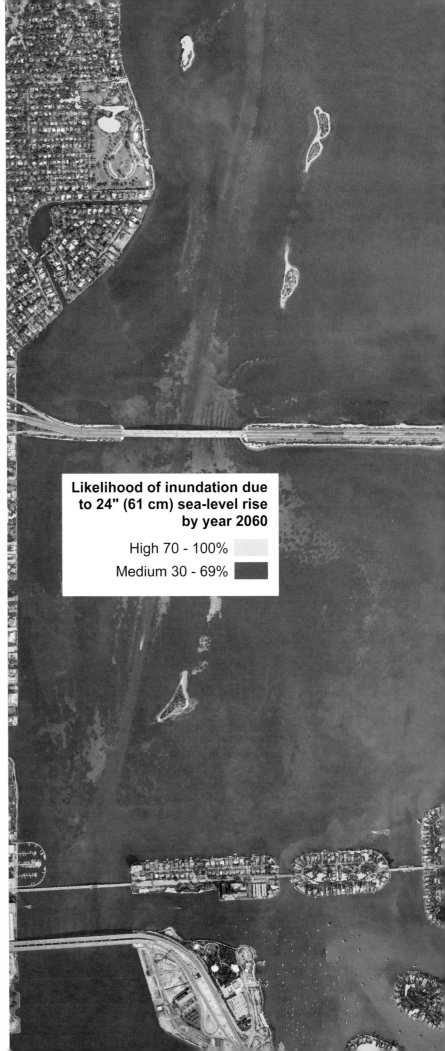

Likelihood of inundation due to 24" (61 cm) sea-level rise by year 2060

High 70 - 100%
Medium 30 - 69%

Biscayne Bay

Miami Beach

Emergency Operations Center Maps

City of Scottsdale
Scottsdale, Arizona, USA
By Mele D. Koneya

Contact
Mele D. Koneya
mkoneya@scottsdaleaz.gov

Software
ArcGIS 10.2.2 for Desktop, Adobe Illustrator,
Adobe InDesign

Data Source
City of Scottsdale

The City of Scottsdale maintains and staffs an emergency operations center (EOC) which provides operational decision support during weather events, public safety issues, and a variety of activities in Scottsdale and neighboring communities. These maps were created by the city's GIS staff to familiarize EOC staff and others from outside agencies with features within Scottsdale.

Courtesy of City of Scottsdale GIS.

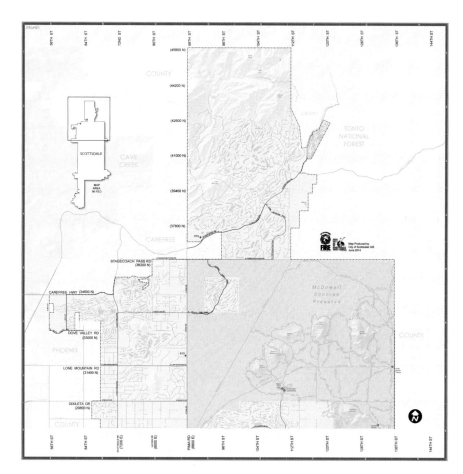

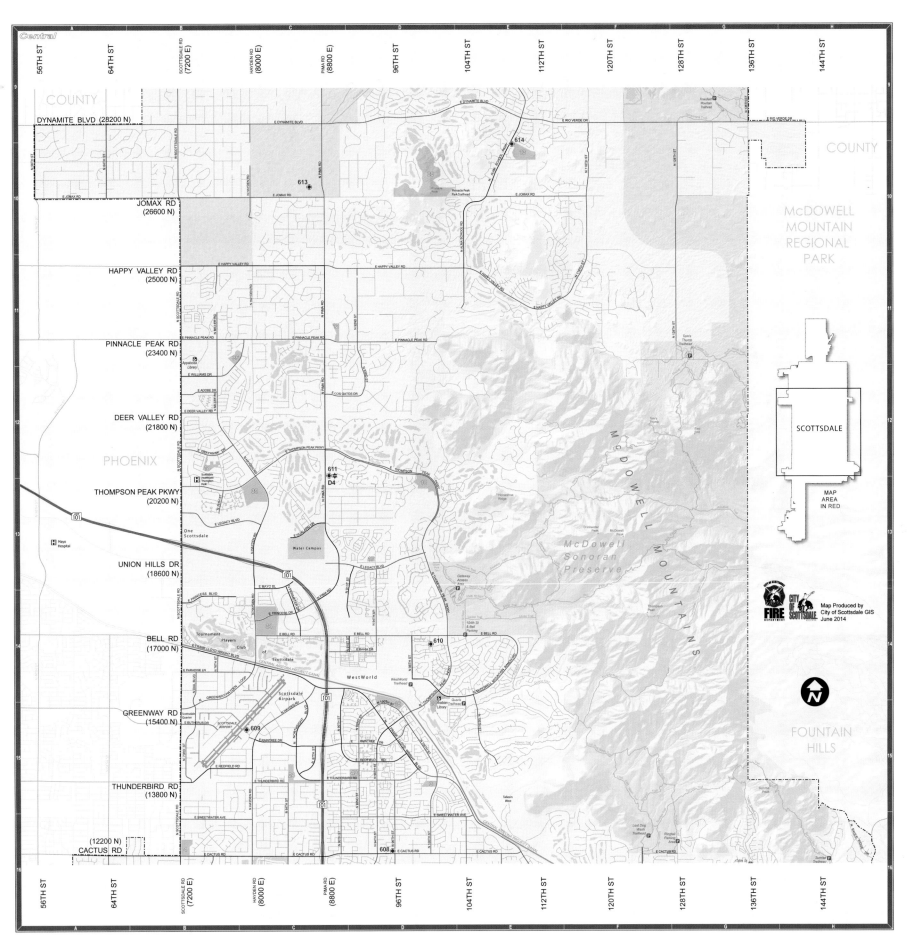

MAP AREA IN RED

SCOTTSDALE

Map Produced by
City of Scottsdale GIS
June 2014

71

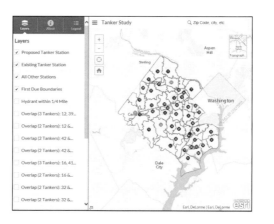

The Fairfax County Fire and Rescue Department's Website

Fairfax County Fire and Rescue Department
Fairfax, Virginia, USA
By Shelby Zelonis, Eric Fisher, and Keg Good

Contact
Shelby Zelonis
shelby.zelonis@fairfaxcounty.gov

Software
ArcGIS 10.2 for Desktop, ArcGIS Online

Data Source
The County of Fairfax, Virginia

The Fairfax County Fire and Rescue Department's (FRD) GIS team fills mapping and spatial data requests from all FRD personnel. A common problem is the time-sensitive nature of fire and rescue operations. Stations are staffed at all times and the GIS team is not always available to address issues when they arise. Firefighters need to be able to quickly access maps and spatial data. Many of the datasets are dynamic and constantly updated.

Maps on the Fairfax County ArcGIS Online website provide personnel with the tools they need to quickly access commonly requested GIS data. All FRD staff has access to the site for viewing a suite of web mapping applications from any web browser at any time. Personnel can view, collect, and map ever-changing data such as first due response areas for each station, estimated travel time data, and fire hydrant locations. Staff can also access planning and analysis tools, take a map tour of the FRD stations across the county, and perform area familiarization training exercises.

Courtesy of the Fairfax County, Virginia, Fire and Rescue Department.

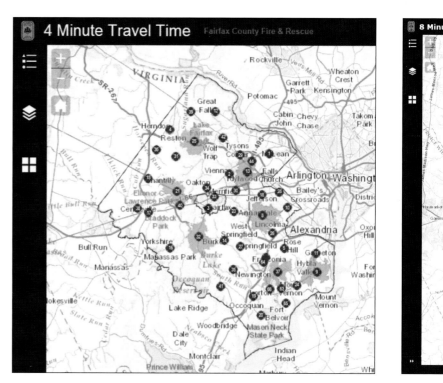

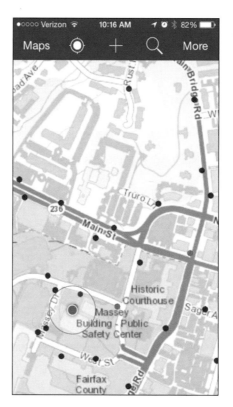

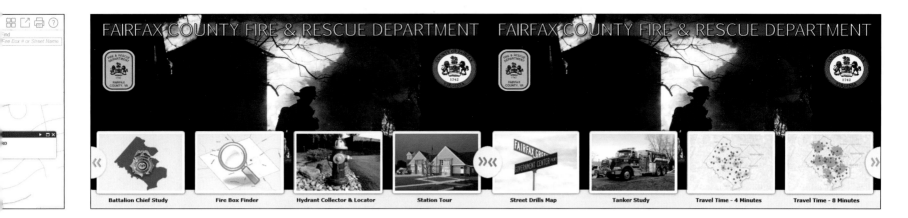

Battalion Chief Study   Fire Box Finder   Hydrant Collector & Locator   Station Tour   Street Drills Map   Tanker Study   Travel Time – 4 Minutes   Travel Time – 8 Minutes

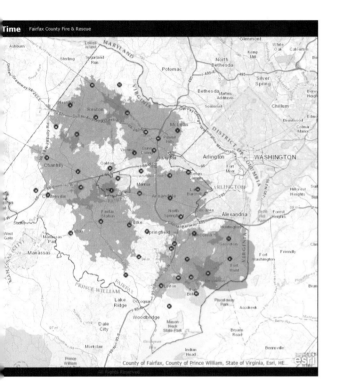

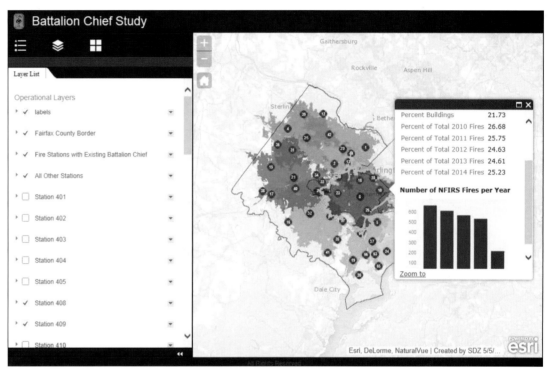

Battalion Chief Study

Layer List

Operational Layers

- ✓ labels
- ✓ Fairfax County Border
- ✓ Fire Stations with Existing Battalion Chief
- ✓ All Other Stations
- ☐ Station 401
- ☐ Station 402
- ☐ Station 403
- ☐ Station 404
- ☐ Station 405
- ✓ Station 408
- ✓ Station 409
- ☐ Station 410

County of Fairfax, County of Prince William, State of Virginia, Esri, HE...

Percent Buildings	21.73
Percent of Total 2010 Fires	26.68
Percent of Total 2011 Fires	25.75
Percent of Total 2012 Fires	24.63
Percent of Total 2013 Fires	24.61
Percent of Total 2014 Fires	25.23

Number of NFIRS Fires per Year

Zoom to

Esri, DeLorme, NaturalVue | Created by SDZ 5/5/...

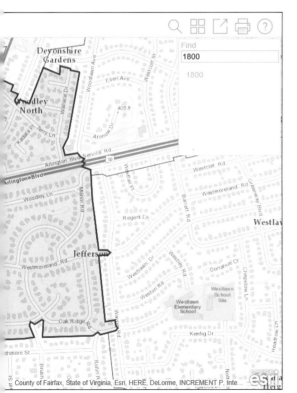

Find
1800
1800

County of Fairfax, State of Virginia, Esri, HERE, DeLorme, INCREMENT P, Inte...

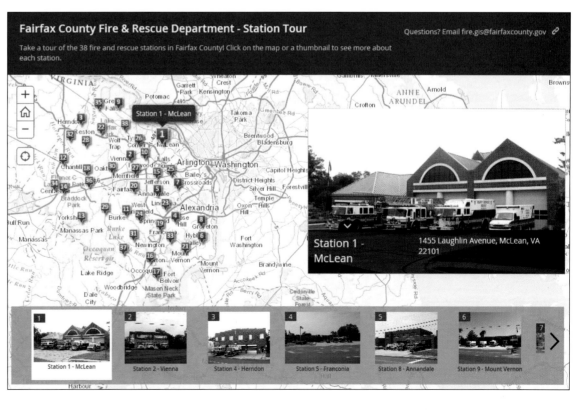

Fairfax County Fire & Rescue Department - Station Tour

Questions? Email fire.gis@fairfaxcounty.gov

Take a tour of the 38 fire and rescue stations in Fairfax County! Click on the map or a thumbnail to see more about each station.

Station 1 - McLean

Station 1 - McLean   1455 Laughlin Avenue, McLean, VA 22101

Station 1 - McLean   Station 2 - Vienna   Station 4 - Herndon   Station 5 - Franconia   Station 8 - Annandale   Station 9 - Mount Vernon

Siting Fire Units: Where to Place Air Compressors

Fairfax County, Virginia
Fairfax, Virginia, USA
By Keg Good

Contact

Keg Good
keg.good@fairfaxcounty.gov

Software

ArcGIS 10.2.1 for Desktop, ArcGIS Network Analyst

Data Source

Fairfax County, Virginia

A firefighter depends on a self-contained breathing apparatus (SCBA) in hazardous environments. Under duress,
each SCBA air tank provides air for only 10 to 30 minutes.
Because of daily testing, the SCBA tanks can become less
than full. Fairfax County studied the placement of mobile and
stationary air compressors used to fill SCBA tanks. The goal
was to minimize the distance and time traveled by firefighters
to top off their tanks.

Using the origin-destination cost matrix analysis within ArcGIS
Network Analyst, the existing locations were reviewed, as
well as the minimal number and optimal placement of air
compressors required for all firefighters to refill their tanks
within 7 to 10 minutes of travel time.

With the current placement of eleven air compressors, firefighters from two stations must travel an unacceptable 10
minutes or more to top off. Moving the locations of the
mobile units gives all firefighters access within 10 minutes of
travel time. By optimizing ten air compressor sites, all firefighters can reach a site within 10 minutes. By optimizing
fifteen air compressor sites, all firefighters can reach a site
within 7 minutes.

Courtesy of Fairfax County, Virginia Fire and Rescue Department.

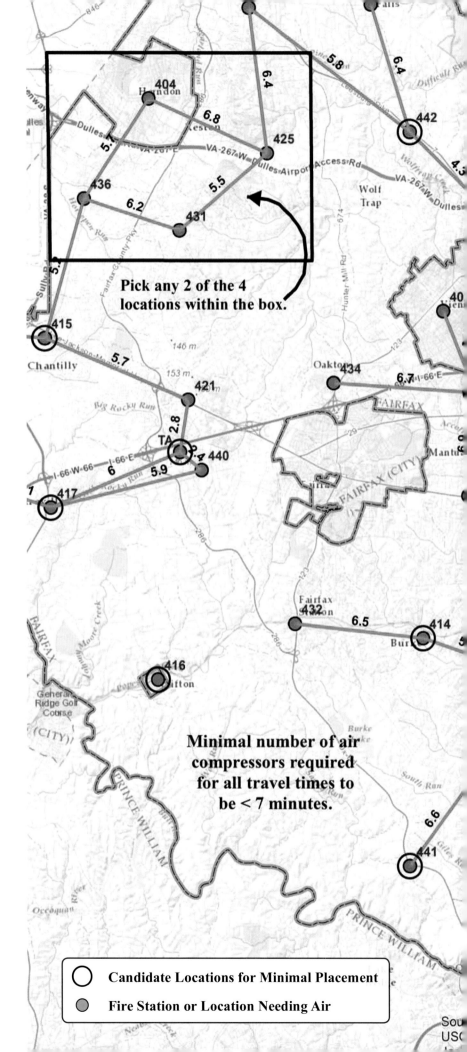

Pick any 2 of the 4 locations within the box.

Minimal number of air compressors required for all travel times to be < 7 minutes.

○ **Candidate Locations for Minimal Placement**

● **Fire Station or Location Needing Air**

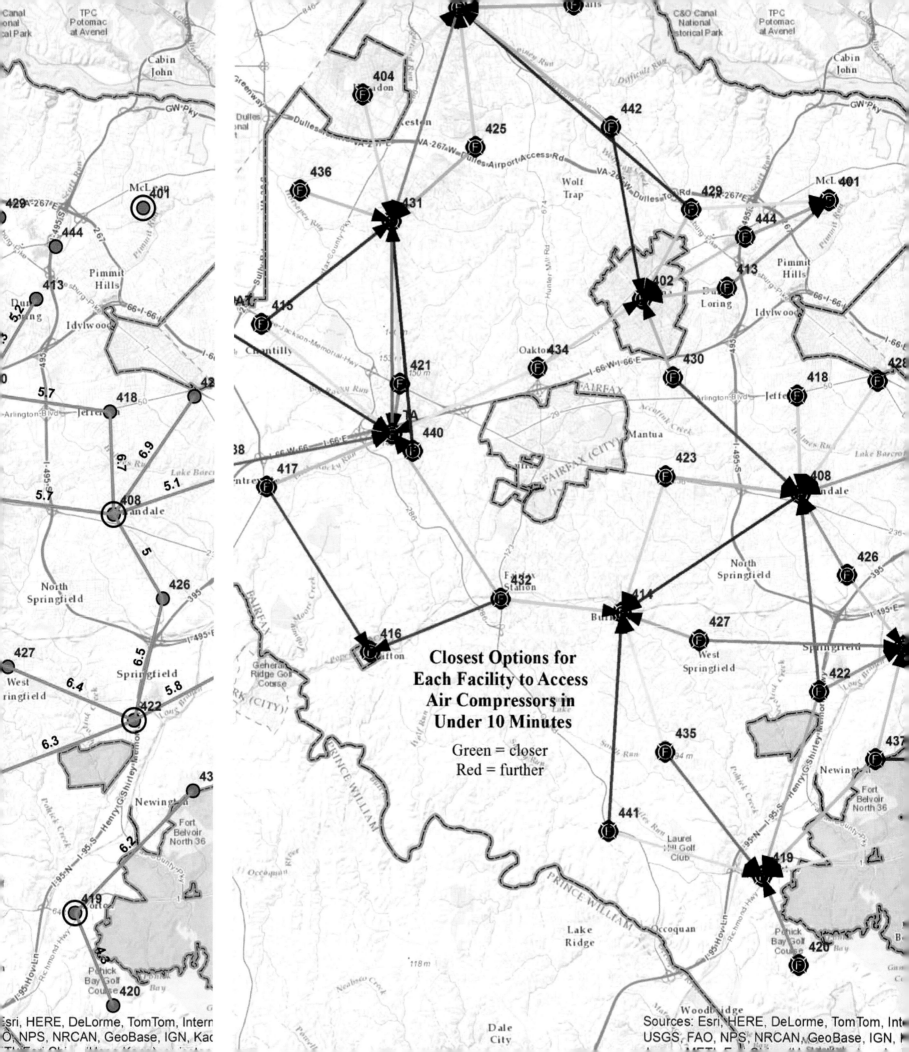

**Closest Options for
Each Facility to Access
Air Compressors in
Under 10 Minutes**

Green = closer
Red = further

Statewide Hazmat Teams' Response Time

California Governor's Office of Emergency Services (Cal OES)
Mather, California, USA
By Hans Frederiksen

Contact

Hans Frederiksen
hans.frederiksen@caloes.ca.gov

Software

ArcGIS 10.3 for Desktop, Adobe Illustrator CS5

Data Source

Certified hazmat teams

The California Governor's Office of Emergency Services (Cal OES) is a cabinet-level agency responsible for overseeing and coordinating emergency preparedness, response, recovery, and homeland security activities within the state. ArcGIS Network Analyst was used to examine service areas around Certified Hazardous Material Team locations throughout California. The result of this analysis provided potential response areas within 15, 30, and 60 minutes. These results offer a summary of Certified Hazardous Materials Team accessibility to locales within the specified response times.

Courtesy of Hans Frederiksen, Cal OES GIS.

1-Hour Response Coverage			
*Calculated in Miles²			
Mutual Region	15 Minutes	30 Minutes	60 Minutes
1	1369	1979	19905
2	1909	2521	32037
3	383	1312	4909
4	630	2697	11391
5	805	3592	12580
6	939	5825	17491

- ⬡ Mutual Aid Region
- County Boundary
- ★ City
- Major Roadway

Certified Haz-Mat Team (01/25/2016)
- ● Type 1
- ● Type 2
- ○ Type 3

Railroad Owner
- Union Pacific
- Burlington Northern Santa Fe
- High Hazard Rail

Response Time
(minutes)

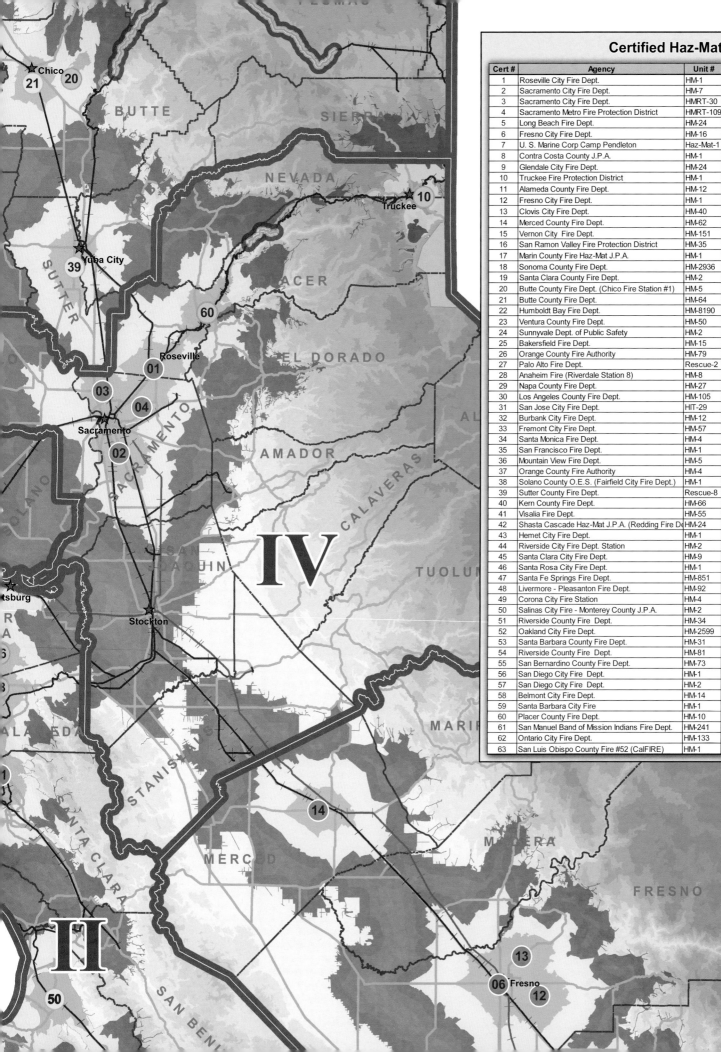

Certified Haz-Mat Teams

Cert #	Agency	Unit #	15 Mins (mi²)	30 Mins (mi²)	45 Mins (mi²)
1	Roseville City Fire Dept.	HM-1	157	550	2302
2	Sacramento City Fire Dept.	HM-7	151	545	2385
3	Sacramento City Fire Dept.	HMRT-30	100	542	2305
4	Sacramento Metro Fire Protection District	HMRT-109	98	478	2165
5	Long Beach Fire Dept.	HM-24	82	426	1348
6	Fresno City Fire Dept.	HM-16	212	732	2537
7	U. S. Marine Corp Camp Pendleton	Haz-Mat-1	8	69	572
8	Contra Costa County J.P.A.	HM-1	132	554	2036
9	Glendale City Fire Dept.	HM-24	171	589	1790
10	Truckee Fire Protection District	HM-1	31	157	439
11	Alameda County Fire Dept.	HM-12	141	616	1747
12	Fresno City Fire Dept.	HM-1	136	484	1996
13	Clovis City Fire Dept.	HM-40	143	447	1902
14	Merced County Fire Dept.	HM-62	122	453	1686
15	Vernon City Fire Dept.	HM-151	185	718	1545
16	San Ramon Valley Fire Protection District	HM-35	88	338	1782
17	Marin County Fire Haz-Mat J.P.A.	HM-1	72	392	1481
18	Sonoma County Fire Dept.	HM-2936	117	399	985
19	Santa Clara County Fire Dept.	HM-2	131	446	1527
20	Butte County Fire Dept. (Chico Fire Station #1)	HM-5	19	135	788
21	Butte County Fire Dept.	HM-64	89	364	1234
22	Humboldt Bay Fire Dept.	HM-8190	52	152	199
23	Ventura County Fire Dept.	HM-50	117	285	881
24	Sunnyvale Dept. of Public Safety	HM-2	157	521	1394
25	Bakersfield Fire Dept.	HM-15	92	441	1267
26	Orange County Fire Authority	HM-79	165	475	1664
27	Palo Alto Fire Dept.	Rescue-2	146	539	1386
28	Anaheim Fire (Riverdale Station 8)	HM-8	152	692	1929
29	Napa County Fire Dept.	HM-27	120	355	1571
30	Los Angeles County Fire Dept.	HM-105	92	326	1961
31	San Jose City Fire Dept.	HIT-29	140	475	1665
32	Burbank City Fire Dept.	HM-12	154	619	1777
33	Fremont City Fire Dept.	HM-57	136	622	1812
34	Santa Monica Fire Dept.	HM-4	105	517	1628
35	San Francisco Fire Dept.	HM-1	119	473	1850
36	Mountain View Fire Dept.	HM-5	147	548	1422
37	Orange County Fire Authority	HM-4	120	418	1495
38	Solano County O.E.S. (Fairfield City Fire Dept.)	HM-1	127	549	2216
39	Sutter County Fire Dept.	Rescue-8	131	516	1850
40	Kern County Fire Dept.	HM-66	145	530	1195
41	Visalia Fire Dept.	HM-55	120	505	1997
42	Shasta Cascade Haz-Mat J.P.A. (Redding Fire De	HM-24	126	388	1037
43	Hemet City Fire Dept.	HM-1	126	418	1508
44	Riverside City Fire Dept. Station	HM-2	163	602	2179
45	Santa Clara City Fire Dept.	HM-9	155	459	1489
46	Santa Rosa City Fire Dept.	HM-1	131	416	1061
47	Santa Fe Springs Fire Dept.	HM-851	153	724	1524
48	Livermore - Pleasanton Fire Dept.	HM-92	120	561	2205
49	Corona City Fire Station	HM-4	116	575	2254
50	Salinas City Fire - Monterey County J.P.A.	HM-2	140	285	869
51	Riverside County Fire Dept.	HM-34	110	380	1542
52	Oakland City Fire Dept.	HM-2599	149	592	1926
53	Santa Barbara County Fire Dept.	HM-31	108	294	654
54	Riverside County Fire Dept.	HM-81	117	320	425
55	San Bernardino County Fire Dept.	HM-73	116	579	2210
56	San Diego City Fire Dept.	HM-1	100	433	1001
57	San Diego City Fire Dept.	HM-2	84	412	969
58	Belmont City Fire Dept.	HM-14	142	496	1414
59	Santa Barbara City Fire	HM-1	64	116	484
60	Placer County Fire Dept.	HM-10	116	425	1795
61	San Manuel Band of Mission Indians Fire Dept.	HM-241	80	341	1772
62	Ontario City Fire Dept.	HM-133	212	922	3059
63	San Luis Obispo County Fire #52 (CalFIRE)	HM-1	97	387	1225

Walkability—City of Manhattan, Kansas

City of Manhattan
Manhattan, Kansas, USA
By Jared Tremblay

Contact

Jared Tremblay
tremblay@cityofmhk.com

Software

ArcGIS 10.3 for Desktop

Data Source

City of Manhattan GIS data, Riley County,
Kansas parcels

Manhattan is a quickly growing university city of 55,000, located in northeast Kansas. The city land-use patterns and developments range from a dense grid network to cul-de-sac suburbia. These developments play a large role in lifestyle, with influences on issues such as transportation, utility usage and needs, social interactions, and mental and physical health. Walkability is a method to measure those issues in a way that clearly shows proximity to services and amenities, while also highlighting how development patterns influence connectivity.

A network dataset was created consisting of sidewalks, trails, and local streets. Data points, representing many amenities used in daily life, were created and awarded scores based on their services offered, usability, diversity, and density. Service areas were run on all amenity layers to create a composite score for each land parcel. A custom color ramp was created to highlight parcel scores on a scale from pedestrian centered to vehicle dependent. The goal of this map was to establish a benchmark score for walkability and then to use it as development occurs to look for ways to improve livability.

Courtesy of the City of Manhattan, Kansas.

ATA Bus Stop   Museum

Bar - Coffee Shop   Restaurant

Gas Station - Convenience   School

Grocery Store   Shopping - Retail Area

K-State Event Center   City Boundary

Library   Park

Major Attraction   K-State Parcel

Miles

0   ¼   ½   ¾   1

City of MHK's Median   City of MHK's Mean (Avg)

Total Walkable Score

0 1 2 3 4 5 6 7 8 9 10 11 12 13 14 15 16 17 18 19 20 21 22 23 24 25 26 27 28 29 30 31 32 33 34 35 36 37 38 39 40 41 42 43 44 45 46 47 48 49 50 51 52 53

Vehicle Dependent   Somewhat Walkable   Pedestrian Centered

20140306_Walkability

A Bright Idea

Springville Power and Light
Springville, Utah, USA
By Johnny Snow

Contact

Johnny Snow
snow@springville.org

Software

ArcGIS 10.3 for Desktop

Data Source

Springville City, Utah Automated Geographic
Reference Center

Street lighting is a fundamental service that Springville Power
and Light provides. LED (light-emitting diode) lighting is an
excellent example of how the utility can provide better service
as well as cut costs. Springville Power and Light is migrating to
LED light fixtures from older technology lights such as metal
halide, high-pressure sodium, and mercury vapor. In addition
to being energy efficient and environmentally friendly, LED
lights cast a larger light footprint.

This map was developed to visualize the street light inventory
and the light footprint that can be expected from each type
of light. It is also helpful in planning where to direct resources
toward installing LED lights. This map clearly shows the
number of LEDs in operation and the increased light footprint
cast by the LEDs.

Courtesy of Johnny Snow, Springville City Power and Light.

244 Mercury Vapor Lights Removed
Replaced Old Street Lighting with
Environmentally Friendly,
Energy Efficent ,
Safer, Brighter,
Lighting

Historic Plat "A"

●	LIGHT EMITTING DIODE	LED	687
○	METAL HALIDE		65
○	HIGH PRESSURE SODIUM		1,333
●	MERCURY VAPOR		0

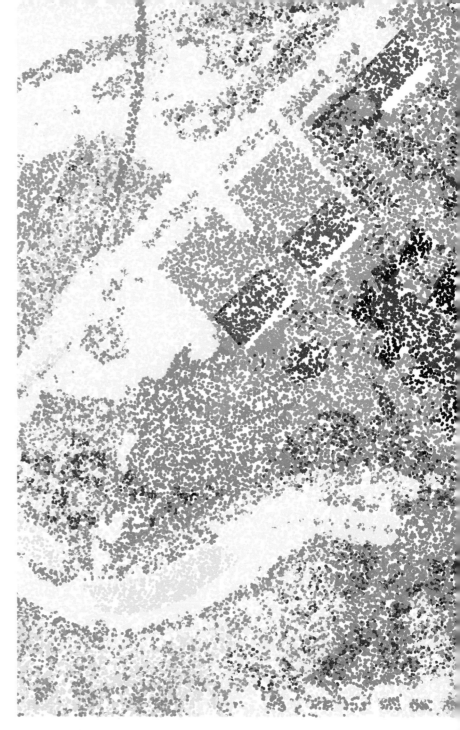

A Thirty-Thousand-Foot Overview of Lidar
InterDev
Atlanta, Georgia, USA
By Michael Edelson, GISP

Contact
Michael Edelson, GIS Manager
medelson@interdev.com

Software
ArcGIS 10.2 for Desktop, ArcGIS 3D Analyst,
ArcGIS Spatial Analyst, SketchUp

Data Sources
US Geological Survey, Op Tech Inc., Colorado
State University, Penn State University, Esri,
University of Georgia, Lidar-UK.com

In December 2012, the City of Brookhaven became Georgia's
newest incorporated city. In Brookhaven's first month of exis-
tence, the city purchased aerial photography and lidar data in
a joint venture with neighboring cities Sandy Springs, Roswell,
Alpharetta, and Dunwoody.

The Brookhaven City Council and staff were well aware of the
potential cost savings and uses for lidar when developing
ground elevation and surface water models. However, the GIS
Department understood that the City Council and staff lacked
an understanding of lidar beyond those very important uses.

Maps were created to promote a better understanding of lidar
for the City Council, city staff, and citizens during GIS Day 2014
activities for DeKalb County, Georgia. The goal was to help the
community better understand how lidar data is being used to
help make communities safer and more efficient.

Courtesy of the City of Brookhaven, Georgia.

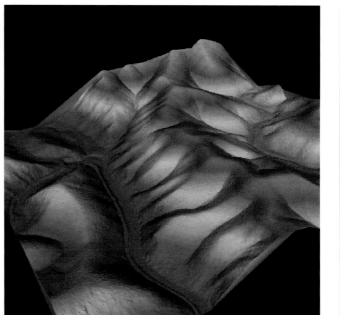

	80m+
	60-80m
	35-60m
	15-35m
	0-15m

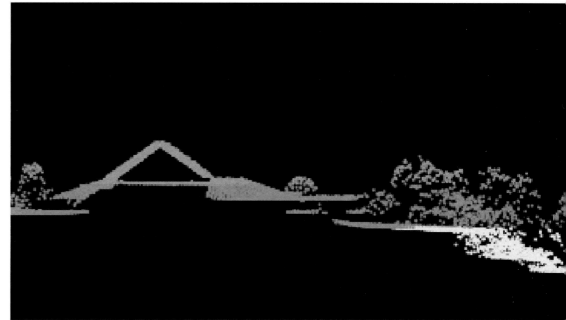
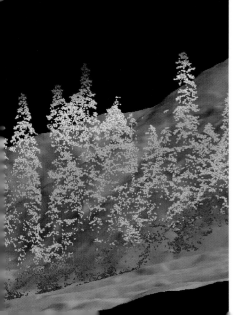

Richmond Gentrification Analysis

Haas Institute for a Fair and Inclusive Society,
University of California, Berkeley
Berkeley, California, USA
By Samir Gambhir and Phuong Tseng

Contact

Samir Gambhir
samirgambhir.2@gmail.com

Software

ArcGIS 10.1 for Desktop

Data Sources

Census 2000, American Community Survey 5-yr
estimates 2009–2013, US Department of Housing
and Urban Development, Esri

The Haas Institute for a Fair and Inclusive Society assessed the
extent of gentrification in Richmond, a city of 107,000 in the
San Francisco Bay area. Researchers analyzed changes in the
demographics and housing market between the years 2000
and 2013.

Gentrification trends in Richmond were analyzed at the neighborhood level by adapting the methodology of previous
analyses of Portland, San Francisco, and Oakland. People
and housing conditions are analyzed across three domains—
vulnerable population, demographic change, and housing
market conditions—to estimate the state of gentrification in
a given city. The analysis is done at the level of the block
group, a set of boundaries created by the US Census that in
Richmond has an average population of 1,428 residents.

*Courtesy of Haas Institute for a Fair and Inclusive Society, University of
California, Berkeley.*

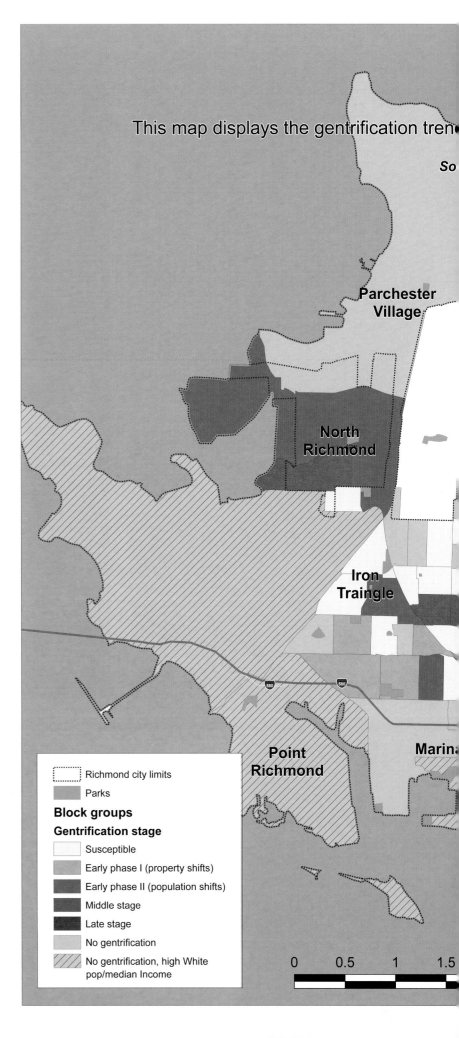

GENTRIFICATION TRENDS
RICHMOND CITY, CALIFORNIA

ased on multiple indicators by block group within the city

Census 2000, ACS 2009-2013 5-yr estimates, ESRI | Date: Feb 12, 2015

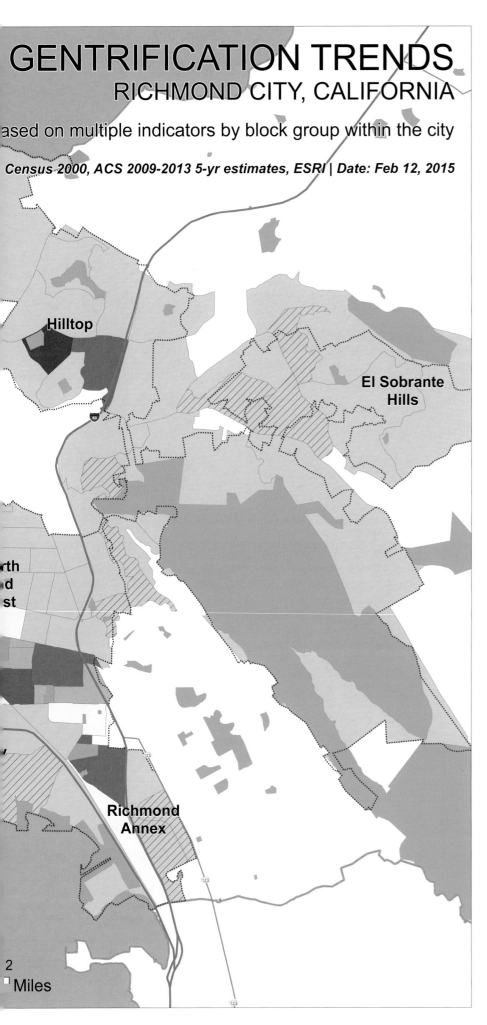

Hilltop

El Sobrante Hills

rth
d
st

Richmond Annex

2

Miles

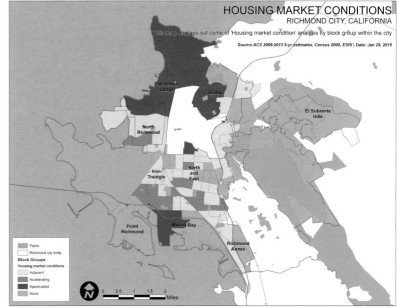

HOUSING MARKET CONDITIONS
RICHMOND CITY, CALIFORNIA
This map displays out come of 'Housing market condition' analysis by block group within the city
Source:ACS 2009-2013 5-yr estimates, Census 2000, ESRI | Date: Jan 29, 2015

Parks
Richmond city limits
Block Groups
Housing market conditions
Adjacent
Accelerating
Appreciated
None

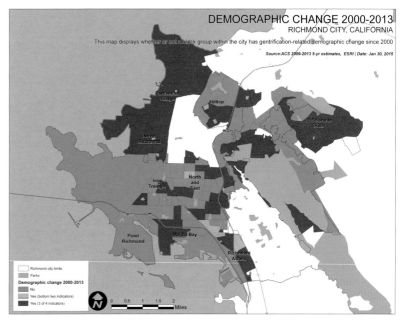

DEMOGRAPHIC CHANGE 2000-2013
RICHMOND CITY, CALIFORNIA
This map displays whether or not a block group within the city has gentrification-related demographic change since 2000
Source:ACS 2009-2013 5-yr estimates, ESRI | Date: Jan 30, 2015

Richmond city limits
Parks
Demographic change 2000-2013
No
Yes (bottom two indicators)
Yes (3 of 4 indicators)

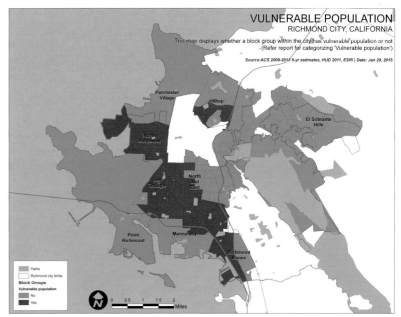

VULNERABLE POPULATION
RICHMOND CITY, CALIFORNIA
This map displays whether a block group within the city has vulnerable population or not
(Refer report for categorizing 'Vulnerable population')
Source:ACS 2009-2013 5-yr estimates, HUD 2011, ESRI | Date: Jan 29, 2015

Parks
Richmond city limits
Block Groups
Vulnerable population
No
Yes

Interactive Kirkland Maps

City of Kirkland
Kirkland, Washington, USA
By Kirkland GIS, Latitude Geographics Group Ltd.

Contact

Kirkland GIS
GISHelp@kirklandwa.gov

Software

ArcGIS 10.2 for Desktop, Geocortex Essentials

Data Sources

City of Kirkland GIS, Permit System, Maintenance Management System, Document Management System, King County GIS, US Census Bureau

In 2015, the City of Kirkland retooled its successful internal GIS web browser with Kirkland Maps, an intuitive, public-facing GIS portal. City staff originally proposed this project as an efficiency measure because an inordinate amount of effort was routinely consumed responding to customer requests for record searches, data, maps, and general information. A simple calculation suggested that both staff and customers would benefit immensely from a well-designed public GIS browser that could reduce a large proportion of these requests.

Kirkland Maps provides standard navigation tools and access to most of the city's primary GIS data layers. It also contains analytical and sketch tools, plus the ability to view and download engineering drawings, historic permit records, and related city documents. The browser conveniently links to external Internet sites such as King County Assessor, King County Recorder, MyBuildingPermit.com (regional online permit application), and City of Kirkland web pages for parks class registration, utility bills, and engineering drawing templates.

Courtesy of City of Kirkland GIS.

Santa Clara County Diversity

County of Santa Clara
San Jose, California, USA
By Douglas Schenk

Contact

Douglas Schenk
douglas.schenk@isd.sccgov.org

Software

ArcGIS 10.0 for Desktop

Data Source

County of Santa Clara

The 2010 US Census population of Santa Clara County is presented as a unique composition of the racial/ethnic diversity of each urban census block. The census block is the smallest unit of geography available from the US Census and most closely represents the characteristics of the local block neighborhoods in a community.

Each unique composition has been symbolized on the map based on the percentage of each of the four major racial/ethnic groups when compared to the total population in the block, mixing the four color components (C–Cyan, M–Magenta, Y–Yellow, and K–Black) in the same proportions present in the population. The closer the color is to gray, the more diversity in the block. The county of Santa Clara is in the top 1 percent of all US counties when measuring diversity using the Shannon-Weiner Diversity Index.

Courtesy of Douglas Schenk, County of Santa Clara.

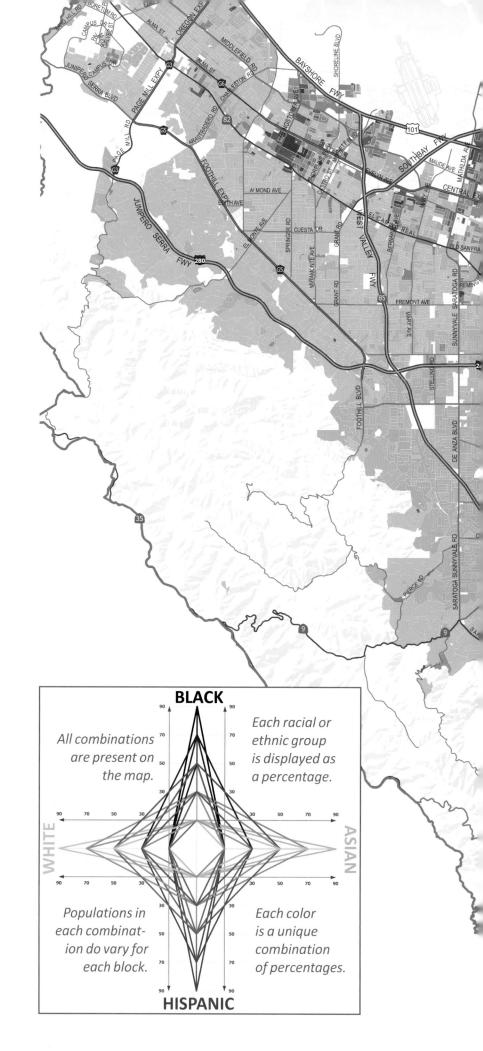

Interpolating ACS Data Using an Adaptive Bandwidth Grid

Portland State University
Portland, Oregon, USA
By Richard Lycan

Contact

Richard Lycan
lycand@pdx.edu

Software

ArcGIS 10.2.1 for Desktop, True Basic Gold,
Microsoft Excel 2010, Adobe Illustrator CS6

Data Sources

US Census, American Community Survey

For a study of rural public transportation needs, researchers needed information on persons with disabilities living in rural areas and small communities. The funding agency, Oregon Department of Transportation, asked for Census Urban Areas to be used for the analysis. The American Community Survey (ACS) provides data on persons with disabilities by broad age groups for Urban Areas, Urban Clusters, and for the remaining Rural areas, but the data's value is compromised by large standard errors, particularly for smaller Urban Clusters and Rural remnants.

To help overcome the sample size limitations of the data, a grid density map generalized the disability rates in space. Researchers calculated density for population and disability for each grid cell on the maps based on a distance weighted average of census block group data within a given radius. They explored two ways of defining given radius or bandwidth: The first used a fixed bandwidth grid with a distance radius from each grid cell. Two examples (maps A and B) illustrate the difficulty of finding an appropriate bandwidth when population density varies considerably. The second way was an adaptive bandwidth grid where the bandwidth is sufficient to include a given population, say one thousand persons age 65 plus (maps 1, 2, and 3). Researchers currently are evaluating the use of generalization using adaptive bandwidth for tabulating and mapping of ACS data for neighborhoods.

Courtesy of Portland State University.

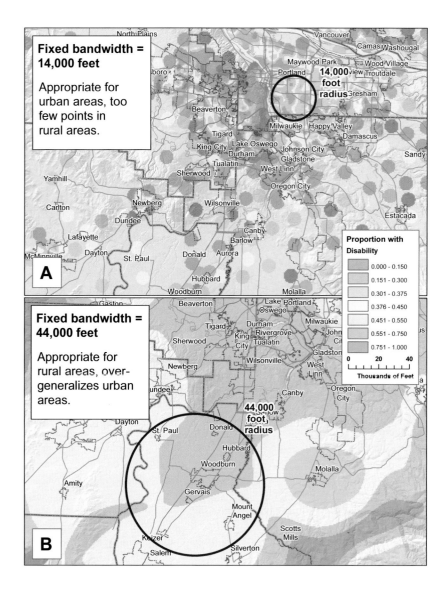

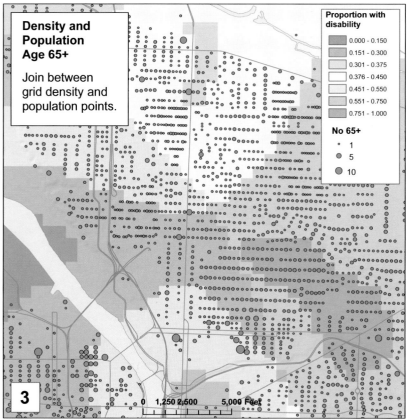

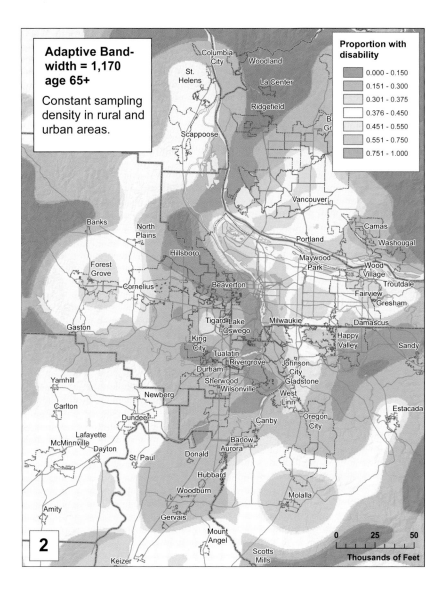

Adaptive Band-width = 1,170 age 65+

Constant sampling density in rural and urban areas.

Proportion with disability

- 0.000 - 0.150
- 0.151 - 0.300
- 0.301 - 0.375
- 0.376 - 0.450
- 0.451 - 0.550
- 0.551 - 0.750
- 0.751 - 1.000

2

0   25   50
Thousands of Feet

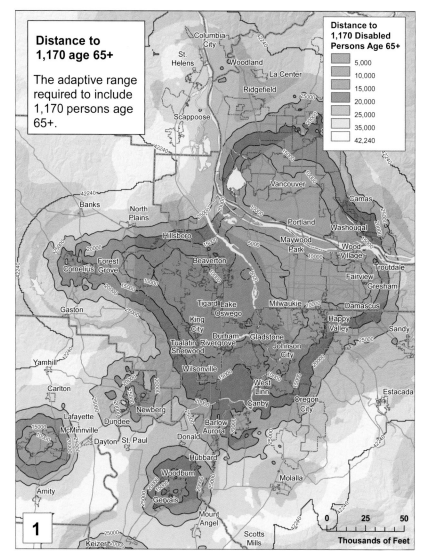

Distance to 1,170 age 65+

The adaptive range required to include 1,170 persons age 65+.

Distance to 1,170 Disabled Persons Age 65+

- 5,000
- 10,000
- 15,000
- 20,000
- 25,000
- 35,000
- 42,240

1

0   25   50
Thousands of Feet

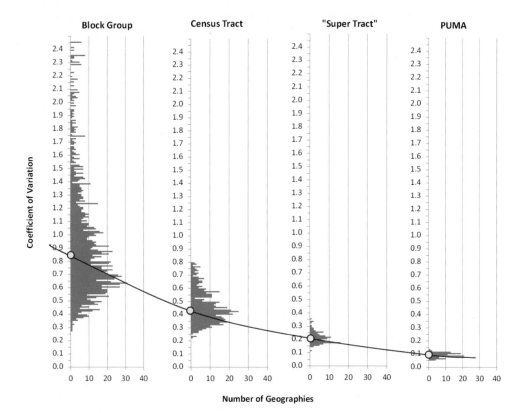

Block Group | Census Tract | "Super Tract" | PUMA

Coefficient of Variation

Number of Geographies

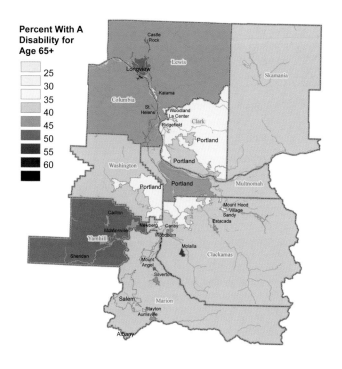

Percent With A Disability for Age 65+

- 25
- 30
- 35
- 40
- 45
- 50
- 55
- 60

91

3D Map of Rio's Favelas—Borel's Case Study
Instituto Pereira Passos (Pereira Passos Institute [IPP])
Rio de Janeiro, Rio de Janeiro, Brazil
By Maira Pinheiro

Contact
Maira Pinheiro
mairasoares.arq@hotmail.com

Software
ArcGIS 10.3 for Desktop, ArcGIS Online, Esri
CityEngine

Data Source
Prefeitura da Cidade do Rio de Janeiro

The Instituto Pereira Passos (IPP) is the research department
for Rio de Janeiro's City Government involved in strategic
planning and public policies integration, mapping, cartographic production, and geotechnology application. The IPP
works to improve living conditions, make public management
more efficient, and promote sustainable urban development.

This 3D map from Borel, one of the favelas (Brazilian slums)
of Rio de Janeiro, shows the potential of 3D maps to intui-
tively explore different levels of information when modeled as
part of urban form. The navigation potential in a 3D model is
better than 2D because of the user's visual identification with
urban forms.

Courtesy of the City of Rio de Janeiro.

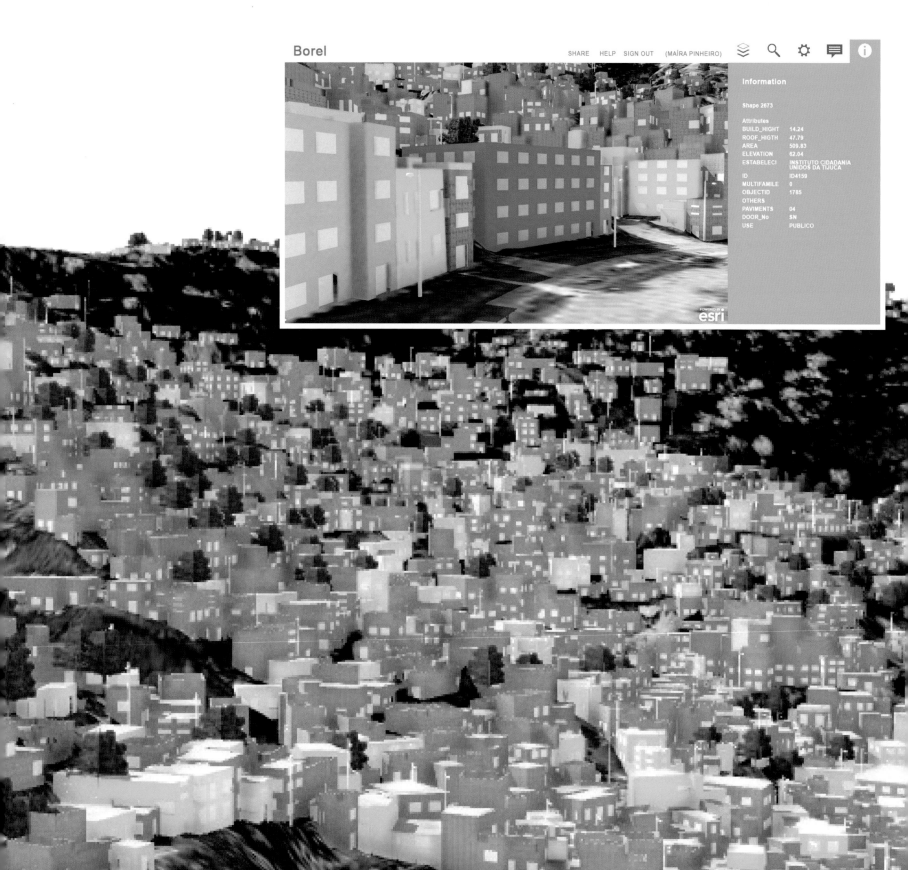

Borel

SHARE   HELP   SIGN OUT   (MAÍRA PINHEIRO)

Information

Shape 2673

Attributes
BUILD_HIGHT   14.24
ROOF_HIGTH   47.79
AREA   509.83
ELEVATION   62.04
ESTABELECI   INSTITUTO CIDADANIA
                   UNIDOS DA TIJUCA
ID   ID4159
MULTIFAMILE   0
OBJECTID   1785
OTHERS
PAVIMENTS   04
DOOR_No   SN
USE   PUBLICO

POWERED BY
esri

Mayor's Poverty Reduction Initiative Priority Area–Census Tract 10.01

City of Durham
Durham, North Carolina, USA
By Toya Merritt

Contact

Toya Merritt
toya.merritt@durhamnc.gov

Software

ArcGIS 10.1 for Desktop

Data Source

City of Durham GIS SDE layers

This map was created to be a visual representation of the current state of a high poverty rate, low per capita income, and high unemployment area in Durham, North Carolina. Durham Mayor William V. "Bill" Bell created an initiative to combat the distressed area defined by the US Department of Housing and Urban Development as Census Tract 10.01, Block Groups 2 and 3 (the focus area).

The map was used to plan for the mayor's initiative by identifying property owners and other property information, community assets, and deficits within the target area. Six task forces—education, finance, health, housing, jobs, and public safety—were formed out of the initiative. Action plans were created by each task force.

Courtesy of the City of Durham, North Carolina, Neighborhood Improvement Services Department.

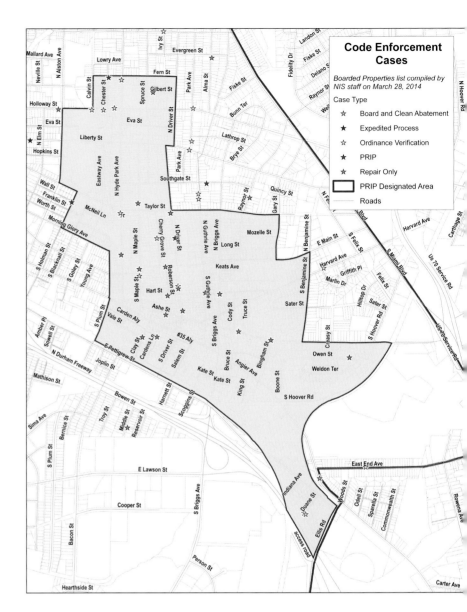

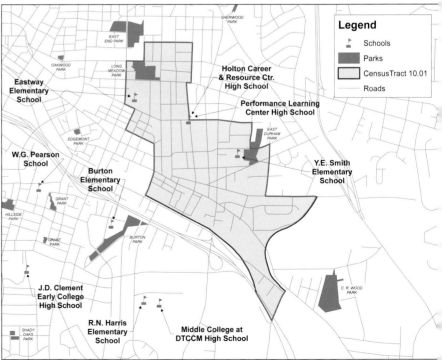

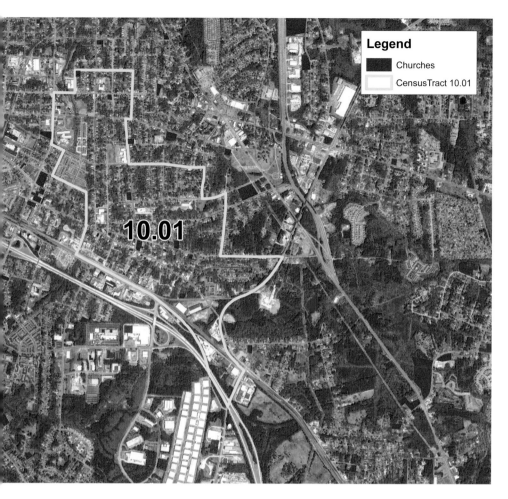

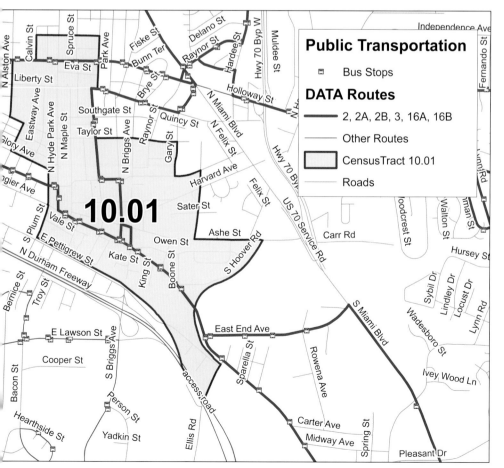

Legend

◼ Churches

☐ CensusTract 10.01

10.01

10.01

10.01

Public Transportation

▣ Bus Stops

DATA Routes

━━━ 2, 2A, 2B, 3, 16A, 16B

──── Other Routes

▭ CensusTract 10.01

──── Roads

Zoning

Landuse Description

Within focus area*

◼ COMMERCIAL*

◼ DOWNTOWN DESIGN-SUPPORT 2

☐ INDUSTRIAL*

◼ OFFICE INSTITUTIONAL*

◼ RESIDENTIAL HIGH DENSITY*

◼ RESIDENTIAL MEDIUM DENSITY*

☐ Census Tract 10.01

Single-Family Residential Housing Changes—City of Houston

City of Houston
Houston, Texas, USA
By Sona Ann Zechariah

Contact

Sona Ann Zechariah
sona.sunny@houstontx.gov

Software

ArcGIS 10.2.2 for Desktop

Data Sources

City of Houston GIS, Harris County Appraisal District

This map shows how the single-family residential housing taxable values in Houston have changed over the last five years. Taxable value is the value after exemptions have been deducted. According to the Harris County Appraisal District, in 2014 single-family homes made up 40 percent of the county's tax base. Areas in green on the map represent an increase in taxable values, red specifies decreasing values, and yellow shows no change in value. There are some areas that even had an increase greater than 20 percent.

Houston is growing not only in size but also in high-income residents. Employment centers scattered throughout the Houston region are attracting not only workers but also homebuyers. This map shows how Houston's booming economy is impacting property values.

Courtesy of the City of Houston.

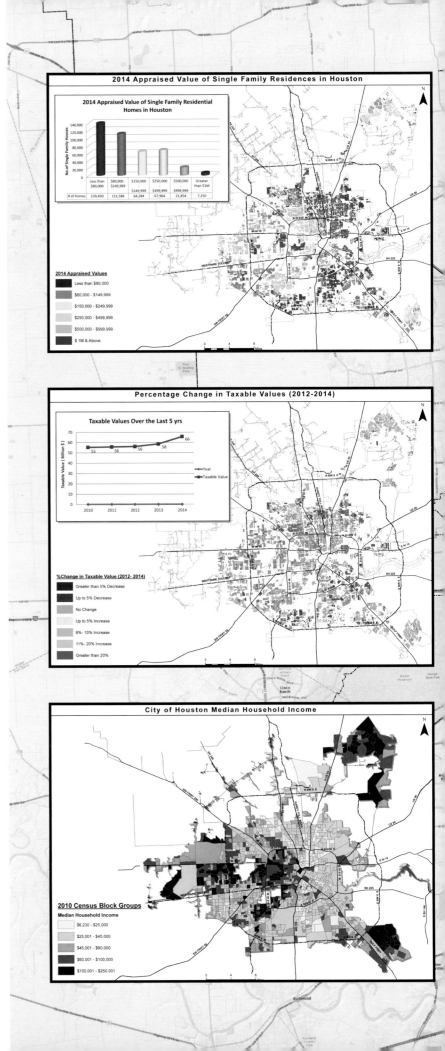

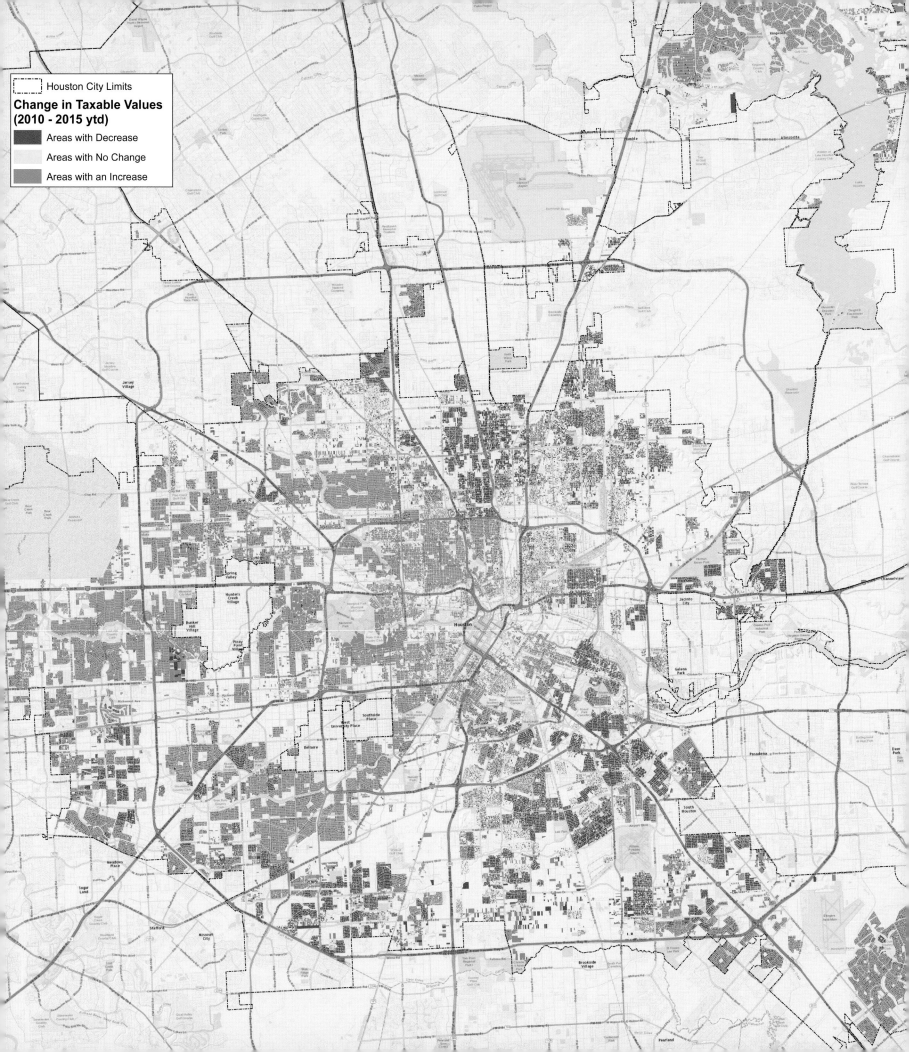

Houston City Limits

**Change in Taxable Values
(2010 - 2015 ytd)**

Areas with Decrease

Areas with No Change

Areas with an Increase

Network Analysis for Access to Drinking Establishments in the United States, 2013

Centers for Disease Control and Prevention (CDC)
Atlanta, Georgia, USA
By Hua Lu, Xingyou Zhang, James B. Holt, Dafna Kanny, and Janet B. Croft

Contact
Hua Lu
hgl6@cdc.gov

Software
ArcGIS 10.2.1 for Desktop

Data Sources
Census 2010, Homeland Security Infrastructure Program GOLD 2013, Esri Data and Maps 10.2

Excessive alcohol consumption is responsible for 88,000 deaths annually in the United States and accounted for $249 billion in economic costs in 2010. The Community Preventive Services Task Force recommended regulating alcohol outlet density for the prevention of excessive alcohol consumption and related harms.

The Centers for Disease Control and Prevention measured alcohol outlet density using an approach based on GIS analysis to quantify the geographic access potential for each populated census block to its nearest seven drinking establishments. The ArcGIS Network Analyst origin-destination cost matrix tool was used to calculate the nearest seven drinking establishments for each populated census block, from which researchers averaged the driving distances and times for the census blocks.

These results can be further used to analyze the relationship between binge drinking and geographic access to drinking establishments. The results of such an analysis can help inform policy makers on defining thresholds for alcohol outlet density for their jurisdictions.

Courtesy of Centers for Disease Control and Prevention.

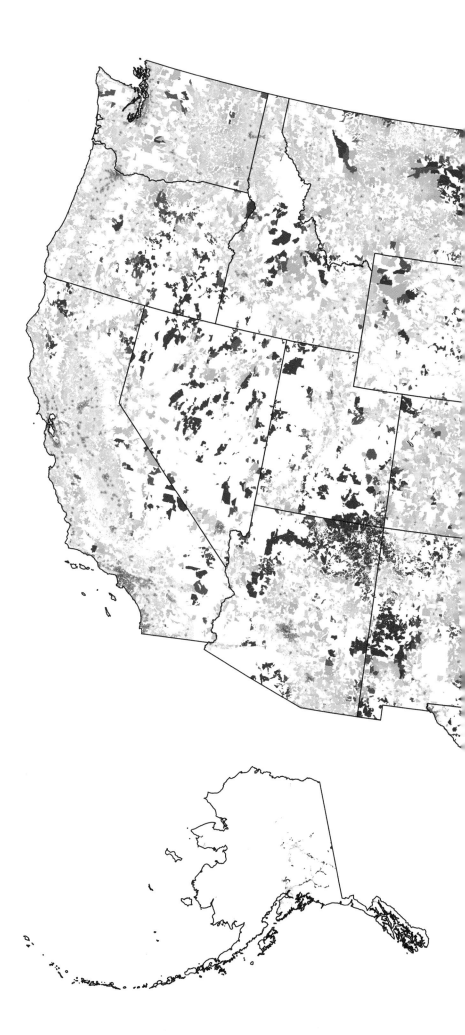

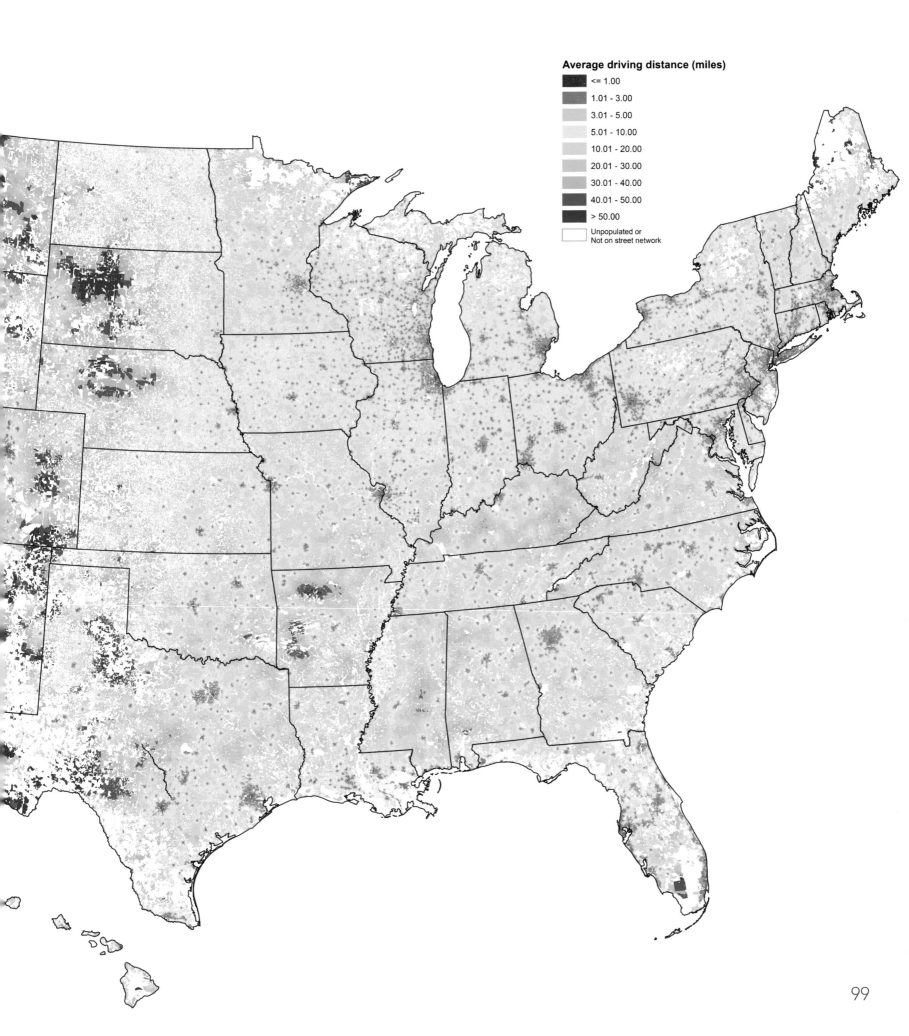

Average driving distance (miles)

■	<= 1.00
■	1.01 - 3.00
■	3.01 - 5.00
■	5.01 - 10.00
■	10.01 - 20.00
■	20.01 - 30.00
■	30.01 - 40.00
■	40.01 - 50.00
■	> 50.00
☐	Unpopulated or Not on street network

Evaluating Malaria Treatment Accessibility in Western Kenyan Highlands

University of California, Irvine
Irvine, California, USA
By Ming-Chieh Lee, Amruta Dixit, and Guiyun Yan

Contact

Ming-Chieh Lee
mingchil@uci.edu

Software

ArcGIS 10.3 for Desktop

Data Sources

University of California, Irvine; Kenya Medical Research Institute

In the western Kenya highlands, distance contributes to the time required to access health care facilities and antimalarial drug retail stores. Delay in seeking malaria treatment usually leads to severe health consequences and a poor cost-benefit ratio. Various socioeconomic factors contribute to the health-seeking behavior of local residents, but the relationship between house location, health facility location, and health-seeking behavior is not clear. The objective of this research was to determine the effect of social, economic, and geographic barriers to access timely treatment for malaria.

Spatial details on population, health care facilities, drug retailers, and topographic features influencing access time were digitized. The analysis took into account different terrain situations, traveling methods, and the presence or absence of surface impedance. A geospatial accessibility model was established to estimate travel speeds and access time for the population to the nearest facilities offering antimalarial medical service.

The maps show the estimated access time to the nearest facilities by different traveling methods for seeking malaria treatment from surveyed villages in Kakamega and Vihiga County in western Kenya. These results provide more realistic scenarios to describe the local residents' health-seeking behaviors and a better way to estimate the access time to malaria treatment facilities and antimalarial retailers.

Courtesy of University of California, Irvine.

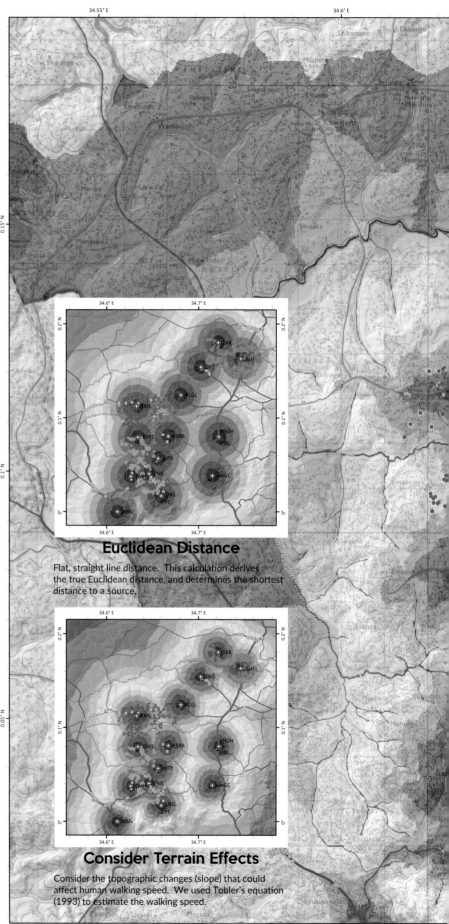

Euclidean Distance

Flat, straight line distance. This calculation derives the true Euclidean distance, and determines the shortest distance to a source.

Consider Terrain Effects

Consider the topographic changes (slope) that could affect human walking speed. We used Tobler's equation (1993) to estimate the walking speed.

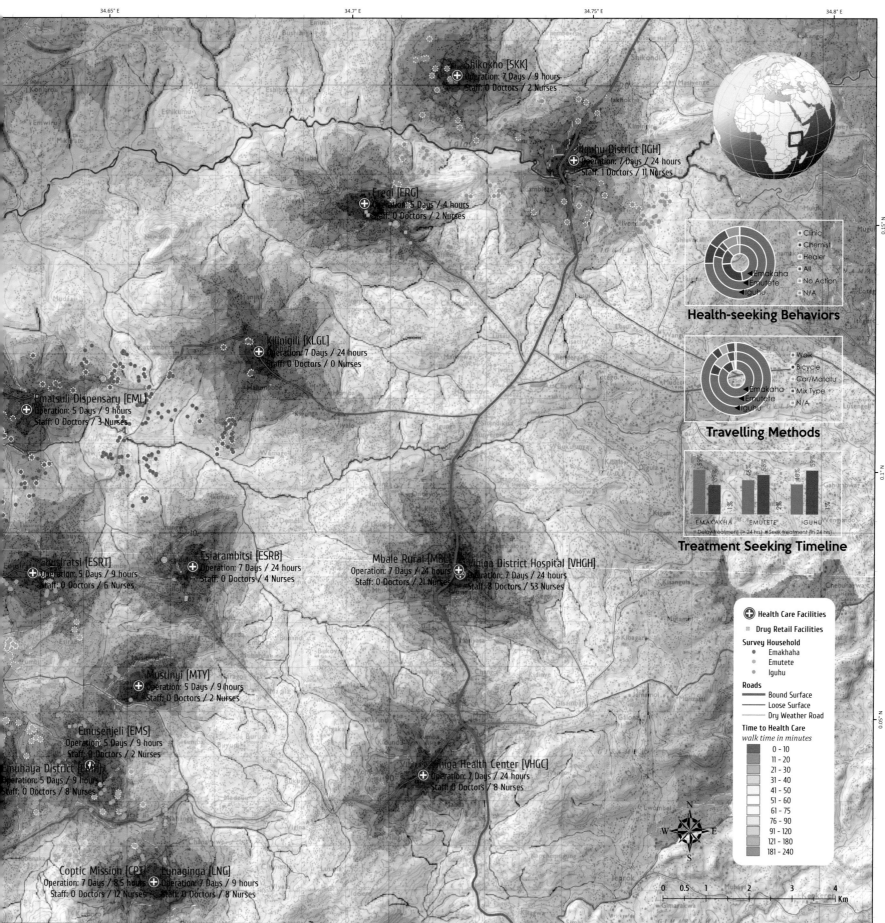

Shikokho [SKK]
Operation: 7 Days / 9 hours
Staff: 0 Doctors / 2 Nurses

Iguhu District [IGH]
Operation: 7 Days / 24 hours
Staff: 1 Doctors / 11 Nurses

Eregi [ERG]
Operation: 5 Days / 4 hours
Staff: 0 Doctors / 2 Nurses

Kilinigili [KLGL]
Operation: 7 Days / 24 hours
Staff: 0 Doctors / 0 Nurses

Ematsuli Dispensary [EML]
Operation: 5 Days / 9 hours
Staff: 0 Doctors / 3 Nurses

Esiratsi [ESRT]
Operation: 5 Days / 9 hours
Staff: 0 Doctors / 6 Nurses

Esiarambitsi [ESRB]
Operation: 7 Days / 24 hours
Staff: 0 Doctors / 4 Nurses

Mbale Rural [MBL]
Operation: 7 Days / 24 hours
Staff: 0 Doctors / 21 Nurses

Vihiga District Hospital [VHGH]
Operation: 7 Days / 24 hours
Staff: 8 Doctors / 53 Nurses

Mustinyi [MTY]
Operation: 5 Days / 9 hours
Staff: 0 Doctors / 2 Nurses

Emusenjeli [EMS]
Operation: 5 Days / 9 hours
Staff: 0 Doctors / 2 Nurses

Emuhaya District [EMH]
Operation: 5 Days / 9 hours
Staff: 0 Doctors / 8 Nurses

Vihiga Health Center [VHGC]
Operation: 7 Days / 24 hours
Staff: 0 Doctors / 8 Nurses

Coptic Mission [CPT]
Operation: 7 Days / 8.5 hours
Staff: 0 Doctors / 12 Nurses

Lynaginga [LNG]
Operation: 7 Days / 9 hours
Staff: 0 Doctors / 8 Nurses

Health-seeking Behaviors

- Clinic
- Chemist
- Healer
- All
- No Action
- N/A

Emakaha
Emutete
Iguhu

Travelling Methods

- Walk
- Bicycle
- Car/Matatu
- Mix Type
- N/A

Emakaha
Emutete
Iguhu

Treatment Seeking Timeline

EMAKAKHA EMUTETE IGUHU

■ Delay treatment (> 24 hrs) ■ Seek treatment (in 24 hrs)

Legend

⊕ Health Care Facilities

▪ Drug Retail Facilities

Survey Household
- Emakhaha
- Emutete
- Iguhu

Roads
— Bound Surface
— Loose Surface
— Dry Weather Road

Time to Health Care
walk time in minutes
- 0 – 10
- 11 – 20
- 21 – 30
- 31 – 40
- 41 – 50
- 51 – 60
- 61 – 75
- 76 – 90
- 91 – 120
- 121 – 180
- 181 – 240

0 0.5 1 2 3 4 Km

Happiness Map of Japan: Geographical Differences in Internet Slang for Laughing and Emoticons of Smiling Faces

The University of Tokyo
Kashiwa, Chiba, Japan
By Takashi Kirimura

Contact

Takashi Kirimura
kirimura@csis.u-tokyo.ac.jp

Software

ArcGIS 10.2.2 for Desktop

Data Source

Twitter feeds

Twitter's geotagged data, a type of social networking service log data, provides a source of knowledge on local geographic differentiations in linguistic representations. The data comes from geotagged tweets posted between February 2012 and April 2015 in Japan, during which time more than 300 million geotagged tweets were posted. Of these, approximately 250 million were posted from Twitter's official apps for mobile devices. Because the geotags assigned by these apps correspond to users' whereabouts, the tweets posted from the apps can be used for mobile devices.

To construct the map, tweets including "笑," corresponding to "lol" (laughing out loud in English) and emoticons of smiling faces were extracted from the geotagged tweet data. Two maps show the number of tweets including "lol" and the emoticons of smiling faces per 100,000 geotagged tweets for each municipality. Tweets using "笑" are posted more frequently in western and northeastern Japan, and tweets using the emoticons of smiling faces are posted more often in middle and western Japan.

In this way, geographic differences in linguistic representations of happiness can be visualized using geotagged data. People living in western and northeastern Japan tweet "笑" and emoticons of smiling faces more often, suggesting that they are relatively happy. However, people living in Tokyo, where both metrics are below the national average, are not likely to be unhappy. Instead, this suggests that various other expressions of happiness, besides "笑" and the smiling face emoticons, are used in Tokyo.

Courtesy of Takashi Kirimura, Center for Spatial Information Science, the University of Tokyo.

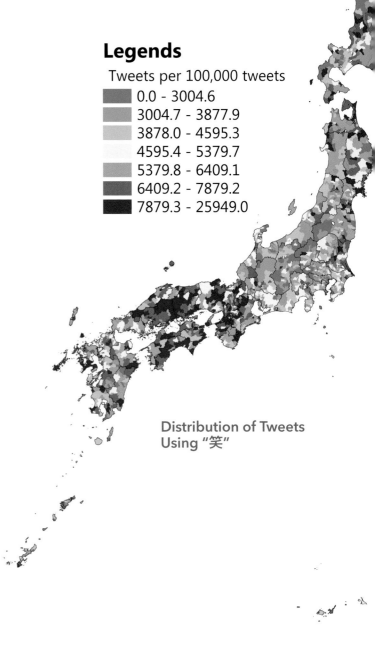

Legends

Tweets per 100,000 tweets

	0.0 - 3004.6
	3004.7 - 3877.9
	3878.0 - 4595.3
	4595.4 - 5379.7
	5379.8 - 6409.1
	6409.2 - 7879.2
	7879.3 - 25949.0

Distribution of Tweets Using "笑"

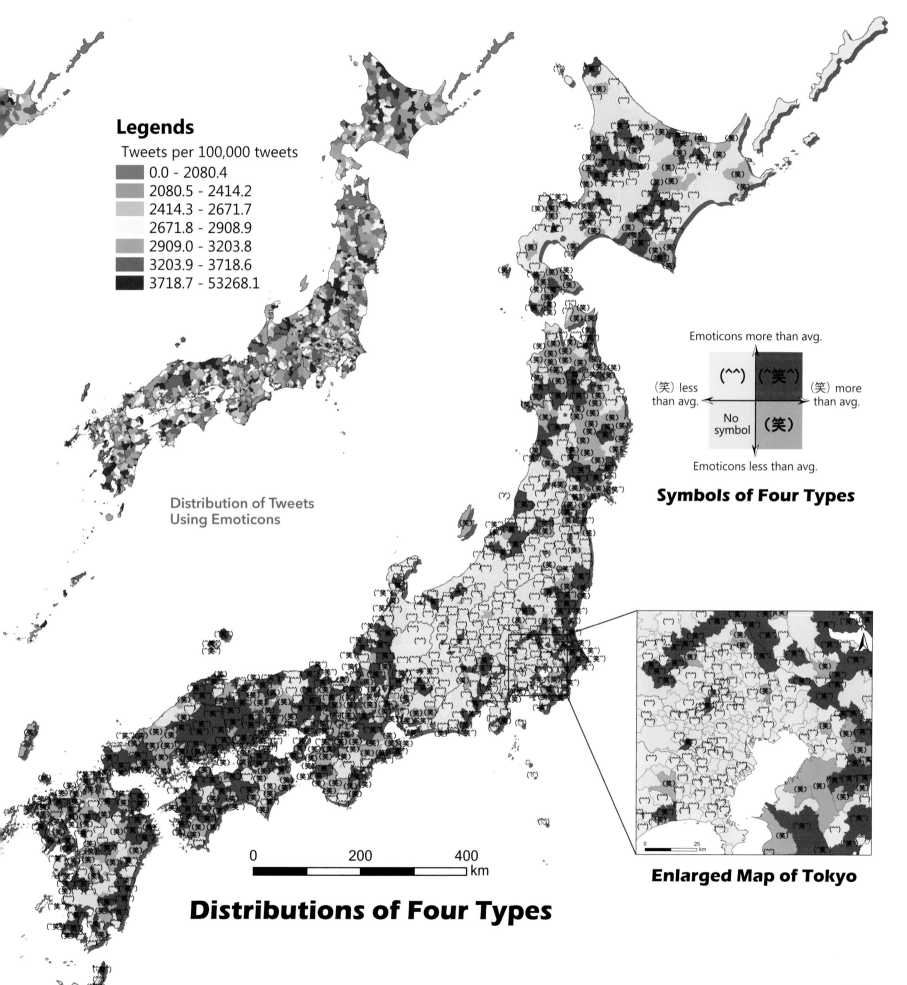

Legends

Tweets per 100,000 tweets

- 0.0 - 2080.4
- 2080.5 - 2414.2
- 2414.3 - 2671.7
- 2671.8 - 2908.9
- 2909.0 - 3203.8
- 3203.9 - 3718.6
- 3718.7 - 53268.1

Distribution of Tweets
Using Emoticons

Emoticons more than avg.

(^^) | (^笑^)

（笑）less
than avg. ← → （笑）more
than avg.

No
symbol | （笑）

Emoticons less than avg.

Symbols of Four Types

Enlarged Map of Tokyo

Distributions of Four Types

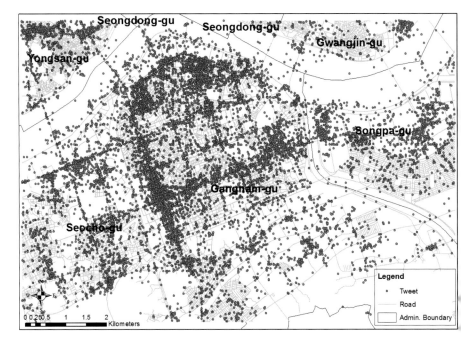

Hot Spots of Tweets Related to Food, Entertainment, Work, and Study in Gangnam Area of Seoul, Korea

University of Southern California
Los Angeles, California, USA
By Woojin Park, Yao-Yi Chiang, Su Jin Lee, and Kiyun Yu

Contact
Su Jin Lee
sujinlee@usc.edu

Software
ArcGIS for Desktop

Data Source
Social media data (Twitter, http://api.twitter.com)

People's main interests and where the interests appear in the city are important in understanding the physical environment and social phenomena. Social media text contents and location information provide valuable answers to these questions. Researchers applied text mining and spatial analysis methods in this study, collecting Twitter data with geotags in the Gangnam district of Seoul, South Korea, in August 2013.

Keywords are extracted from tweets with categories such as food, entertainment, and work and study, and are then selected and classified. Spatial clustering is conducted for the tweets containing keywords in each category. Clusters of each category are compared with benchmark buildings in the same location.

There was high consistency between the clusters in the food category and large-scale commercial areas. Clusters in the entertainment category corresponded with theaters, art centers, and sports complexes. Clusters of work and study showed high consistency with areas where private institutes and office buildings concentrate.

Courtesy of the University of Southern California.

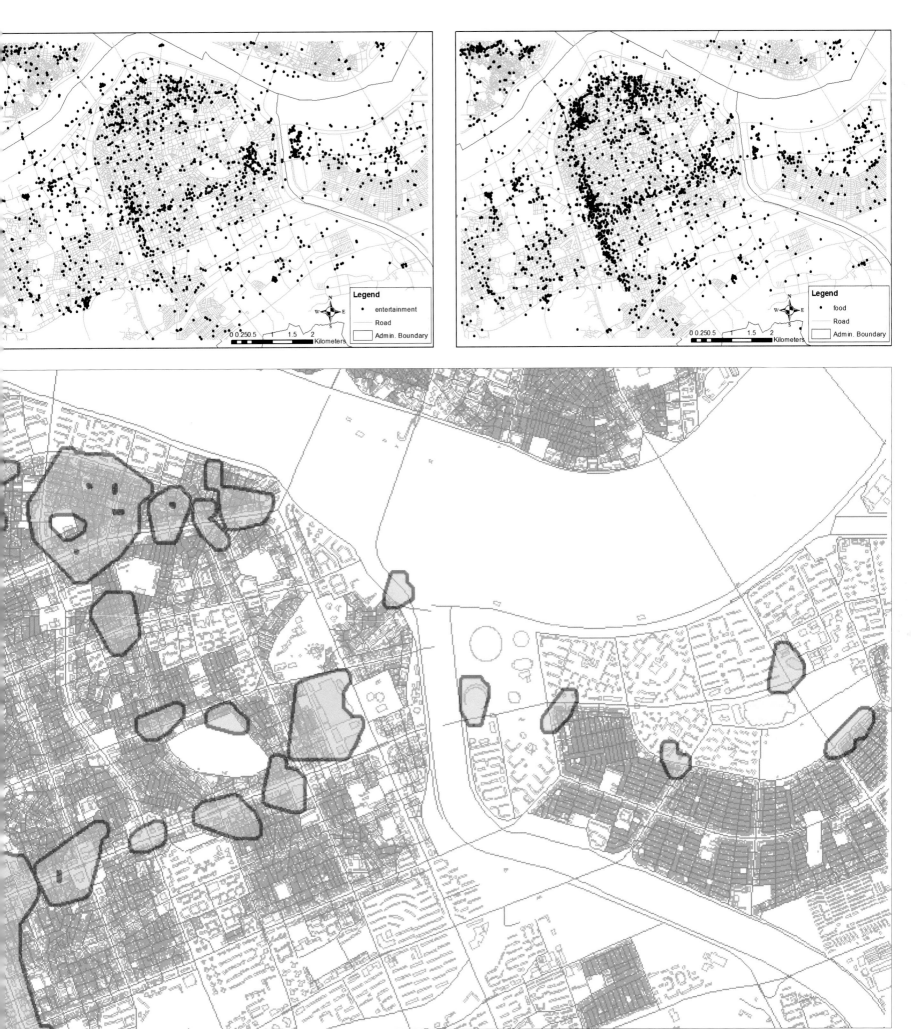

The Syrian Conflict and Migration of Refugees

Community College of Baltimore County
Catonsville, Maryland, USA
By Kevin McMahon

Contact
Scott Jeffrey
sjeffrey@ccbcmd.edu

Software
ArcGIS 10.1 for Desktop, ArcGIS Pro, Affinity
Designer

Data Source
United Nations High Commissioner for Refugees

This map identifies areas of conflict throughout Syria and highlights the tracks of refugees from the conflict zones to international refugee centers and beyond. In addition, estimates of the number, ethnic composition, and the damage to cities within the conflict zones are presented and provide a comprehensive picture of the level of the human tragedy that is the Syrian Civil War.

Since the beginning of armed conflict in Syria in 2011, more than 2.39 million people have become refugees. The speed and intensity with which the Syrian refugee crisis unfolded throughout 2013, and the growth of the refugee population in the region exceeding four million by the end of 2014, confirmed that this refugee crisis is the largest, most complex, and most profound in several decades. The influx of Syrian refugees is causing substantial pressure on the daily lives of host country populations that are seeing dramatic increases in housing prices, spikes in unemployment, depressed wage rates, and limited employment opportunities.

Copyright © Community College of Baltimore County Geospatial Applications Program.

Turkey

Syria

Raqqa

Deir Ez Zor

Lebanon

Palestine

Israel

Jordan

Egypt

Crop Planting Frequency Data Layers (2008–2014) for Corn, Cotton, Soybeans, and Wheat

US Department of Agriculture (USDA), National
Agricultural Statistics Service (NASS)
Fairfax, Virginia, USA
By Claire Boryan, Zhengwei Yang, Patrick Willis,
and Lee Ebinger

Contact

Lee Ebinger
Lee.Ebinger@nass.usda.gov

Software

ArcGIS 10.0 for Desktop, ERDAS Imagine 11

Data Sources

National Agricultural Statistics Service Cropland
Data Layers, Farm Service Agency Common Land
Unit data

Information on future crop-specific planting is valuable for
improving agricultural survey estimates and critical for agricultural production planning, agricultural product commodity
inventory control, natural resource allocation, and conservation.
However, future crop planting details are generally unavailable.

The National Agricultural Statistics Service (NASS) Crop
Planting Frequency Data Layers (CPFDL), generated from
2008–2014 Cropland Data Layers, can be used as indicators to indirectly provide information regarding future crop
planting. National-scale corn, soybeans, wheat, and cotton
CPFDLs are illustrated in the maps. The accuracies of the
national-scale CPFDLs are 91.00 percent for corn, 90.13
percent for cotton, 87.67 percent for soybeans, and 85.96
percent for wheat as assessed using Farm Service Agency
Common Land Unit Data (Boryan et al. 2014).

Boryan, C. G., Z. Yang, and P. Willis. 2014. "US Geospatial
Crop Frequency Data Layers." Proceedings of the Third
International Conference on Agro-Geoinformatics (Agro-
Geoinformatics 2014), Beijing, China, August 11–14.
DOI:10.1109/Agro-Geoinformatics.2014.6910657.

Courtesy of USDA NASS.

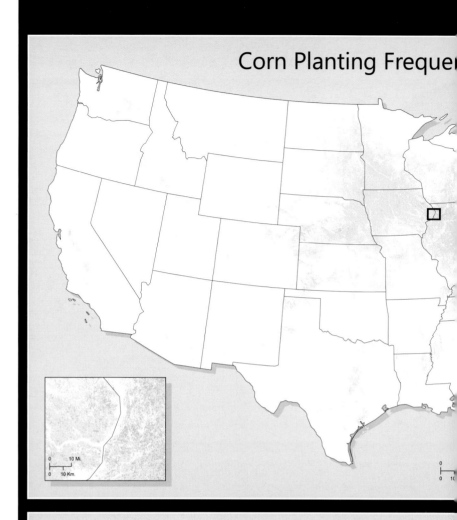

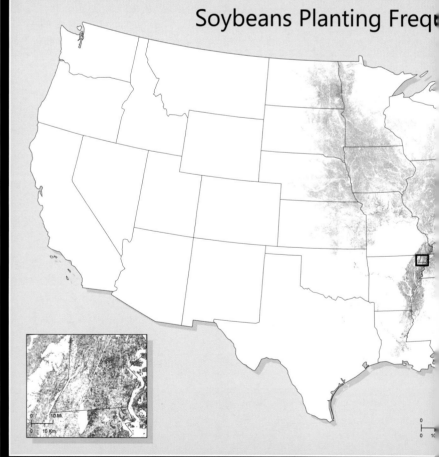

Crop-Specific Frequency Data Layers

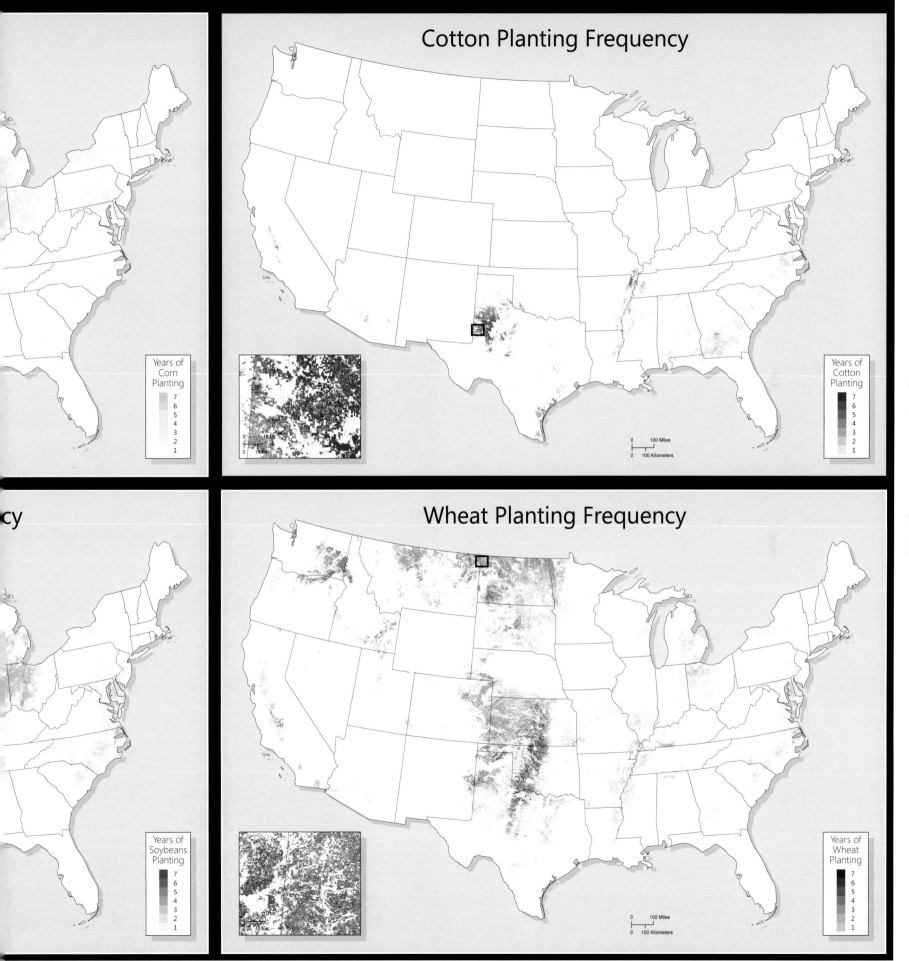

Cotton Planting Frequency

Years of
Corn
Planting

7
6
5
4
3
2
1

Years of
Cotton
Planting

7
6
5
4
3
2
1

0   100 Miles

0   100 Kilometers

Wheat Planting Frequency

Years of
Soybeans
Planting

7
6
5
4
3
2
1

Years of
Wheat
Planting

7
6
5
4
3
2
1

0   100 Miles

0   100 Kilometers

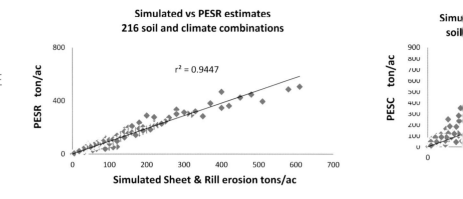

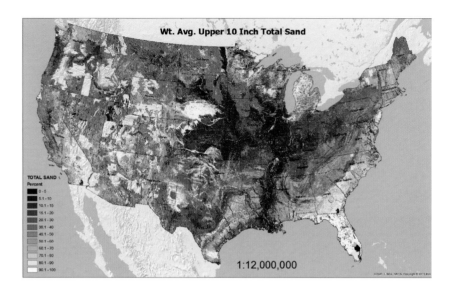

A National Relative Index for Potential Water and Wind Erosion

US Department of Agriculture (USDA) Natural Resources Conservation Service (NRCS)
Fort Worth, Texas, USA
By Joel Poore and W. Dwain Daniels

Contact
Waylon Daniels
dwain.daniels@ftw.usda.gov

Software
ArcGIS 10.2 for Desktop

Data Sources
Gridded Soil Survey Geographic data soil properties, Annual R and Estimated Wind Energy Climate factors

General erosion index values are used by the Natural Resources Conservation Service (NRCS) to identify and compare site-specific risks of wind- and water-induced soil erosion. Relative erosion indices are useful to NRCS for focusing conservation planning and technical and financial assistance to areas with the greatest risk of erosion-related resource concerns.

Erosion simulations using current erosion prediction models with current climate and soil data variables were used to develop equations to quantify the relative risk for various types of erosion. Raster data input layers for climate and soil were used to calculate the erosion index values for areas within the conterminous United States. Georeferenced layer products can be used for relative comparisons for the risk of the different types of erosion at a specific location and comparing one type of erosion for multiple locations.

Courtesy of USDA Natural Resources Conservation Service.

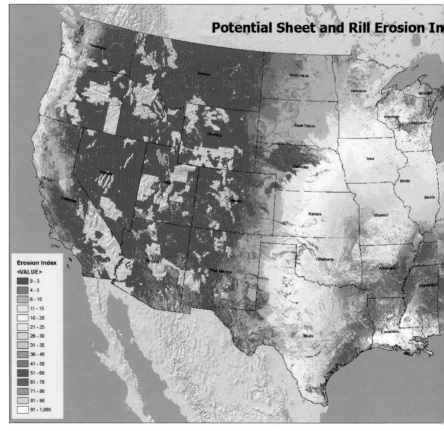

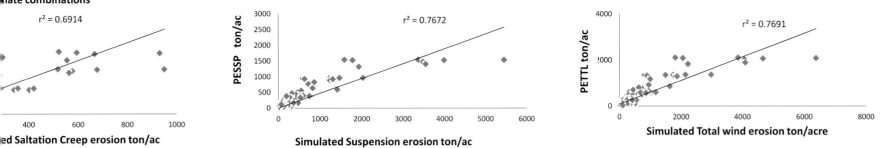

PESC estimates 216
climate combinations

r² = 0.6914

...ed Saltation Creep erosion ton/ac

Simulated vs PESSP estimates

r² = 0.7672

PESSP   ton/ac

Simulated Suspension erosion ton/ac

Simulated vs PETTL estimates

r² = 0.7691

PETTL ton/ac

Simulated Total wind erosion ton/acre

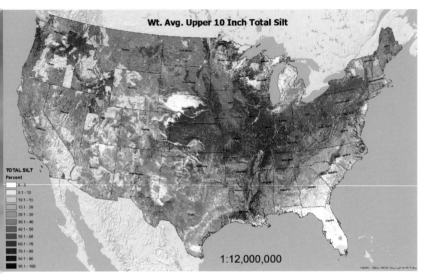

Wt. Avg. Upper 10 Inch Total Silt

1:12,000,000

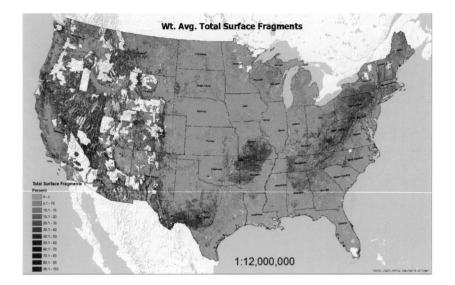

Wt. Avg. Total Surface Fragments

1:12,000,000

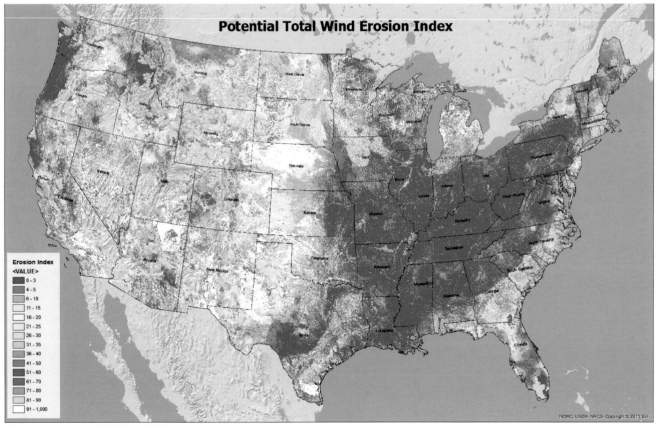

Potential Total Wind Erosion Index

Erosion Index
<VALUE>
0 - 3
4 - 5
6 - 10
11 - 15
16 - 20
21 - 25
26 - 30
31 - 35
36 - 40
41 - 50
51 - 60
61 - 70
71 - 80
81 - 90
91 - 1,000

1:12,000,000

Groundwater Vulnerability in Wheat-Growing Regions of the United States

Stone Environmental
Montpelier, Vermont, USA
By Lauren Padilla, Michael Winchell, Natalia Peranginangin, Shanique Grant, Charlie Hoffman, and Katie Budreski

Contact
Lauren Padilla
lpadilla@stone-env.com

Software
ArcGIS 10.2.2 for Desktop

Data Sources
Soil Survey Geographic database, Cropland Data Layer, US Department of Agriculture AgCensus, Solar and Meteorological Surface Observational Network, US Geological Survey Groundwater Data for the Nation

Groundwater vulnerability to herbicides varies throughout the wheat-growing regions across the nation. Variability is a function of soil types, weather patterns, depth to groundwater, and wheat cultivation practices. National datasets including the Soil Survey Geographic database and Cropland Data Layer can be used in conjunction with groundwater models to capture the range in vulnerability.

Copyright 2015 Stone Environmental, Inc., and Sygenta Crop Protection.

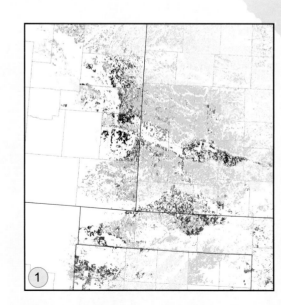

Groundwater Mode▮

Groundwater modeling was condu▮
with the Pesticide Root Zone Mode▮
combinations of soil types, weather▮
cultivation practices assuming a sh▮
meters. Model-predicted concentra▮
shallow aquifer varied throughout▮
variability, locations of wheat fields▮
concentrations are shown at left for▮
New Mexico, Texas, and Oaklahom▮
concentrations are symbolized from▮

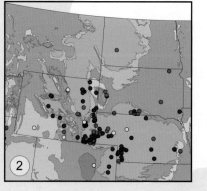

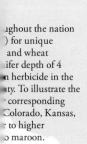

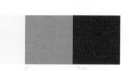

Less than 4 meters | 4 to 20 meters | Greater than 20 meters

Aquifer Depth

Although groundwater modeling was conducted with a constant aquifer depth of 4 meters from the surface, the shallow aquifer depth in wheat-growing regions varies widely throughout the United States. Predicted groundwater herbicide concentrations are sensitive to the aquifer depth. Deeper aquifers generally have lower exposure to herbicides via movement through the soil profile over a given time period. Groundwater depth data from wells (blue dots at left) in the Principal Aquifers of the United States (USGS) were used to identify more vulnerable locations for subsequent analysis. The Principal Aquifers are mapped at left and above.

Exposure Calculation

The map above shows, at the county level, the relative exposure to groundwater from an herbicide applied to wheat. Exposure scores are the product of county-average model-predicted herbicide concentrations in the shallow aquifer and the fraction of the county growing wheat. Low exposure counties are shown as lighter red and higher exposure counties are shown as darker red. To standardize the basis of comparison, all counties are assumed to have the same depth to shallow aquifer (4 meters).

ughout the nation
) for unique
and wheat
ifer depth of 4
n herbicide in the
ty. To illustrate the
corresponding
Colorado, Kansas,
to higher
o maroon.

Modeling Tree Canopy Cover for Coastal Alaska

US Department of Agriculture (USDA) Forest Service
Salt Lake City, Utah, USA
By Vicky Johnson and Robert Benton

Contact
Kevin Megown
kamegown@fs.fed.us

Software
ArcGIS 10.0.5 for Desktop

Data Source
USDA Forest Service

The National Land Cover Database 2011 percent canopy cover layer is sponsored by the Multi-Resolution Land Characteristics Consortium and prepared by the USDA Forest Service. Percent canopy cover data is useful for monitoring change in tree cover in both forested lands and in areas not traditionally considered forest.

Knowing where trees are is an important first step in managing tree resources and quantifying carbon sequestration. It is an essential measure for assessing forest health and watershed condition and it is critical input for fire behavior modeling. Percent canopy cover is also an important data element for characterizing habitat fragmentation, one of the primary threats to biodiversity in forests.

Courtesy of USDA Forest Service.

sat 5 False Color Composite
(Bands 7,4,3)

011 Tree Canopy Cover

Percent Tree Canopy Cover

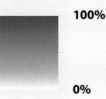

100%

0%

Locator Map

Miles

0   25   50   100   150   200

Existing Vegetation Mapping on the Caribou-Targhee National Forest

US Department of Agriculture (USDA) Forest Service
Salt Lake City, Utah, USA
By Wendy Goetz

Contact
Paul Maus
pmaus@fs.fed.us

Software
ArcGIS 10.0 for Desktop, Adobe Creative Suite CS6

Data Source
USDA Forest Service

The Caribou-Targhee National Forest encompasses over 3.1 million acres and stretches across southeastern Idaho along the Montana, Utah, and Wyoming borders. Vegetative communities include grasslands, shrublands, woodlands, riparian ecosystems, coniferous forests, and deciduous forests. These diverse communities provide wildlife habitat, livestock forage, stable watersheds, and recreational opportunities.

For this project, three maps were produced to show vegetation type, canopy cover, and tree size. The purpose of the project was to provide land managers with baseline vegetation maps that would support assessment of forest health, timber availability, wildlife habitat, and environmental change. The Caribou-Targhee National Forest maps provide current and complete information about vegetative communities and structure across the landscape.

Courtesy of USDA Forest Service.

VEGETATION TYPE

1. Acquire and Assemble Geospatial Data

2. Perform Image Segmentation to Develop Modeling Units

3. Collect Reference Data to Train Models

4. Run Classification Models Using Random Forests™

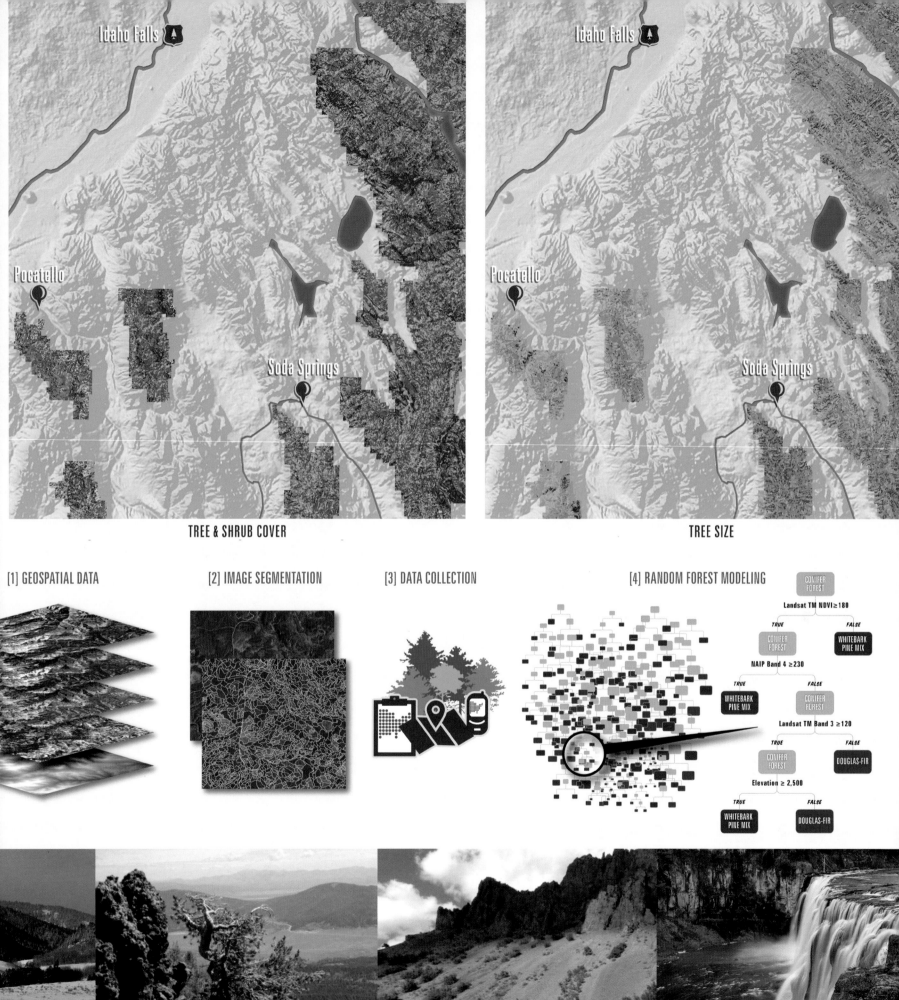

TREE & SHRUB COVER

TREE SIZE

[1] GEOSPATIAL DATA

[2] IMAGE SEGMENTATION

[3] DATA COLLECTION

[4] RANDOM FOREST MODELING

CONIFER FOREST

Landsat TM NDVI ≥ 180

TRUE — CONIFER FOREST

FALSE — WHITEBARK PINE MIX

NAIP Band 4 ≥ 230

TRUE — WHITEBARK PINE MIX

FALSE — CONIFER FOREST

Landsat TM Band 3 ≥ 120

TRUE — CONIFER FOREST

FALSE — DOUGLAS-FIR

Elevation ≥ 2,500

TRUE — WHITEBARK PINE MIX

FALSE — DOUGLAS-FIR

NATURAL RESOURCES—FORESTRY

Zambia—Change Detection

US Department of Agriculture (USDA) Forest Service
Salt Lake City, Utah, USA
By Ian Housman and Mark Finco

Contact
Kevin Megown
kamegown@fs.fed.us

Software
ArcGIS for Desktop

Data Source
USDA Forest Service

Zambia is one of the nine original pilot countries for the UN-REDD/REDD+ Programme, which provides economic incentives for reducing deforestation and forest degradation rates and maintaining healthy forests. Part of the UN REDD/REDD+ requirement is that countries understand baseline levels of deforestation and forest degradation.

This map depicts forest cover changes in Zambia's Eastern Province between 1990 and 2010. It was developed by remote-sensing specialists from RedCastle Resources under contract to the USDA Forest Service and USAID/Zambia using a time series of Landsat imagery and ancillary geospatial data. The paucity of the Landsat data records in Africa limited the types of change analysis techniques that could be applied, necessitating the application of an innovative technique based on regression analysis. The map was delivered at two workshops in 2013 to stakeholders from the Zambian Forestry Department, other Zambian governmental ministries and departments, representatives from nongovernmental organizations, and Zambian universities.

Courtesy of USDA Forest Service.

Area 1: Chipata District and nearby Forest Reserves

Area 2: International border with Malawi adjacent to National Park

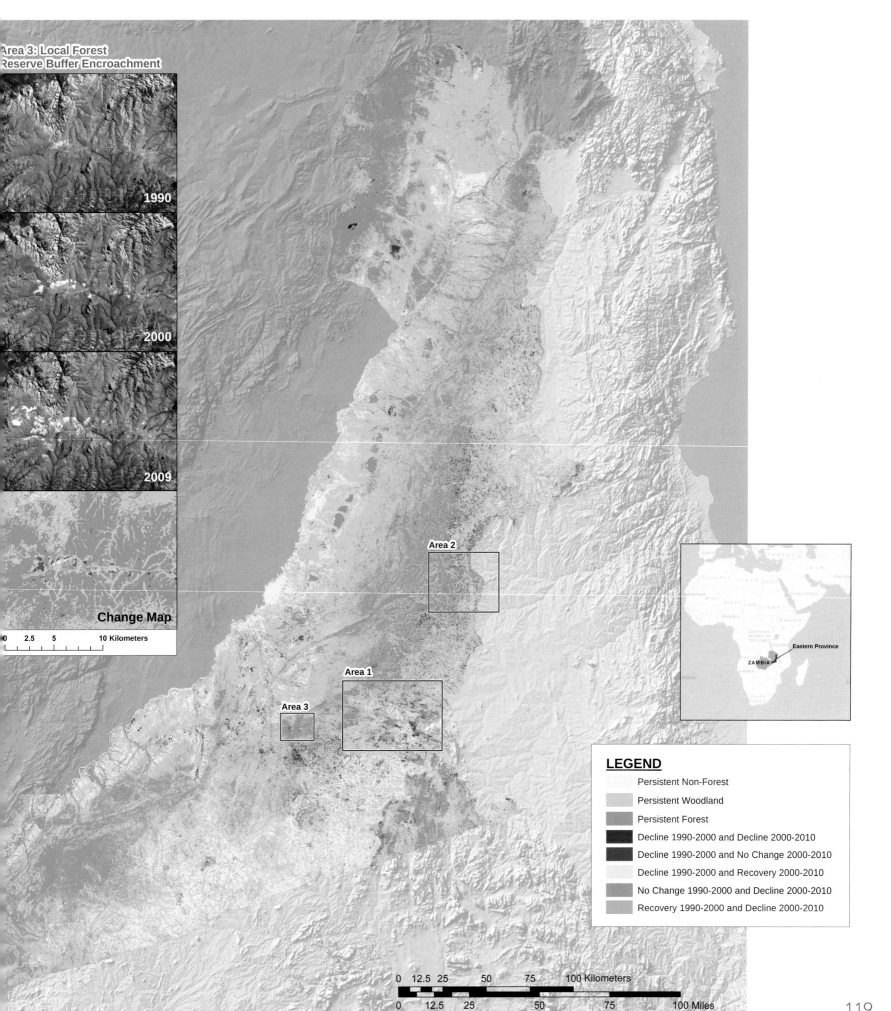

Area 3: Local Forest Reserve Buffer Encroachment

1990

2000

2009

Change Map

0   2.5   5   10 Kilometers

Area 2

Area 1

Area 3

Eastern Province

ZAMBIA

LEGEND

Persistent Non-Forest

Persistent Woodland

Persistent Forest

Decline 1990-2000 and Decline 2000-2010

Decline 1990-2000 and No Change 2000-2010

Decline 1990-2000 and Recovery 2000-2010

No Change 1990-2000 and Decline 2000-2010

Recovery 1990-2000 and Decline 2000-2010

0   12.5   25   50   75   100 Kilometers

0   12.5   25   50   75   100 Miles

Conservation International works directly with in country partners and understand the challenges users face managing fire risk and fire incidence.

Firecast: A Near Real-Time Monitoring System Improving Forest Management in the Tropics

Conservation International
Arlington, Virginia, USA
By Karyn Tabor and Carlos Andrés Cano Alvarez

Contact
Carlos Andrés Cano Alvarez
ccano@conservation.org

Software
ArcGIS for Server, Microsoft Publisher 2010

Data Sources
National Aeronautics and Space Administration; MODIS Active Fire and Burned Area Products; Giglio, L., J. Descloitres, C. O. Justice, Y. Kaufman. 2003. "An Enhanced Contextual Fire Detection Algorithm for MODIS." *Remote Sensing of Environment* 87:273–282; Steininger, M. K., K. Tabor, J. Small, C. Pinto, J. Soliz, E. Chavez. 2013. "A Satellite Model of Forest Flammability." *Environmental Management* 52(1):136–150.

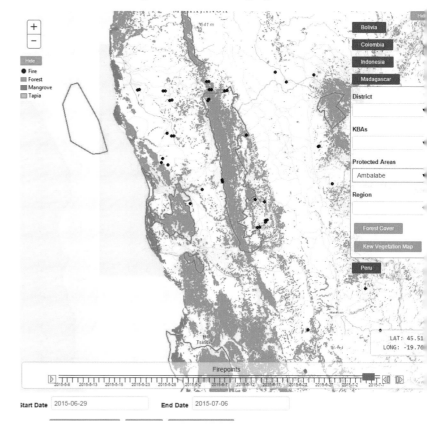

The loss of the world's natural habitat through timber extraction, wildland fires, and agricultural expansion is causing wide-ranging environmental and economic impacts. Projected increases in frequency and intensity of drought conditions will increase the incidence of wildland fires. Drought and fire cause economic strain, displacement, and food insecurity while also impacting biodiversity and ecosystem services such as water availability, water quality, and pollination. In addition, fire disasters cause health problems from poor air quality and spread of disease.

In response to these challenges, Conservation International built an innovative early warning system called Firecast to empower local stakeholders with timely monitoring and forecasting information. The web-based system captures from MODIS and VIIRS sensors daily fire and fire risk information in an interactive web map and a dashboard while also delivering email alerts with near real-time detection of fires, drought, and deforestation. The system is already being used by decision makers in Peru, Bolivia, Colombia, Indonesia, and Madagascar to assist fire disaster prevention, forest conservation, Reducing Emissions from Deforestation and Forest Degradation (REDD+) project implementation, and sustainable livelihoods in the tropics.

Courtesy of Conservation International.

LOW

Fire Season Severity Forecasting

decision makers to

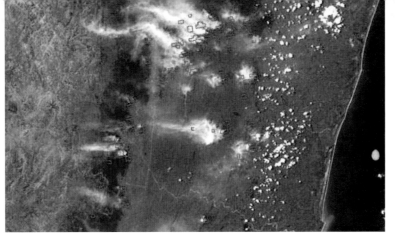

Fires in Madagascar on October 19th, 2008. Images from NASA's Aqua satellite show detected active fires (in red) and smoke plumes.

Near real time Earth Observation inputs include: MODIS active fire, TRMM 3B42RT, MODIS Atmospheric profiles, and VIIRS.

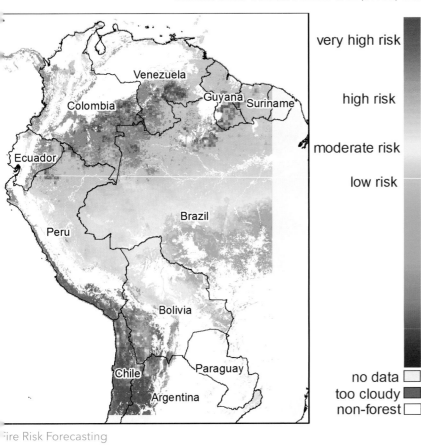

very high risk

high risk

moderate risk

low risk

no data
too cloudy
non-forest

Fire Risk Forecasting

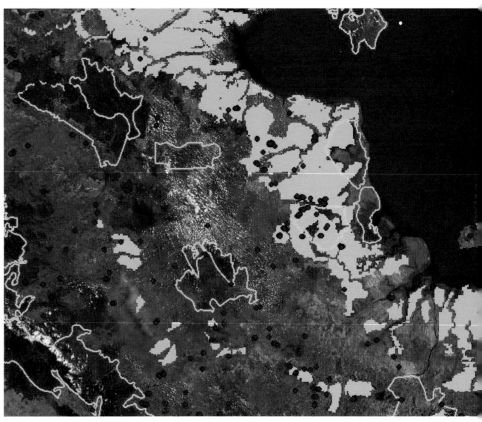

Active Fire Alerts

Illegal deforestation and habitat loss are rapidly degrading ecosystems and the benefits they provide to people (photo by Trond Larsen).

Community education and outreach for fire risk in Bolivia (photo by FAN).

Park rangers patrolling the Alto Mayo Protected Forest in Perú (photo by Thomas Muller).

Monitoring Trends in Burn Severity in the Western United States, 1984–2012

US Department of Agriculture (USDA) Forest Service Remote Sensing Applications Center Salt Lake City, Utah, USA

By Linda Smith, Mark Finco, Jennifer Lecker, and Brad Quayle

Contact
Brad Quayle
bquayle@fs.fed.us

Software
ArcGIS 10.0 for Desktop, Adobe Creative Suite 6

Data Source
USDA Forest Service

The Monitoring Trends in Burn Severity (MTBS) project, conducted jointly by the USDA Forest Service and US Geological Survey, maps the location, extent, and burn severity of documented large fires in the United States from 1984 to present. This map displays forest fires in the western United States mapped by MTBS between the years 1984 and 2012, including their size and time of occurrence. Associated statistical summaries illustrate the observed trends in fire frequency, area, and severity during this twenty-nine-year period.

Courtesy of USDA Forest Service.

1. Douglas fir/Western hemlock, Oregon
(*Pseudotsugamenziesii/Tsuga heterophylla*)

3. Lodgepole pine, Colorado
(*Pinus contorta*)

2. Subalpine fir/Englemann spruce, Idaho
(*Abies lasiocarpa/ Picea engelmannii*)

4. Pinyon pine/Utah juniper, Utah
(*Pinus edulis/Juniperus utahensis*)

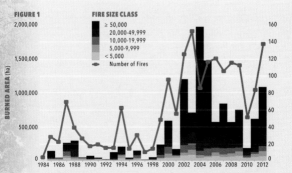

5. Ponderosa pine, Arizona
(*Pinus ponderosa*)

FIGURE 1

FIRE SIZE CLASS

- ≥ 50,000
- 20,000-49,999
- 10,000-19,999
- 5,000-9,999
- < 5,000
- Number of Fires

BURNED AREA (ha)

2,000,000

1,500,000

1,000,000

500,000

160

140

120

100

80

60

40

20

0

1984 1986 1988 1990 1992 1994 1996 1998 2000 2002 2004 2006 2008 2010 2012

KILOMETERS

750   1,000

Ground Subsidence Hazard Map of Underground Coal Mine Area in Samcheok, South Korea

Seoul National University
Gwanak-gu, Seoul, Republic of South Korea
By Jin Son, Jangwon Suh, Daeun Yun, Myeongchan Oh, Hyeong-Dong Park, Seungho Lee

Contact
Jin Son
stynerkhal@snu.ac.kr

Software
ArcGIS 10.2 for Desktop

Data Source
Mine Reclamation Corporation

This map illustrates the ground subsidence hazard indices of the underground coal mine area in Samcheok, South Korea. The objective of this map was to enhance the accuracy of statistical analysis on subsidence hazard assessment by considering the area of subsidence influence. Drift distance, drift depth, drift density, slope, and flow accumulation were selected as triggering factors. The whole factors were extracted from the digital elevation model, mine drift maps, and ground subsidence inventory data distributed by Mine Reclamation Corporation (MIRECO) of South Korea.

Ground subsidence hazard maps can be composed by frequency ratio method, specifying the hazard-inducing characteristics of training areas which include the area of subsidence influence. This work was supported by the Mine Reclamation Technology Development Project funded by the MIRECO.

Courtesy of Seoul National University.

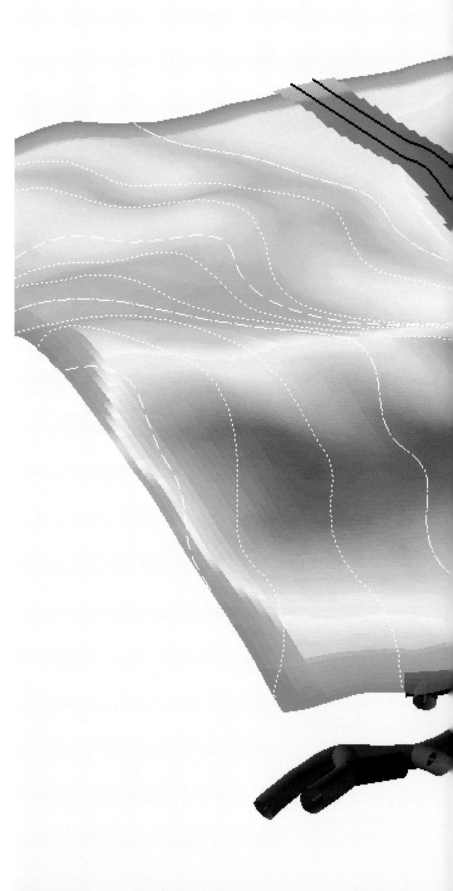

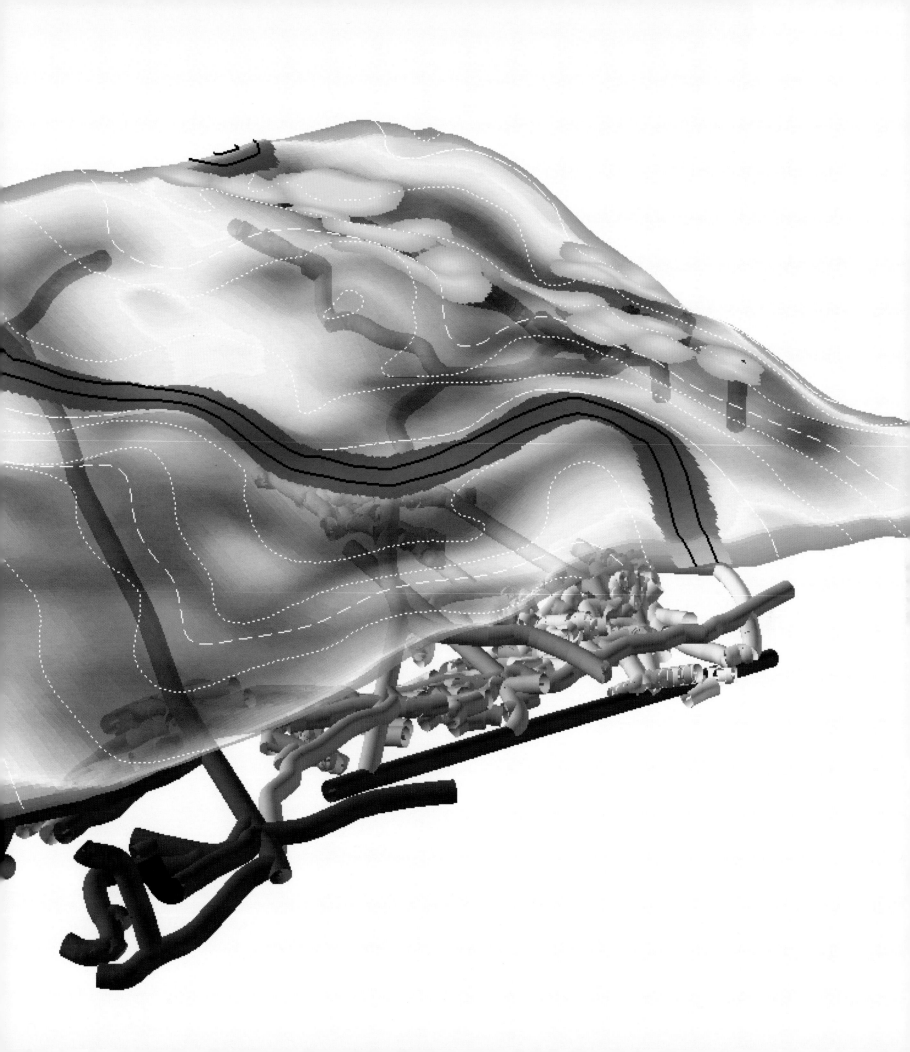

Pathway and Tendency of Heavy Metal Releases from Abandoned Mine Tailings in South Korea

Seoul National University
Gwanak-gu, Seoul, Republic of South Korea
By Da-eun Yun, Sung-Min Kim, Jin Son,
Myeongchan Oh, Hyeong-Dong Park, and
Seungho Lee

Contact
Da-eun Yun
daeun@snu.ac.kr

Software
ArcGIS 10.1 for Desktop

Data Source
Mine Reclamation Corporation

Environmental pollution problems at abandoned mine areas occur continually and are especially associated with heavy metal releases from tailings. These problems affect soils, rivers, cultivated lands, and residents who live near abandoned mine areas. This map describes the result of multidirectional flow accumulation and the distribution of hexavalent chromium (Cr^{6+}) concentration at the abandoned gold and silver mine in Jeollanam-do, South Korea.

This study focused on leaching behaviors of heavy metal associated with flow accumulation over a wide area. Hydrology analysis was used to decide the pathway of metal releases. As cumulative values of flow accumulation increase, metal concentrations increase. Also, values of concentration in the main flow are higher than those in other flows. The main flow starts from the tailings and is the largest flow on the left side of the map. The tendency is the same in the case of arsenic.

This analysis will be useful to find areas susceptible to heavy metal contaminants from tailings and to decide the priority of reclamation. This work was supported by the Mine Reclamation Technology Development Project funded by Mine Reclamation Corporation of Korea.

Courtesy of Seoul National University.

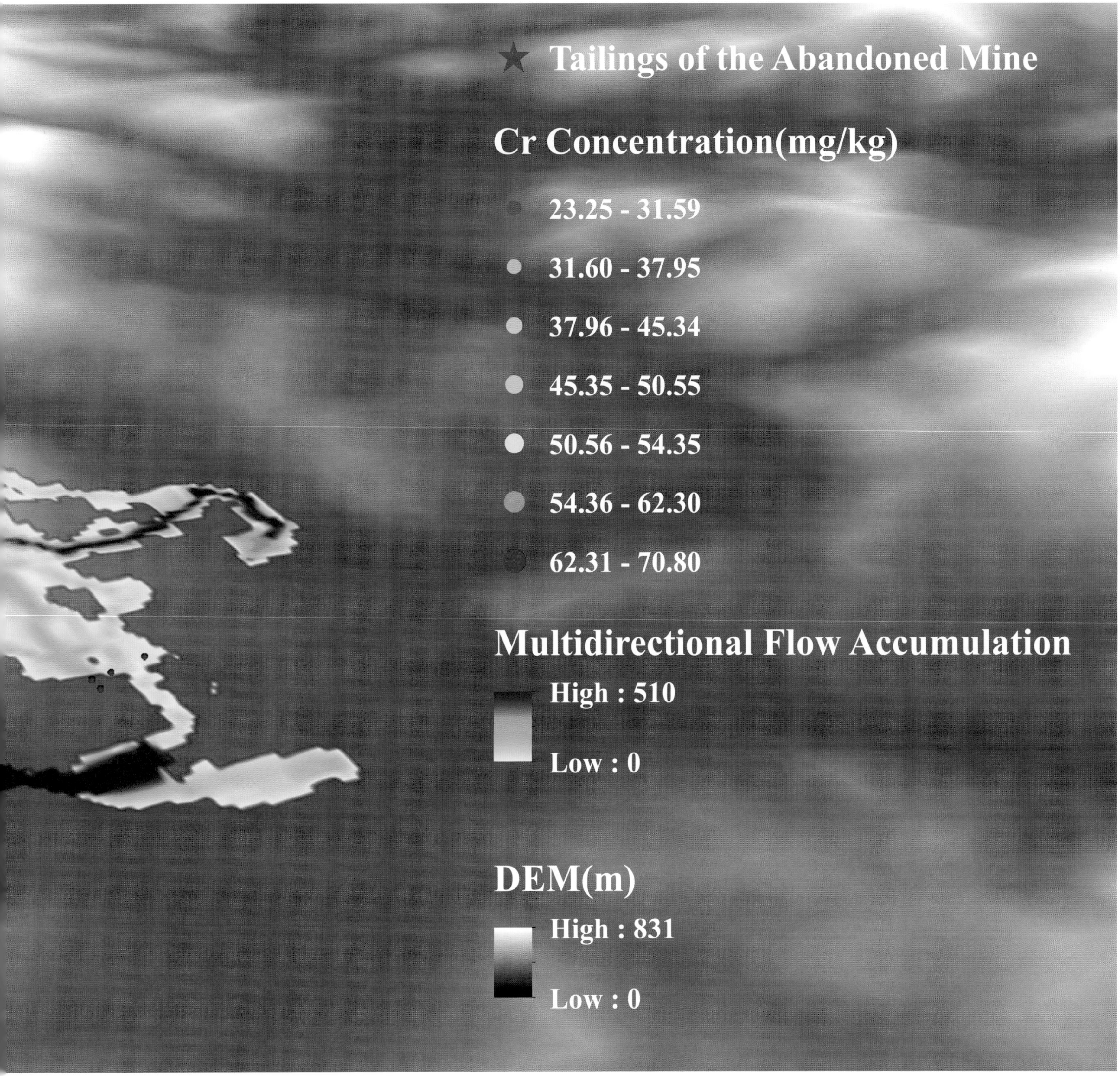

Tailings of the Abandoned Mine

Cr Concentration(mg/kg)

- 23.25 - 31.59
- 31.60 - 37.95
- 37.96 - 45.34
- 45.35 - 50.55
- 50.56 - 54.35
- 54.36 - 62.30
- 62.31 - 70.80

Multidirectional Flow Accumulation

High : 510

Low : 0

DEM(m)

High : 831

Low : 0

What Lies Beneath: Spatial Trend Analysis to Reduce Subsurface Uncertainty in the Gulf of Mexico

US Department of Energy, National Energy Technology Laboratory (NETL)
Albany, Oregon, USA
By Roy Miller III, MacKenzie Mark-Moser, Kelly Rose, and Jennifer Bauer

Contact
Roy Miller III
roy.miller@netl.doe.gov

Software
ArcGIS 10.2.2 for Desktop, Adobe Illustrator

Data Source
Bureau of Ocean Energy Management

Uncertainty is a major challenge in subsurface resource evaluations, as they rely on disparate and discontinuous datasets collected from often diverse and disparate sources. The National Energy Technology Laboratory's (NETL) Subsurface Trend Analysis (STA) is a hybrid deductive-probabilistic approach that combines geologic systems information with GIS and spatiotemporal statistical methods, supporting subsurface property characterization and uncertainty reduction.

Potential uses for this approach include petroleum resource or risk assessments, groundwater evaluation, and subsurface environmental assessments. This map illustrates an application of the STA approach used for the Gulf of Mexico. Domains defined using the STA approach in this evaluation offer improved insight into key subsurface properties such as pressure, temperature, depth, permeability, and porosity. Using the STA's hybrid deductive-probabilistic approach helps reduce uncertainty and better constrain the likely range and distribution of these key properties relative to each domain.

Copyright 2015 NETL.

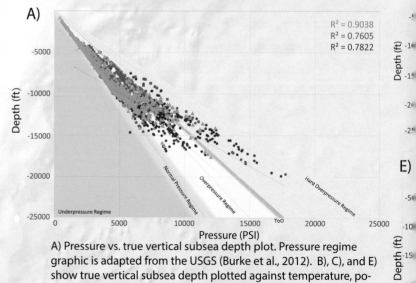

*Gradient domain boundaries represent uncertainty

Statistical Analysis of Example Domain

A) Pressure vs. true vertical subsea depth plot. Pressure regime graphic is adapted from the USGS (Burke et al., 2012). B), C), and E) show true vertical subsea depth plotted against temperature, porosity, and permeability respectively. F) shows log permeability versus porosity. E) shows termperature versus pressure. G) is a ternary diagram displaying the contribution of the geologic processes of structure, deposition, and diagenesis to domain 7's trends. Each chronozone is plotted individually according to the influence of the processes on that chronozone's attributes.

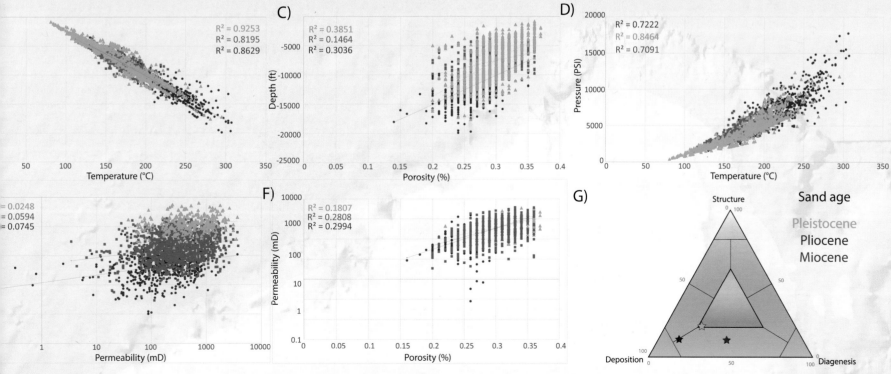

What is Autocorrelation?

Spatial or temporal autocorrelation occurs when the value of a property at one point can, at least in part, be predicted by knowledge of the value of that property at another point (Jones, in prep).

Spatial autocorrelation can be seen in elevation.

C)

R² = 0.9253
R² = 0.8195
R² = 0.8629

R² = 0.3851
R² = 0.1464
R² = 0.3036

D)

R² = 0.7222
R² = 0.8464
R² = 0.7091

Temperature (°C)

Depth (ft)

Porosity (%)

Pressure (PSI)

Temperature (°C)

= 0.0248
= 0.0594
= 0.0745

F)

R² = 0.1807
R² = 0.2808
R² = 0.2994

G)

Permeability (mD)

Porosity (%)

Structure

Sand age

Pleistocene
Pliocene
Miocene

Deposition

Diagenesis

' is within a shelf minibasin region structurally and is depositionally dominated by deltaic and delta-fed apron sedimentation. The Red Fault System is situated in this orresponding to a lateral boundary between fluid overpressured compartments. Pressure and depth show heteroskedasticity. Depth and temperature are well-correlated.

Global Hurricane Tracks

EEC Environmental
Orange, California, USA
By Jinho Kang

Contact
Jinho Kang
jinho.kang@outlook.com

Software
ArcGIS 10.2.2 for Desktop

Data Source
Unisys weather data

The map was created to effectively visualize spatial big data. Hurricane records from 2000 to 2013 were collected from an open source data website and a spatial database was created based on the collected information. Different visual methodologies—projection system and quantitative/qualitative symbology—have been applied not only to understand the large-scale data's spatial patterns, but also to design visually aesthetic models.

Courtesy of Jinho Kang, EEC Environmental.

Indian

Atlantic

America-Pacific

Asia-Pacific

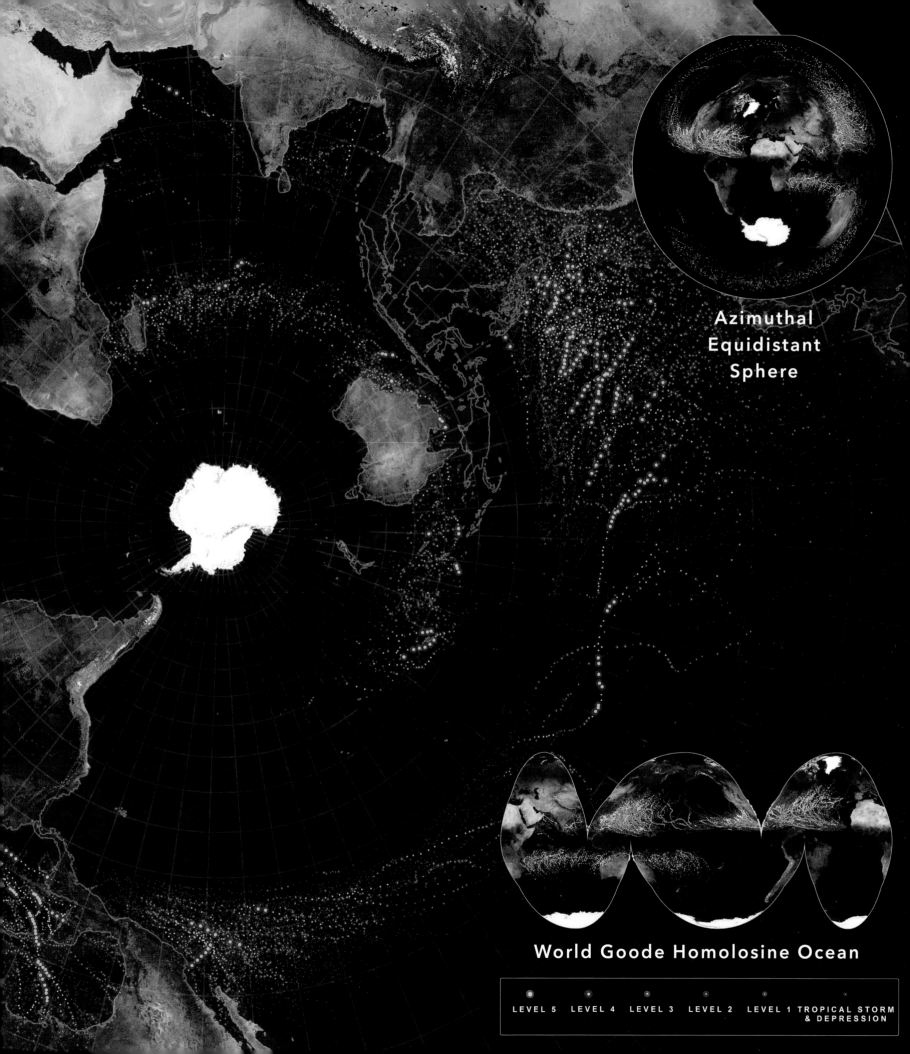

Azimuthal
Equidistant
Sphere

World Goode Homolosine Ocean

LEVEL 5   LEVEL 4   LEVEL 3   LEVEL 2   LEVEL 1 TROPICAL STORM
& DEPRESSION

Edwards Aquifer Rainfall Comparative Study

Edwards Aquifer Authority

San Antonio, Texas, USA

By Mark Hamilton, Jenna Pace, and Sarah Eason

Contact

Sarah Eason Watson

swatson@edwardsaquifer.org

Software

ArcGIS 10.2.2 for Desktop, ArcGIS Spatial Analyst

Data Sources

US Geological Survey; Vieux & Associates, Inc.; National Oceanic and Atmospheric Administration; NEXRAD; Edwards Aquifer Authority

The Edwards Aquifer in Texas is a karst formation, which is created from the dissolution of limestone, dolomite, and gypsum. The Edwards Aquifer serves the domestic, industrial, and agricultural needs of 2 million people and is the primary source of water for San Antonio, the nation's eighth-largest city. It is home to more than 40 million species, eight of which are endangered or threatened. The system consists of three segments: the drainage area, recharge zone, and artesian zones.

Recharge to the aquifer originates as precipitation over the drainage area and recharge zone or as interformational flow from adjacent aquifers. The drainage area actually acts as a drain allowing water to run down into the recharge area. It does not hold the water for long or in vast amounts for sustainability. In the recharge zone, the Edwards limestone is on the surface of the ground. Water soaks into the rock's fractures, faults, cavities, and sinkholes, where it flows into the artesian zone. The artesian zone is where the water is stored in quantities large enough for sustainability purposes.

This project explored the relationship between precipitation and recharge by comparing estimated recharge in wet and dry years. It shows that more than half of the recharge in eleven years occurred in just two of those years and demonstrates the vast amount of recharge that is possible with enough rain and the lack of recharge without.

Courtesy of Edwards Aquifer Authority.

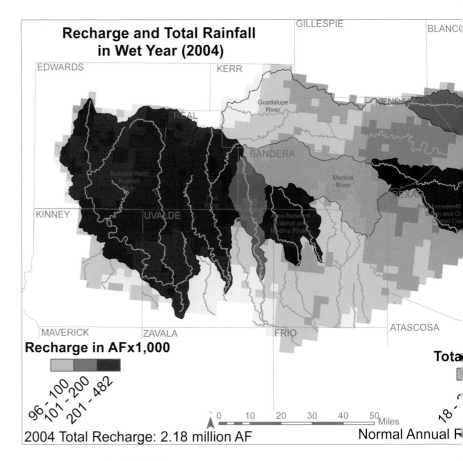

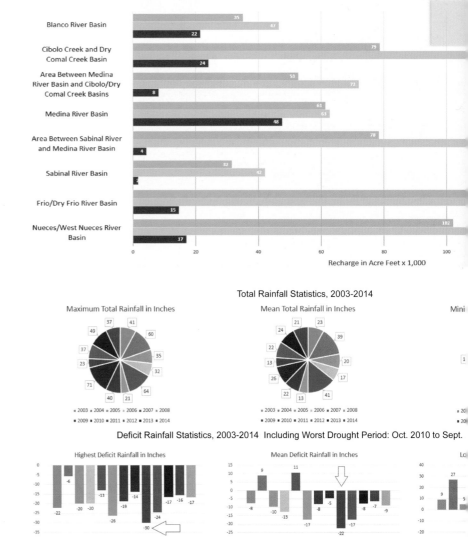

A Comparison of Actual Rainfall to 30 Year Average with a Resulting Deficit Across the Edwards Aquifer Region 2003-2014

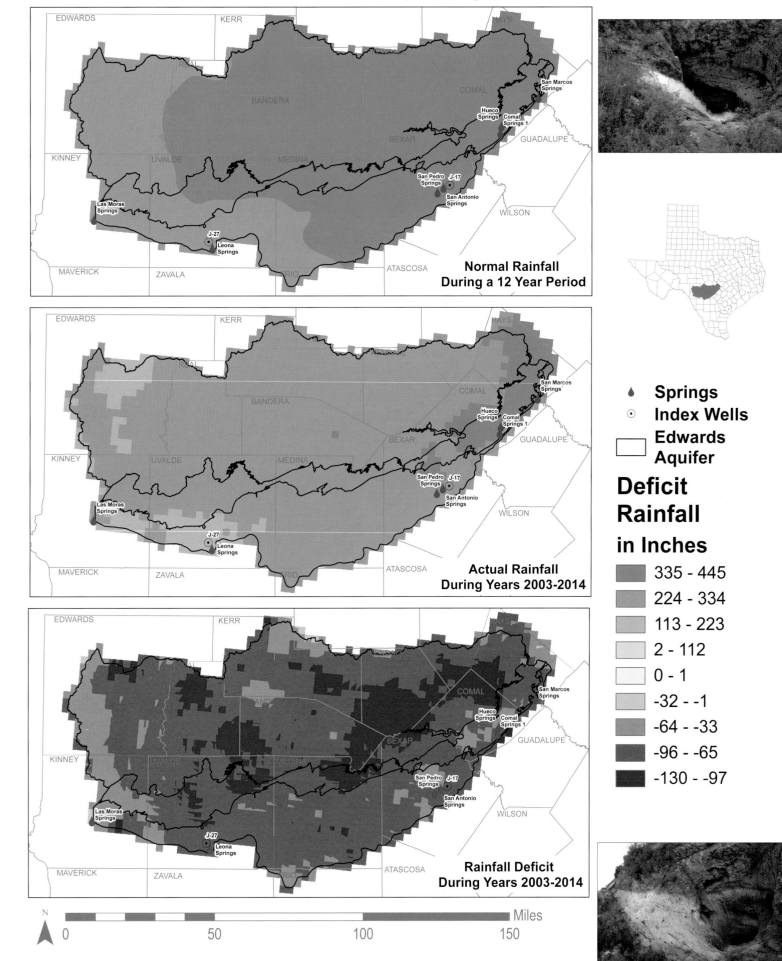

Normal Rainfall During a 12 Year Period

Actual Rainfall During Years 2003-2014

Rainfall Deficit During Years 2003-2014

Springs
Index Wells
Edwards Aquifer

Deficit Rainfall in Inches

	335 - 445
	224 - 334
	113 - 223
	2 - 112
	0 - 1
	-32 - -1
	-64 - -33
	-96 - -65
	-130 - -97

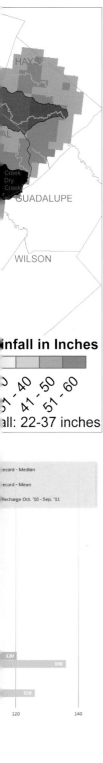

infall in Inches

41 - 50 51 - 60

all: 22-37 inches

Assessment of Enhanced Aquifer Recharge Potential—Twin Cities Metro Area

HDR
Minneapolis, Minnesota, USA
By Sean Tuohey and Adam Kessler

Contact
Sean Tuohey
stuohey@hdrinc.com

Software
ArcGIS 10.3 for Desktop

Data Sources
Metropolitan Council, Minnesota Geological Survey, Natural Resources Conservation Service, Minnesota Department of Natural Resources, Minnesota Department of Health, US Census, National Hydrography Dataset (HDR)

The Metropolitan Council contracted with HDR to perform a regional feasibility assessment, which includes a process to identify opportunities for enhanced groundwater recharge within the Twin Cities metropolitan area. The primary goal of the enhanced recharge analysis was to identify locations where water applied at the surface could infiltrate the subsurface efficiently, ultimately recharging permeable bedrock formations without creating unacceptable impacts to public drinking water supplies, groundwater contaminant plumes, and current land use.

Courtesy of HDR and the Metropolitan Council.

2040 Model-projected Drawdown / Recovery: Prairie du C

Drawdown (ft)	Recovery (ft)
0 - 2	40+
2 - 4	20 - 40
4 - 6	10 - 20
6 - 10	6 - 10
10 - 20	4 - 6
20 - 40	2 - 4
40+	0 - 2

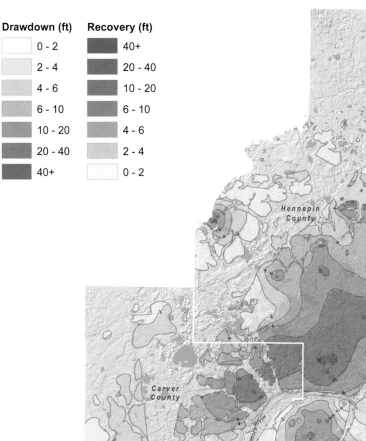

Enhanced Recharge Criteria

Vertical Infiltration Rate - Top 5 Feet (NRCS)

10 ft/day (or greater) is preferred for maximizing vertical infiltration; 10 ft/day corresponds with hydraulic conductivity of silty sand to clean sand (Freeze and Cherry, 1979).

1 ft/day was chosen as a reasonable minimum rate to effectively transmit water vertically away from an infiltration basin; 1 ft/day corresponds with hydraulic conductivity of silty sand (Freeze and Cherry, 1979).

Composite Hydraulic Conductivity (MGS)

10 ft/day (or greater) is preferred for maximizing vertical infiltration; 10 ft/day corresponds with hydraulic conductivity of silty sand to clean sand.

1 ft/day was chosen as a reasonable minimum rate to effectively transmit water vertically away from an infiltration basin; 1 ft/day corresponds with hydraulic conductivity of silty sand.

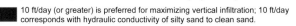

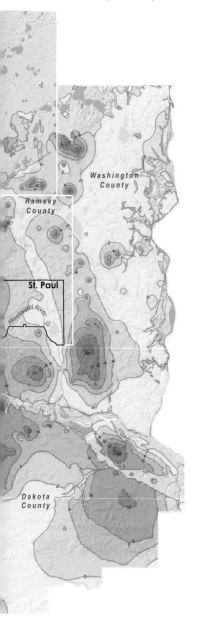

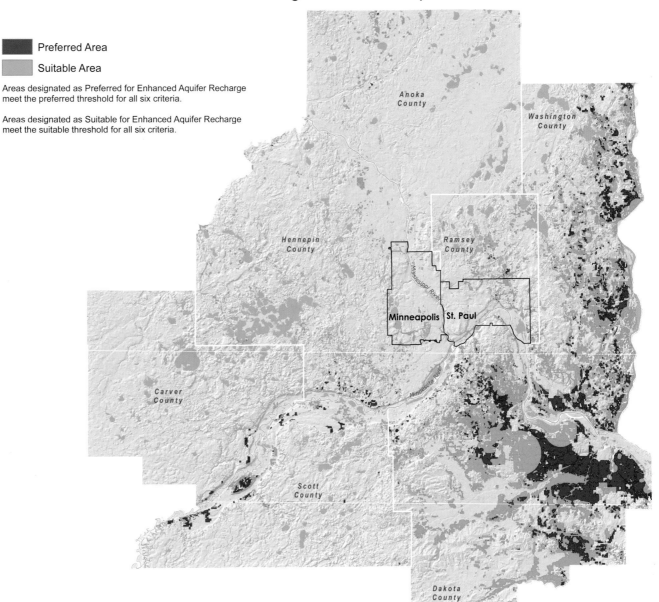

Preferred Area

Suitable Area

Areas designated as Preferred for Enhanced Aquifer Recharge meet the preferred threshold for all six criteria.

Areas designated as Suitable for Enhanced Aquifer Recharge meet the suitable threshold for all six criteria.

Depth to Water Table (MCES)

50 feet (or greater) unsaturated thickness is preferred for maximizing infiltration.

15 feet was chosen as a reasonable minimum unsaturated thickness over which water from an infiltration basin can build a sufficient vertical gradient to effectively drive infiltration.

Land Use (MCES)

Agricultural, parks, and undeveloped areas may have land available and are considered preferred for locating large infiltration basins.

All other types of land use are considered unsuitable since the land is already developed.

Natural Resources (MN DNR)

Areas outside of Calcareous Fens, Trout Streams, NPC, AMA, WMA, Federal Land/Easement, SNA, State Parks, USDA NRCS Easement, Nature Conservancy, and RNRA are preferred for locating infiltration basins.

T&E Species Areas and Game Refuges are considered suitable for locating. infiltration basins at this time based on low potential for impact to those areas.

Drinking Water Protection/Contamination Sites (MDH)

Preffered areas are located outside of Drinking Water Supply Management Areas and MDA Investigation Sites. MDH guidance (MDH, 2007) specifies stormwater infiltration should not occur where less than 100 feet of unconsolidated sediments separate fractured bedrock (e.g., Prairie du Chien dolomite) from the ground surface within a vulnerable DWSMA. This guidance is in place to protect vulnerable public supply wells from potential pathogens.

MDA investigation boundaries indicate areas that may be contaminated and are deemed unsuitable for recharge.

Mapping Storm Water Plume Interactions with Southern California Marine Protected Areas

Southern California Coastal Water Research Project
Costa Mesa, California, USA
By Steven Steinberg, Ph.D., GISP, and Abel Santana

Contact

Steven Steinberg

steves@sccwrp.org

Software

ArcGIS 10.2 for Desktop

Data Source

Southern California Coastal Water Research Project

Marine protected areas (MPAs) are potentially subject to pollutant effects of storm water plumes, particularly in California's south coast region, where 20 million people live within an hour's drive of the ocean. The Southern California Coastal Water Research Project conducted a screening study to quantify which MPAs are at greatest risk from storm water plume impingement. Impingement risk was estimated as a function of how often and how widespread plume exposure was within an MPA.

Dana Point, Swami's, and Crystal Cove MPAs, all of which are situated directly in front of urban watersheds, had the greatest potential risk of storm water plume impingement. Matlahuayl, Point Dume, San Diego-Scripps, and South La Jolla MPAs had a large extent of exposure, but plume frequencies were much lower, resulting in lower risk.

This study estimates storm water plume exposure, but does not quantify storm water effects, which will also be a function of the water quality from the discharge watersheds. A logical next step would be to quantify storm water concentrations and loads to assess pollutant exposure and examine biological responses to the potential water quality impacts.

Courtesy of the Southern California Coastal Water Research Project.

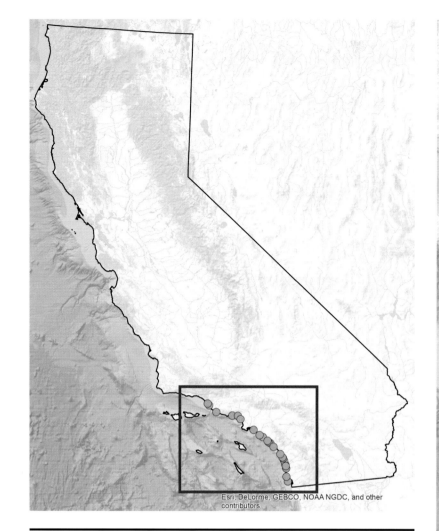

Esri, DeLorme, GEBCO, NOAA NGDC, and other contributors

Location	Debris Before	Debris After	% Change
Leo Carrillo	23	–	–
Zuma	921	262	-72%
Malibu	63	60	-5%
Santa Monica	2614	2855	+8%
Dockweiler	3876	1169	-70%
Redondo	282	234	-17%
Cabrillo	215	191	-11%

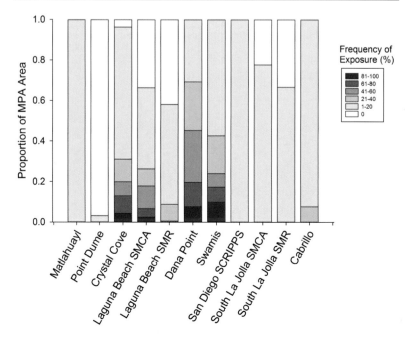

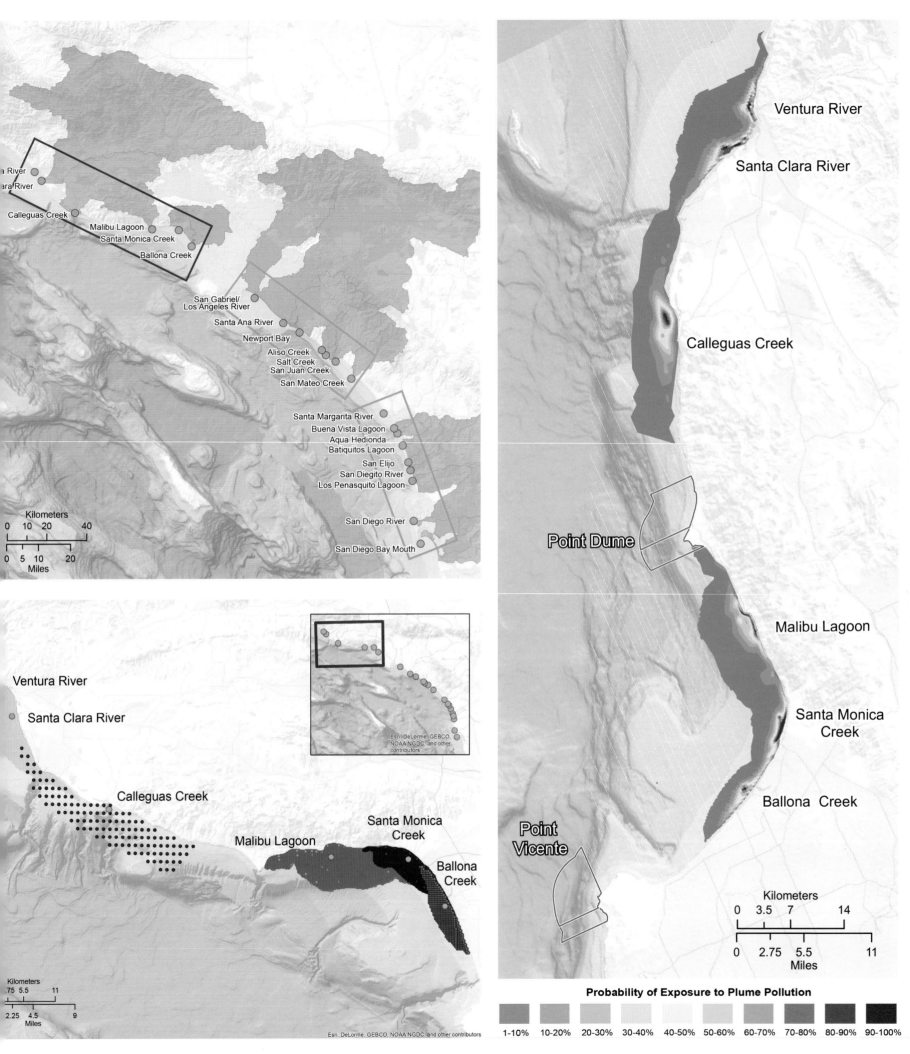

a River
ara River

Calleguas Creek

Malibu Lagoon
Santa Monica Creek
Ballona Creek

San Gabriel/
Los Angeles River

Santa Ana River

Newport Bay

Aliso Creek
Salt Creek
San Juan Creek

San Mateo Creek

Santa Margarita River
Buena Vista Lagoon
Aqua Hedionda
Batiquitos Lagoon
San Elijo
San Diegito River
Los Penasquito Lagoon

San Diego River

San Diego Bay Mouth

Kilometers
0   10 20   40

0 5 10   20
Miles

Ventura River

Santa Clara River

Calleguas Creek

Malibu Lagoon

Santa Monica
Creek

Ballona Creek

Ventura River
Santa Clara River

Calleguas Creek

Malibu Lagoon

Santa Monica
Creek

Ballona
Creek

Point Dume

Point
Vicente

Esri, DeLorme, GEBCO,
NOAA NGDC, and other
contributors

Kilometers
75 5.5   11

2.25   4.5   9
Miles

Kilometers
0   3.5   7   14

0   2.75   5.5   11
Miles

Probability of Exposure to Plume Pollution

1-10% 10-20% 20-30% 30-40% 40-50% 50-60% 60-70% 70-80% 80-90% 90-100%

Esri, DeLorme, GEBCO, NOAA NGDC, and other contributors

Drought, Drops, and Dots—Declining Groundwater Levels Across California

California Department of Water Resources (DWR)
Sacramento, California, USA
By Christina Boggs and William Brewster

Contact
Christina Boggs
christina.boggs@water.ca.gov

Software
ArcGIS 10.2 for Desktop

Data Sources
California Department of Water Resources Data Library

The California Department of Water Resources (DWR) monitors groundwater elevations and collects groundwater data through the California Statewide Groundwater Elevation Monitoring Program and other data collection efforts. All of this data comes together allowing the DWR to take a look at groundwater level change from a statewide perspective. This map shows how the recent drought in California is being reflected in changing groundwater levels across the state.

Courtesy of California Department of Water Resources.

Yearly

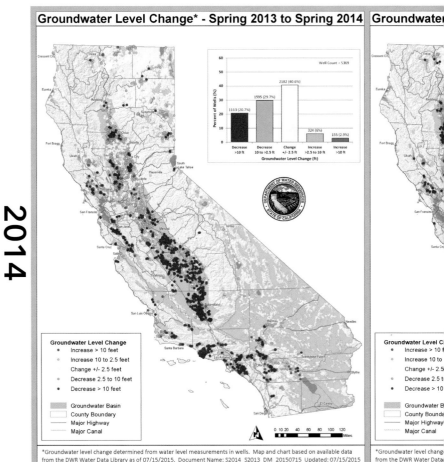

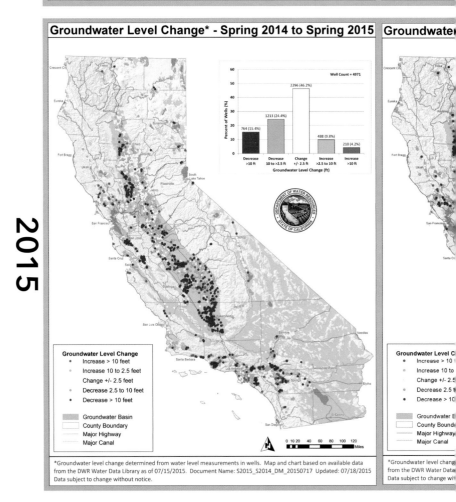

3-Year

5-Year

10-Year

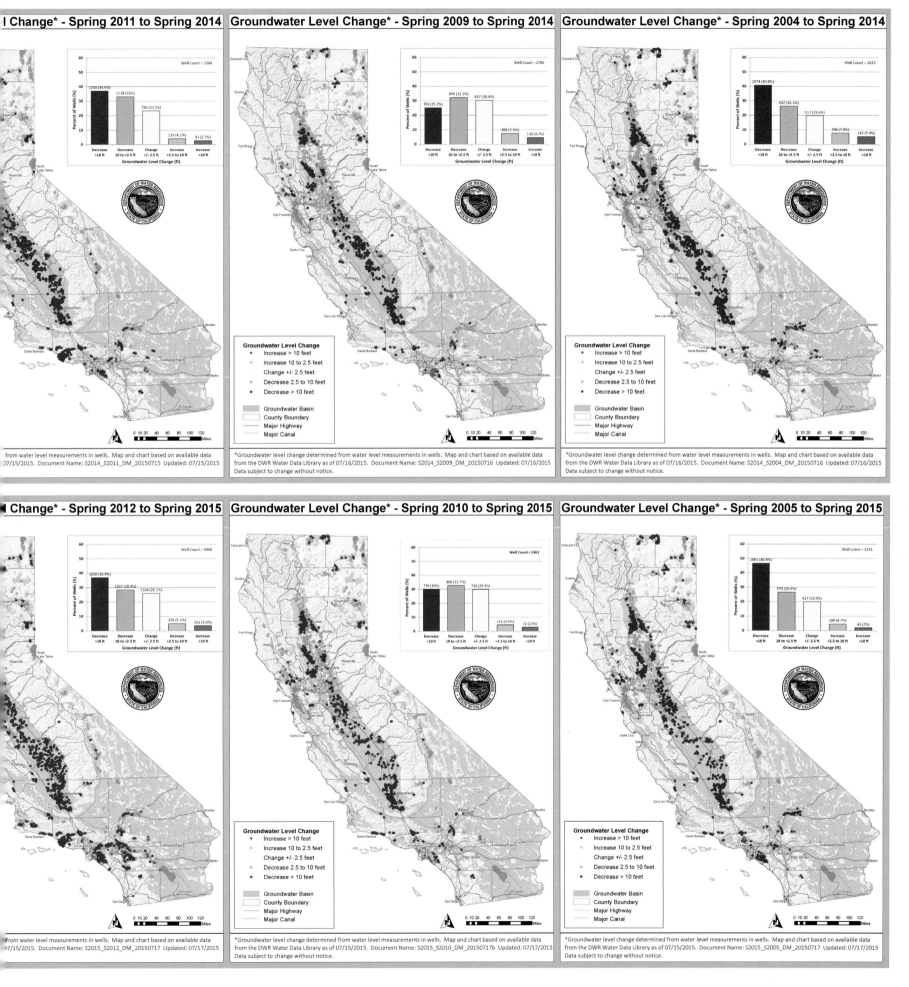

I Change* - Spring 2011 to Spring 2014

Groundwater Level Change* - Spring 2009 to Spring 2014

Groundwater Level Change* - Spring 2004 to Spring 2014

Change* - Spring 2012 to Spring 2015

Groundwater Level Change* - Spring 2010 to Spring 2015

Groundwater Level Change* - Spring 2005 to Spring 2015

Groundwater Particle Tracking: Using GIS to Calculate the Path of Groundwater Contamination

Langan Engineering & Environmental Services
Philadelphia, Pennsylvania, USA
By Michael Hagan

Contact
Michael Hagan
mhagan@langan.com

Software
ArcGIS 10.3 for Desktop

Data Source
Langan Engineering & Environmental Services

The effects of groundwater contamination on ecological health are becoming increasingly evident. To treat contaminated groundwater, it is essential to determine the contaminant's source location as well as the direction of groundwater flow. This map illustrates how, by using the ArcGIS Groundwater toolset, users are able to track groundwater particles to better understand the travel time, distance, and concentration of a particular contaminant, which can lead to more effective ways in remediating groundwater contamination.

Courtesy of Langan Engineering & Environmental Services.

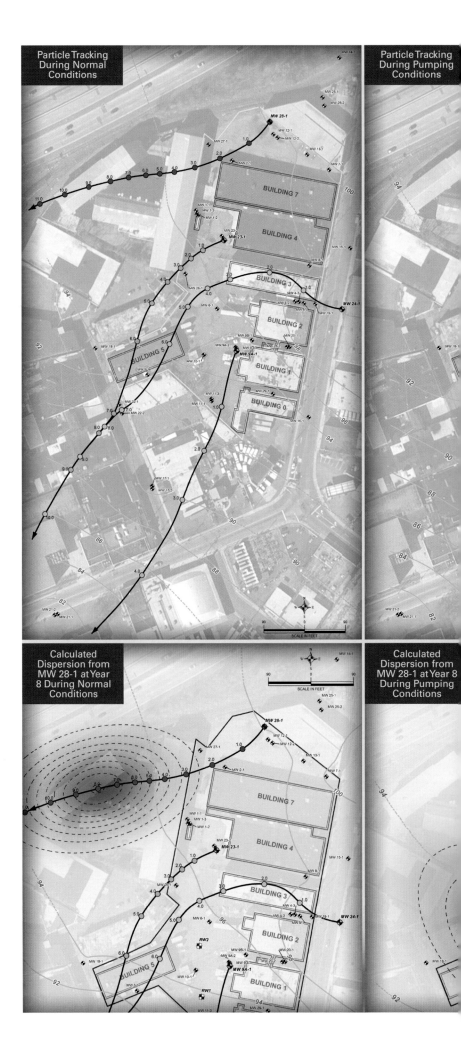

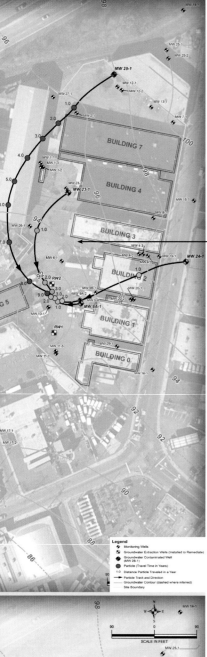

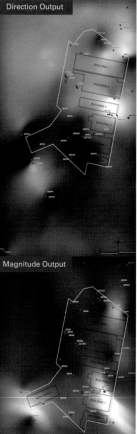

Groundwater Head Elevation Raster

Direction Output

Magnitude Output

Use "Particle Track" which follows the path of advection through the flow field from a point source

Input Files:
- Groundwater Direction Raster (generated using Darcy Flow)
- Groundwater Magnitude Raster (generated using Darcy Flow)

Output Files:
- Particle Track ASCII file
- Particle Track Polyline

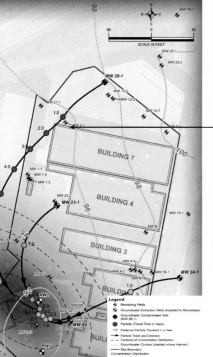

Use "Porous Puff" which calculates the hydrodynamic dispersion of an instantaneous point release for a constituent as it is advected along the flow path

Input Files:
- Particle Track ASCII file
- Porosity Raster
- Saturated Thickness Raster
- Mass

Output Files:
- Mass Raster

Use "Darcy Flow" which generates a groundwater flow velocity field from geologic data

Input Files:
- Groundwater Head Elevation Raster
- Effective Formation Porosity Raster
- Saturated Thickness Raster
- Formation Transmissivity Raster

Output Files:
- Groundwater Volume Balance Residual Raster (measure difference between groundwater flow in/out of each cell)
- Groundwater Direction Raster
- Groundwater Magnitude Raster (velocity at center of cell)

Napa Quake 2014 and Primary Water Release

DCSE Inc.
Laguna Hills, California, USA
By Hugh Dittrich

Contact

Hugh Dittrich
writeswater@gmail.com

Software

ArcGIS Pro

Data Sources

primarywaterinstitute.org, Rivers.gov, Cal Water

Primary water is sourced from deep in the mantle where hydrogen and oxygen are synthesized. Pressure forces vapors to the surface, where cooling and state change take place, to create liquid water. Primary water reaches the surface through the crust's weakest formations, resulting in aquifers and springs. New sources of primary water can reach the surface as a result of earthquakes. The 6.0 Napa earthquake in 2014 filled local rivers with 200,000 gallons of water a day in the dry season.

Courtesy of DCSE Inc.; illustration courtesy of Primary Water Institute.

Napa Quake 201
Primary Water R

www.Rivers.gov

Cal Water - Watersheds, Napa County
Watershed
Watershed
Watershed
Watershed

0   15   30   60   90   120
Miles

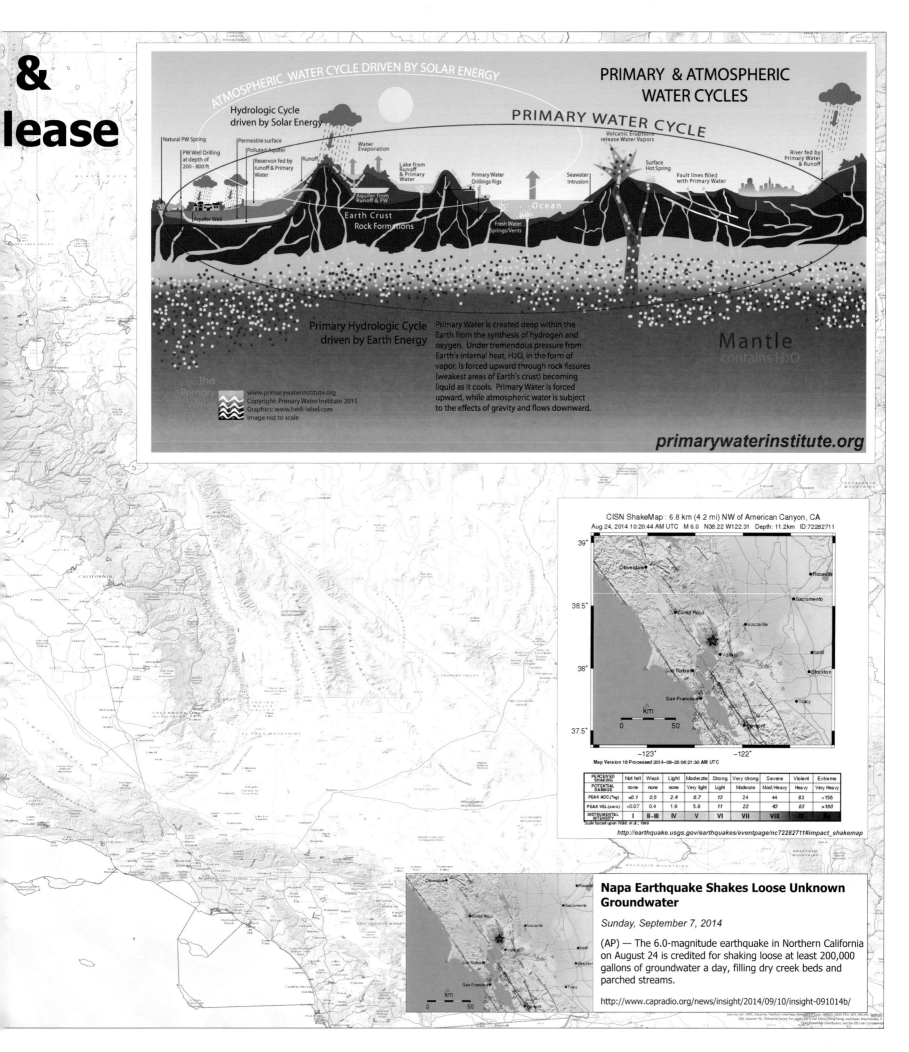

& lease

PRIMARY & ATMOSPHERIC WATER CYCLES

ATMOSPHERIC WATER CYCLE DRIVEN BY SOLAR ENERGY

PRIMARY WATER CYCLE

Hydrologic Cycle
driven by Solar Energy

Natural PW Spring

PW Well Drilling
at depth of
200 - 800 ft

Permeable surface
Polluted Aquifer

Reservoir fed by
runoff & Primary
Water

Aquifer Well

Water
Evaporation

Runoff

Lake from
Runoff &
Primary
Water

Aquifer from
Runoff & PW

Primary Water
Drillings Rigs

Volcanic Eruptions
release Water Vapors

Surface
Hot Spring

Seawater
Intrusion

Ocean

Fresh Water
Springs/Vents

Fault lines filled
with Primary Water

River fed by
Primary Water
& Runoff

Earth Crust
Rock Formations

Primary Hydrologic Cycle
driven by Earth Energy

Primary Water is created deep within the Earth from the synthesis of hydrogen and oxygen. Under tremendous pressure from Earth's internal heat, H2O, in the form of vapor, is forced upward through rock fissures (weakest areas of Earth's crust) becoming liquid as it cools. Primary Water is forced upward, while atmospheric water is subject to the effects of gravity and flows downward.

Mantle
contains H2O

www.primarywaterinstitute.org
Copyright: Primary Water Institute 2015
Graphics: www.hedi-label.com
Image not to scale

primarywaterinstitute.org

CISN ShakeMap : 6.8 km (4.2 mi) NW of American Canyon, CA
Aug 24, 2014 10:20:44 AM UTC M 6.0 N38.22 W122.31 Depth: 11.2km ID:72282711

Map Version 18 Processed 2014-08-25 04:21:30 AM UTC

PERCEIVED SHAKING	Not felt	Weak	Light	Moderate	Strong	Very strong	Severe	Violent	Extreme
POTENTIAL DAMAGE	none	none	none	Very light	Light	Moderate	Mod./Heavy	Heavy	Very Heavy
PEAK ACC (%g)	<0.1	0.5	2.4	6.7	13	24	44	83	>156
PEAK VEL (cm/s)	<0.07	0.4	1.9	5.8	11	22	43	83	>160
INSTRUMENTAL INTENSITY	I	II–III	IV	V	VI	VII	VIII	IX	X+

Scale based upon Wald. et al., 1999

http://earthquake.usgs.gov/earthquakes/eventpage/nc72282711#impact_shakemap

---

Napa Earthquake Shakes Loose Unknown Groundwater

Sunday, September 7, 2014

(AP) — The 6.0-magnitude earthquake in Northern California on August 24 is credited for shaking loose at least 200,000 gallons of groundwater a day, filling dry creek beds and parched streams.

http://www.capradio.org/news/insight/2014/09/10/insight-091014b/

US Army Corps of Engineers Civil Works Projects

US Army Corps of Engineers (USACE)
Kansas City, Missouri, USA
By Charles T. Sellmeyer, GISP

Contact
Charles T. Sellmeyer
charles.t.sellmeyer@usace.army.mil

Software
ArcGIS 10.3 for Desktop

Data Sources
Corps Project Notebook, National Inventory of Dams, and other Corps geospatial datasets

The Civil Works Program is a major component of the US Army Corps of Engineers (USACE) and is dedicated to providing quality and responsive water resource solutions. The Civil Works Program includes projects related to water resource development activities such as flood risk management, navigation, recreation, and infrastructure as well as environmental stewardship.

This map was designed to show the administrative components and active projects of the USACE's Civil Works Program in the fifty states and Puerto Rico. Headquarters, eight divisions, and thirty-eight districts coordinated efforts to rank over five thousand civil works projects for possible inclusion on the map. The primary goal was to locate projects and communicate the USACE's organizational structure. The challenge was in striking a balance between accurately locating and labeling projects in a confined map space while effectively communicating USACE's vast jurisdictional extent.

Courtesy of US Army Corps of Engineers.

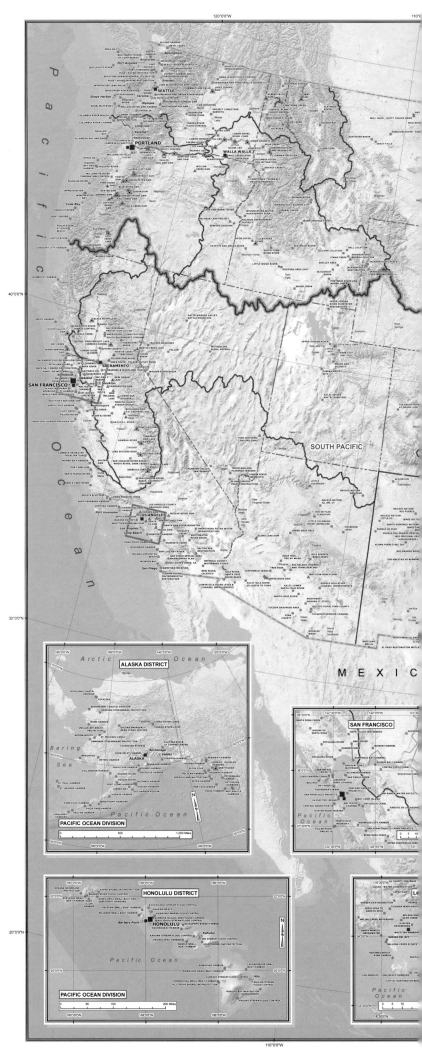

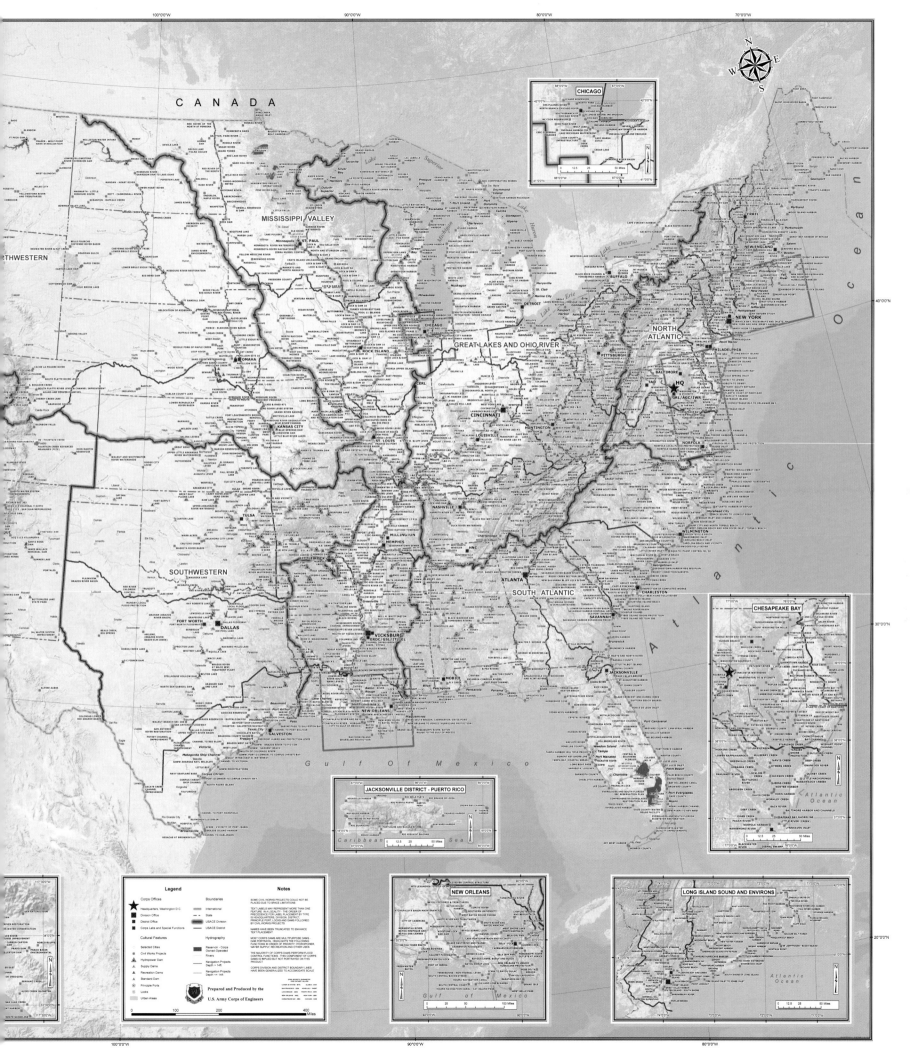

City of Monrovia: Planning for New Development Using ArcGIS and CityEngine

City of Monrovia
Monrovia, California, USA
By Aries Page and Mitch Cochran

Contact

Aries Page
apage@ci.monrovia.ca.us

Software

ArcGIS 10.3.1 for Desktop, Esri CityEngine 2015

Data Sources

City of Monrovia, Esri, Google Earth

This display portrays the City of Monrovia's usage of ArcGIS Desktop and Esri CityEngine software for planning new developments within the city. The Planning Division of the Community Development Department has the ability to look at areas within the city to determine the viability of a project in relation to its surrounding attributes.

Most 2D designs or artist renditions do not portray the specific characteristics of the surrounding neighborhood. The advantage of the 3D viewpoint is that it combines the best elements of the 2D map while also showing its impact on the surrounding neighborhood, including heights of buildings, shadows, and potential line-of-sight issues.

In this example, Monrovia's city staff was able to view two different proposed designs for a piece of land at one of the major intersections within the city. The proposals (one four-story office building versus two one-story commercial buildings) are different in size and stature. The impact on the neighborhood surrounding the proposals can be seen from the 3D views shown.

Courtesy of City of Monrovia.

Business Enterprise   Office/Research & Development/Light Manufacturing   Manufacturing

Corridor Commercial | Planned Development | Public/Quasi Public | Residential Low | Residential Medium 3000/Planned Unit Development | Residential Medium 3500 | Residential High | Residential Medium-High

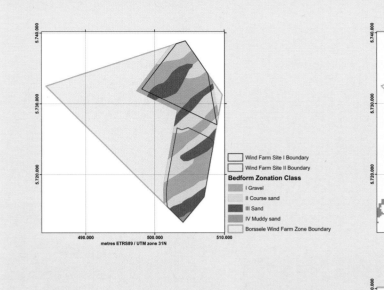

Offshore Wind Energy: The Netherlands

Ministry of Economic Affairs
Utrecht, Utrecht, Netherlands
By Rick van der Heijden, Ruud de Bruijne, Danny
Meus, and Bart Glaap

Contact
Caroline Porsius
GISCC@rvo.nl

Software
ArcGIS 10.2 for Desktop

Data Sources
Netherlands Enterprise Agency (RVO.nl),
Rijkswaterstaat, TenneT, Deltares, Vestigia Coastal
and River Archaeology, REASEuro, Deep BV, Fugro
N.V., Ecofys, KNMI

The Dutch government wants to promote energy conservation and renewable energy. The Energy Agreement
for Sustainable Growth sets out key actions and goals for
energy conservation, boosting energy supply from renewable sources, and job creation. The agreement sets a target
for 14 percent of all energy to be generated from renewable
sources by 2020, rising to 16 percent by 2023.

Offshore wind energy will play a significant role in meeting
the targets. To assist in this, a new market framework and
subsidy support system has been designed in consultation
with the wind energy sector. To help companies fully prepare
competitive bids, the government provides the relevant site
data regarding the physical conditions of the wind farm sites.
The wind farm sites that will be tendered are located in three
designated offshore wind farm zones off the Dutch west coast.

ArcGIS is used to combine collected data in defining parcel
boundaries and to visualize wind speed, bathymetry, unexploded ordnance, and other information. All data is made
available as maps and GIS data on a project website.

Courtesy of Ministry of Economic Affairs.

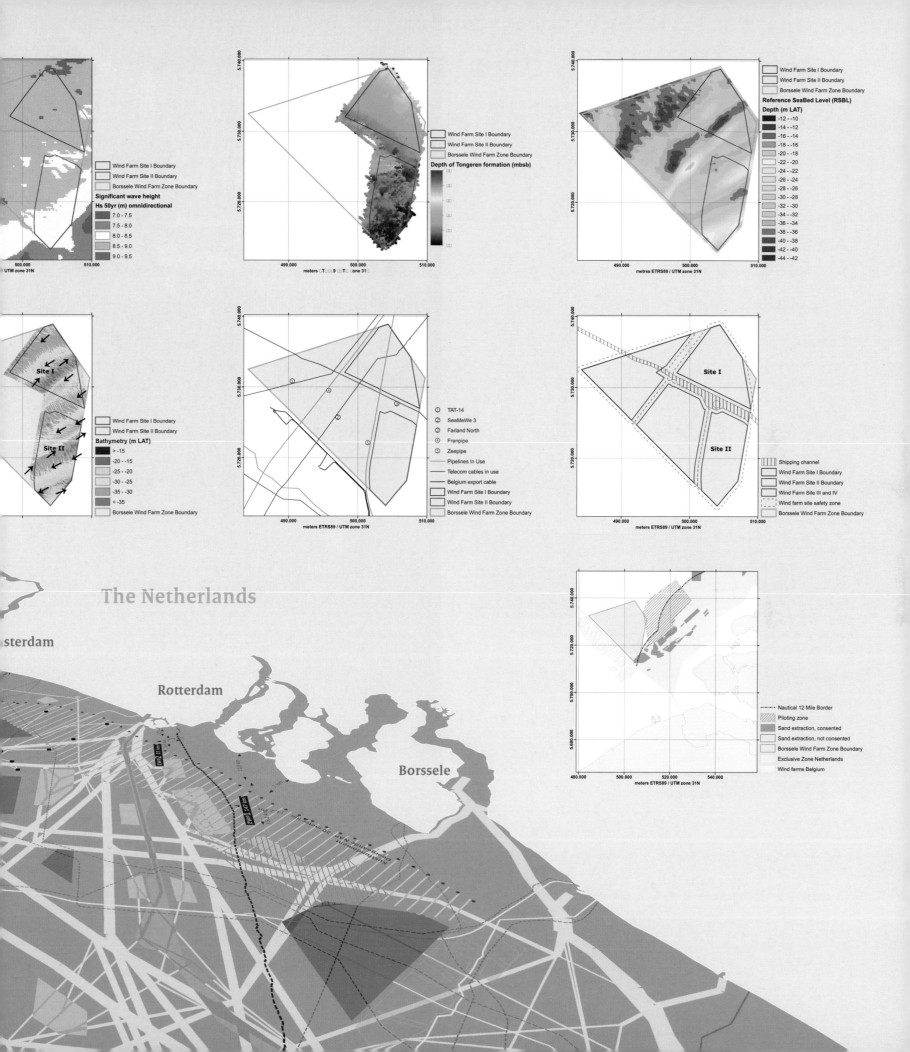

Significant wave height
Hs 50yr (m) omnidirectional
- 7.0 - 7.5
- 7.5 - 8.0
- 8.0 - 8.5
- 8.5 - 9.0
- 9.0 - 9.5

Wind Farm Site I Boundary
Wind Farm Site II Boundary
Borssele Wind Farm Zone Boundary

UTM zone 31N

Depth of Tongeren formation (mbsb)

Wind Farm Site I Boundary
Wind Farm Site II Boundary
Borssele Wind Farm Zone Boundary

meters ETRS89 UTM zone 31

Reference SeaBed Level (RSBL)
Depth (m LAT)
- -12 - -10
- -14 - -12
- -16 - -14
- -18 - -16
- -20 - -18
- -22 - -20
- -24 - -22
- -26 - -24
- -28 - -26
- -30 - -28
- -32 - -30
- -34 - -32
- -36 - -34
- -38 - -36
- -40 - -38
- -42 - -40
- -44 - -42

Wind Farm Site I Boundary
Wind Farm Site II Boundary
Borssele Wind Farm Zone Boundary

metres ETRS89 / UTM zone 31N

Site I
Site II

Bathymetry (m LAT)
- > -15
- -20 - -15
- -25 - -20
- -30 - -25
- -35 - -30
- < -35

Wind Farm Site I Boundary
Wind Farm Site II Boundary
Borssele Wind Farm Zone Boundary

① TAT-14
② SeaMeWe 3
③ Farland North
④ Franpipe
⑤ Zeepipe

Pipelines In Use
Telecom cables in use
Belgium export cable
Wind Farm Site I Boundary
Wind Farm Site II Boundary
Borssele Wind Farm Zone Boundary

meters ETRS89 / UTM zone 31N

Site I
Site II

Shipping channel
Wind Farm Site I Boundary
Wind Farm Site II Boundary
Wind Farm Site III and IV
Wind farm site safety zone
Borssele Wind Farm Zone Boundary

meters ETRS89 / UTM zone 31N

The Netherlands

Amsterdam
Rotterdam
Borssele

Nautical 12 Mile Border
Piloting zone
Sand extraction, consented
Sand extraction, not consented
Borssele Wind Farm Zone Boundary
Exclusive Zone Netherlands
Wind farms Belgium

meters ETRS89 / UTM zone 31N

McCarran International Airport– Airfield Lighting Decoded

Clark County
Las Vegas, Nevada, USA
By Sonya Wilson

Contact
Sonya Wilson
swn@mccarran.com

Software
ArcGIS 10.3.0 for Desktop

Data Source
Clark County Department of Aviation GIS-ERP

This map depicts the runway airfield lighting systems at McCarran International Airport (LAS) in Las Vegas, Nevada. Federal Aviation Administration aviation and airport acronyms can be confusing to nonpilots and nonaviation insiders. Upgraded LED lighting has been installed for enhanced safety and energy efficiency. This map explains the lighting purpose and naming clearly and shows how the airfield looks at night to a pilot. It is also one of the first sights for millions of visitors who touch down at the airport.

Courtesy of Clark County, McCarran International Airport.

McCarran International Airport-Airfield Lighting Decoded

Clark County Department of Aviation
Enterprise Resource Projects-
Geographic Information Systems

Lighting Type & Color

- Taxiway Edge Light, Blue
- Gate Light, Blue
- High Speed Taxiway, Alternating Steady Amber & Green
- Hold Light, Flashing Amber
- Runway End Indicator Light (REIL), Red/Green
- Runway Edge Lights (REL), Steady White
- Runway Edge Lights (REL), Amber to Approach on Last 2000'
- Taxiway Centerline, Steady Green
- Runway Threshold Light (RTL), Amber/Green

Medium Intensity Approach Lighting System with Sequenced Flashers (MALSF)

- MALSF, Green
- MALSF, White

Medium Intensity Approach Lighting System with RAIL (MALSR)

- MALSR, Green
- MALSR, White

Runway Status Lights (RWSL) System:
Red airfield lights automatically illuminate and extinguish as vehicles and aircraft traverse the airfield.

- Runway Entrance Lights (RELs) provide signal to aircraft crossing entering runway from intersecting taxiway
- Takeoff Hold Lights (THLs) provide signal to aircraft in position for takeoff

Taking a Ride on the C&T

Doug Cain
Fort Collins, Colorado, USA
By Doug Cain

Contact

Doug Cain
dcain@fcgov.com

Software

ArcGIS 10.2.1 for Desktop

Data Sources

US Geological Survey, The National Map, Bureau of Land Management, Esri Image Service, C&T Scenic Railroad Map by Osterwald (1975), HistoryColorado.org, www.drgw.net

Riding on the Cumbres & Toltec Scenic Railroad from Chama, New Mexico, to Antonito, Colorado, and viewing a vintage map of the Mississippi River inspired the author to produce this strip map. The railroad is a narrow gauge track (3 feet wide) operated by a steam locomotive.

An 1880s ribbon map—a few inches wide and 11 feet long—shows state lines, towns and cities, plantation owners, and more along the Mississippi River. The map was stored in a canister, intended to be scrolled out while a passenger traveled along the Mississippi on a steamboat. Seeing a digital version of this map inspired the author to create a strip map of the C&T Railroad that could be scrolled up and used in a small space but still cover a large area.

The map uses publicly available data from The National Map Viewer and US Geological Survey digital elevation models to create contours and hillshades that provide a base. Basic transportation, water, and points of interest information added detail to the map.

To collect information specifically about the railroad, the author digitized features such as mile markers, trestle bridges, and water tanks based on resources such as GPS data, C&T Scenic Railroad tourist maps and brochures, and aerial photo services from ArcGIS.

Courtesy of Doug Cain.

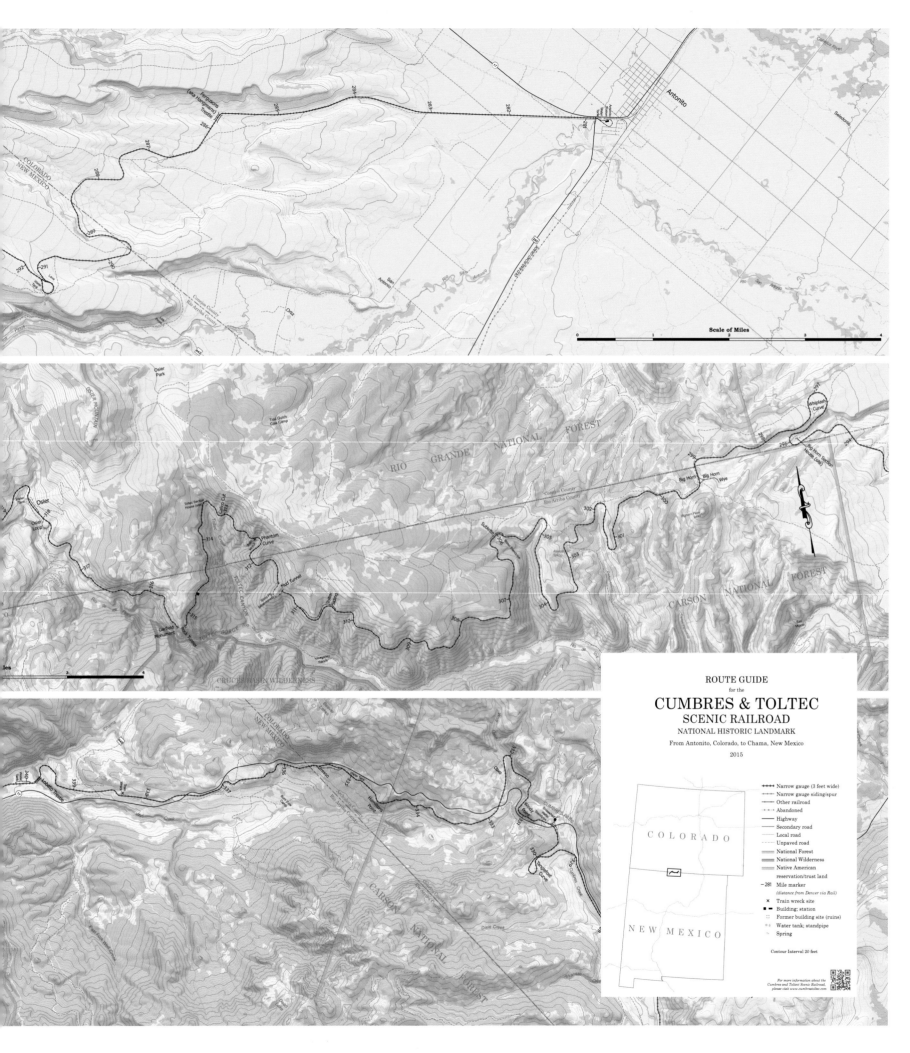

ROUTE GUIDE
for the

CUMBRES & TOLTEC
SCENIC RAILROAD
NATIONAL HISTORIC LANDMARK

From Antonito, Colorado, to Chama, New Mexico

2015

+++++	Narrow gauge (3 feet wide)
	Narrow gauge siding/spur
	Other railroad
	Abandoned
	Highway
	Secondary road
	Local road
	Unpaved road
	National Forest
	National Wilderness
	Native American reservation/trust land
−281	Mile marker *(distance from Denver via Rail)*
×	Train wreck site
■ ▪	Building; station
⁛	Former building site (ruins)
⚲	Water tank; standpipe
⚶	Spring

Contour Interval 20 feet

For more information about the Cumbres and Toltec Scenic Railroad, please visit www.cumbrestoltec.com

Wasatch Back Ski Resorts, Utah

Mapsynergy LLC
Sandy, Utah, USA
By Matt Liapis

Contact
Matt Liapis
matt@mapsynergy.com

Software
ArcGIS 10.3 for Desktop

Data Sources
US Geological Survey (elevation data), Utah Automated Geographic Reference Center (streets and water)

This map details the three Wasatch Back ski resorts of Deer Valley, Park City Mountain Resort, and The Canyons in Utah. Shown are ski lifts with name, capacity, speed, and loading direction, and resort boundaries with separate tree-filled areas and open slope. Also shown are proposed resort improvements, lifts, and boundaries. The map includes the ski slope rating symbols (green circles, blue squares, and black diamonds) and also shows slopes with the easiest way down. Most importantly, elevation characteristics like a background hillshade with 40-foot contour lines are depicted.

Copyright 2015 Mapsynergy LLC.

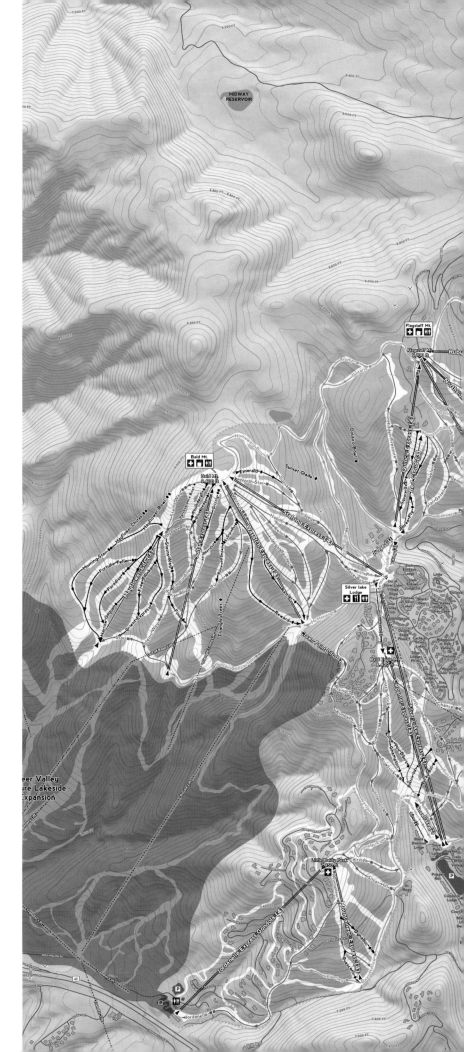

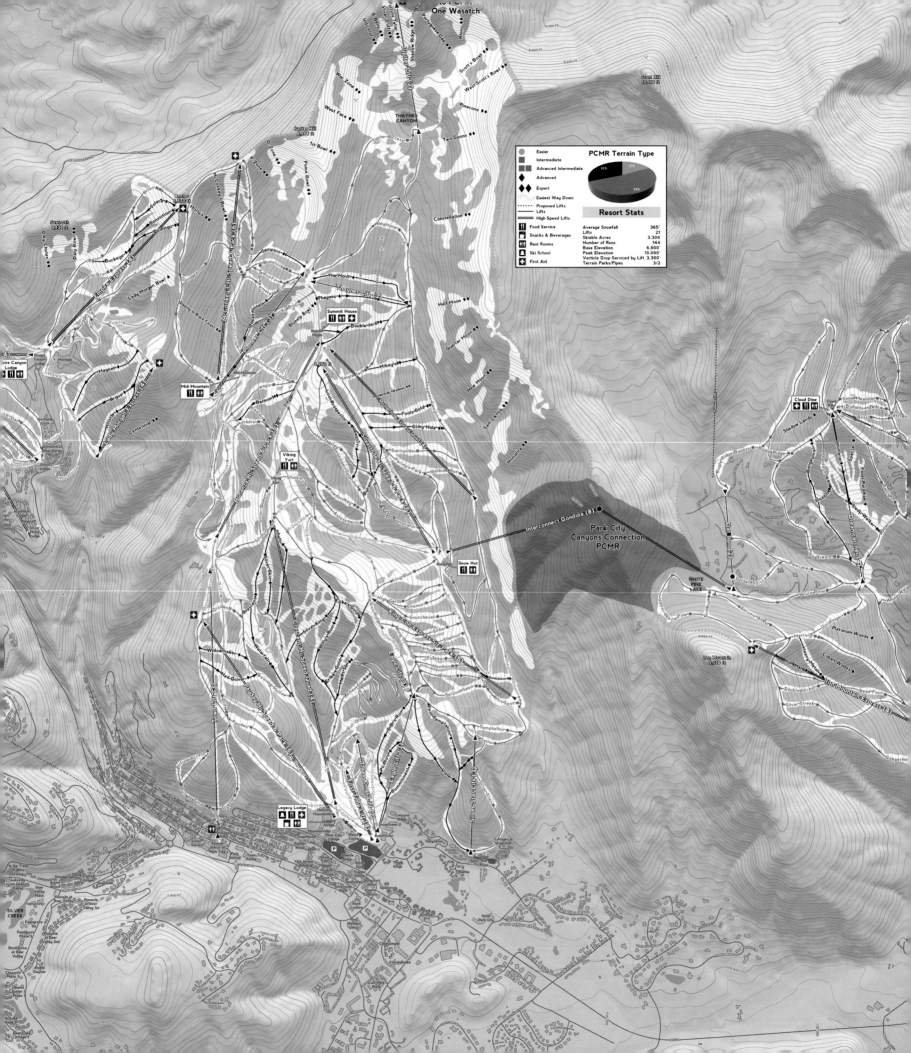

One Wasatch

PCMR Terrain Type

- ● Easier
- ■ Intermediate
- ◼ Advanced Intermediate
- ◆ Advanced
- ◆◆ Expert
- ····· Easiest Way Down
- ----- Proposed Lifts
- —— Lifts
- ═══ High Speed Lifts
- 🍴 Food Service
- 🥤 Snacks & Beverages
- 🚻 Rest Rooms
- 🎿 Ski School
- ✚ First Aid

Resort Stats

Average Snowfall	365'
Lifts	21
Skiable Acres	3,300
Number of Runs	144
Base Elevation	6,900'
Peak Elevation	10,000'
Verticle Drop Serviced by Lift	3,300'
Terrain Parks/Pipes	3/2

Park City
Canyons Connection
PCMR

Interconnect Gondola (8)

WHITE
PINE
LAKE

SILVER
CREEK

Mountain Goat Trail

City of Laguna Niguel
Laguna Niguel, California, USA
By Sean Southwell

Contact

Community Development Department
CommDev@cityoflagunaniguel.org

Software

ArcGIS 10.3 for Desktop

Data Source

City of Laguna Niguel

The City of Laguna Niguel has several hiking trails for its residents. The Mountain Goat Trail is a 1.1-mile loop currently in development by the city's Public Works and Community Development departments. This map was created to visualize the proposed trail, prepare construction cost estimates, and address concerns related to slope and proximity to the adjacent neighborhood.

The proposed route was digitized in the field and the route data was draped over a triangulated irregular network surface to determine the average slope value for route segments. Average slope values were classified into three classes, which were then symbolized based on their relative level of difficulty.

A few additional features were included to complete the visualization of the proposed trail. Background aerial imagery, at 4-inch resolution, shows the trail's location in relation to its surroundings. The distance from the trail to the edge of the nearby neighborhood was measured in a few places to demonstrate the required 200-foot buffer from residentially zoned property.

Courtesy of the City of Laguna Niguel.

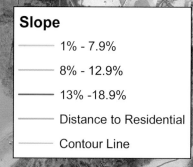

Slope

— 1% - 7.9%

— 8% - 12.9%

— 13% -18.9%

— Distance to Residential

— Contour Line

Rank	Corridor	Borough	# of Pizzerias	# of 4+ Star Pizzerias	Avg Yelp Rating
1	Jamaica Ave	QUEENS	7	4	3.9
2	3rd Ave	BROOKLYN	6	4	3.8
3	7th Ave	BROOKLYN	7	4	3.7
4	Bell Blvd	QUEENS	8	4	3.6
5	Richmond Rd	STATEN ISLAND	6	4	3.6

Pizza Corridors of New York City

Abt SRBI

New York, New York, USA

By Dara Seidl

Contact

Dara Seidl

d.seidl@srbi.com

Software

ArcGIS 10.3 for Desktop

Data Sources

Yelp Search API, New York City Department of Planning, New York City Department of Information Technology and Telecommunications

Where can someone in New York go to get a decent slice of pizza? New York City pizzerias of all kinds (local pizzerias to national franchises) were collected via the Yelp Search API and assigned to the closest street network segment, derived from the NYC LION database. Street segments were dissolved by the street name and ZIP Code to obtain ZIP Code level corridors.

Pizza corridors depicted on this map are home to at least two pizzerias, are colored by the average Yelp rating, and have a line width relative to the frequency of pizzerias in the corridor. The top five pizza corridors are ranked weighting 30 percent to the number of pizzerias, 50 percent to the average Yelp rating, and 20 percent to the number of four-star-plus pizzerias. The top five pizzeria corridors are found in Queens, Brooklyn, and Staten Island. While Manhattan has a high number of pizzerias, the average quality by corridor is relatively low.

Courtesy of Dara Seidl, Abt SRBI.

1,856 total pizzerias rated on yelp⁘

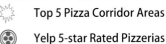

Top 5 Pizza Corridor Areas

Yelp 5-star Rated Pizzerias

Average Corridor Rating

▬▬	1.75 – 2.66
▬▬	2.67 – 3.25
▬▬	3.26 – 3.66
▬▬	3.67 – 4.00
▬▬	4.01 – 4.75

Number of Pizzerias

──	2
──	3
──	4 - 11

Frequency of Pizzerias by Yelp Rating

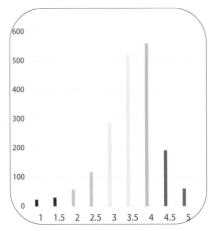

HATTAN

AMS

Pizza Rollio

lio 9C

tonno's Pizzeria

VERNON BOULEVARD

36 AVENUE

Via Caramico

Nonna Lena's Trattoria

DITMARS BOULEVARD

Caffe Rustico

FRANCIS LEWIS BOULEVARD

BELL BOULEVARD

4

Frank & John's

QUEENS

Pizza La Cancha

BEDFORD AVENUE

GRAND AVENUE

Jays Pizza

Gino's Express Pizza

QUEENS BOULEVARD

Kosher Pizzamania

UNION TURNPIKE

La Familia Pizza & Pasta

Fresca Pizza

Feta Pizza

Farmer's Pizza

MYRTLE AVENUE

FRANKLIN AVENUE

argot's Pizza

3

1

JAMAICA AVENUE

Broadway Pizza & Fried Chicken

Angela's Pizzeria

101 Pizza

Domenick Pizza Resturant

Pizzeria Lubrense

Johnny's Original Pizza

Anthony's Restaurant

CROSS BAY BOULEVARD

AVENUE

BROOKLYN

Ya Ya's Pizzeria

Manhattan Pizza

Rami's Pizza Express

Pizza Plus

BEACH 20 STREET

Yellow Cuisine

Annanapoli Pizza & Pastas

The Maryland Appalachian Trail

Maryland Appalachian Trail Shelter Site Assessment

Community College of Baltimore County
Catonsville, Maryland, USA
By Robert Flora

Contact
Scott Jeffrey
sjeffrey@ccbcmd.edu

Software
ArcGIS 10.1 for Desktop

Data Sources
Maryland Department of Information Technology,
Maryland Department of Natural Resources,
Maryland Department of Forestry

The 2,200-mile Appalachian Trail passes through fourteen
states and is said to be the longest hiking-only trail in the
world. This map shows a weighted analysis to determine
the best locations for trail shelters on the Appalachian Trail
in Maryland. Key factors were access to water, roads, and
parking; location relative to existing shelters; land use; and
slope. Several locations were identified and one location
stood out as the best potential site.

*Copyright © Community College of Baltimore County Geospatial
Applications Program.*

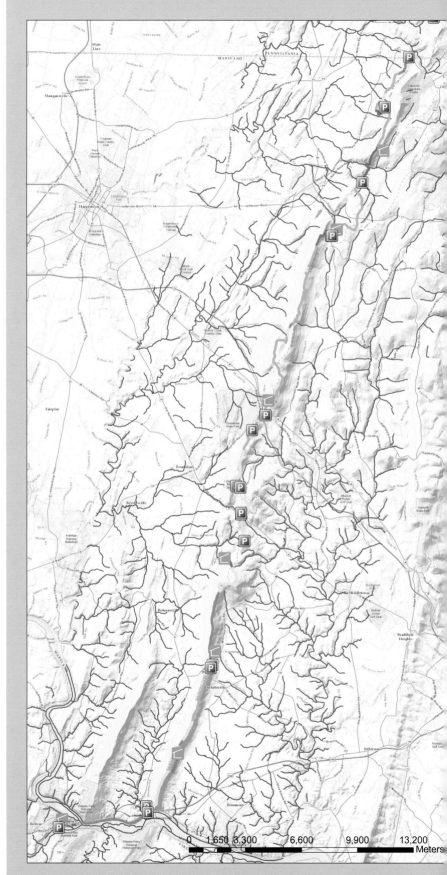

Site Assessment Criteria

Potential Shelter Sites

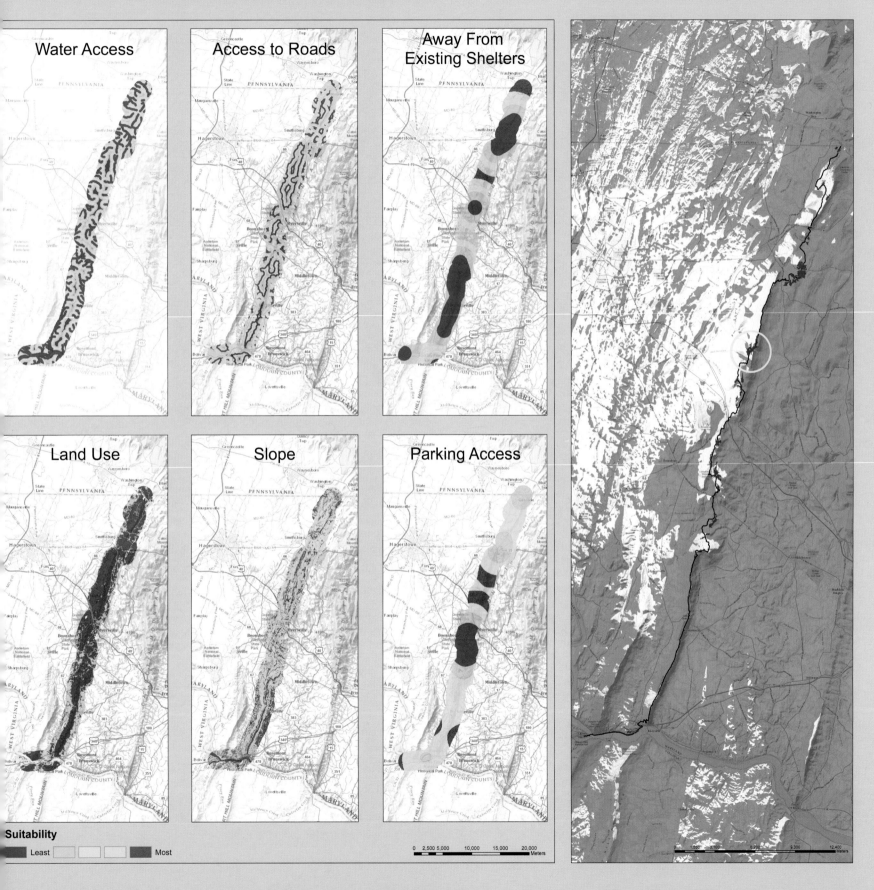

Water Access

Access to Roads

Away From Existing Shelters

Land Use

Slope

Parking Access

Suitability

Least ▢▢▢▢■ Most

0 2,500 5,000 10,000 15,000 20,000
Meters

Parks of Kenton County

Planning and Development Services of
Kenton County
Fort Mitchell, Kentucky, USA
By Louis Hill Jr., Ryan Kent, and Trisha Brush

Contact
Louis Hill Jr.
lhill@pdskc.org, @NKYmapLAB

Software
ArcGIS 10.2.2, CorelDRAW X7

Data Sources
LINK-GIS, Planning and Development Services of
Kenton County, Ohio-Kentucky-Indiana Regional
Council of Governments

This map shows an analysis of walk-time and drive-time
distances to parks throughout Kenton County. For the
purposes of this study, a park was included in the analysis
only if it is a publicly accessible location with active recreation
opportunities. Both analyses calculated the number of households that were located inside each walk-time and drive-
time interval and presented that as a percentage of the total
households in Kenton County.

Northern Kentucky mapLAB (NKYmapLAB), a product of the
Planning and Development Services of Kenton County, aims
to analyze a wide variety of data and present it in a visual
format that facilitates a better understanding by the public
and its elected leaders. Through traditional maps and story
maps, NKYmapLAB has addressed a wide variety of topics
such as the parks analysis shown here.

Courtesy of Planning and Development Services of Kenton County.

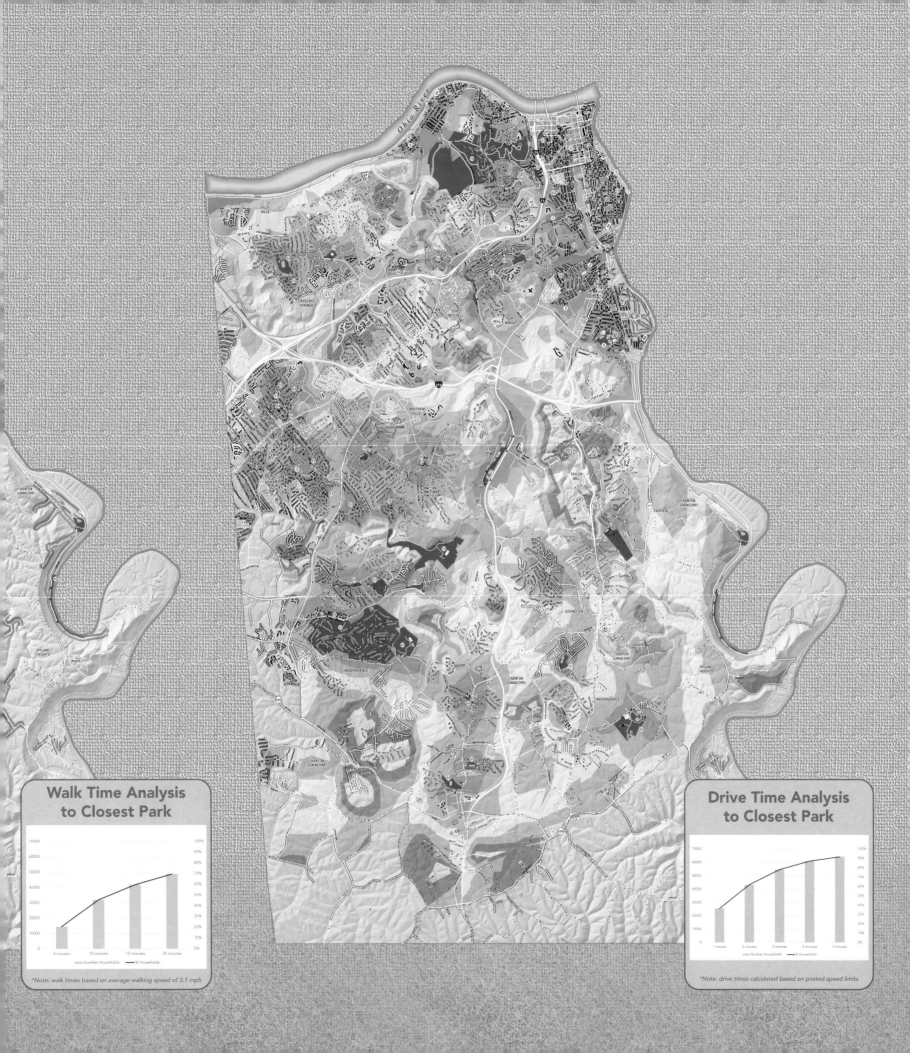

**Walk Time Analysis
to Closest Park**

Note: walk times based on average walking speed of 3.1 mph

**Drive Time Analysis
to Closest Park**

Note: drive times calculated based on posted speed limits

Walkability: Sidewalk Connectivity in Kenton County

Planning and Development Services of
Kenton County
Fort Mitchell, Kentucky, USA
By Louis Hill Jr., Ryan Kent, and Trisha Brush

Contact

Louis Hill Jr.
lhill@pdskc.org, @NKYmapLAB

Software

ArcGIS 10.2.2, CorelDRAW X7

Data Sources

LINK-GIS, Planning and Development Services of
Kenton County, Ohio-Kentucky-Indiana Regional
Council of Governments

This map shows Kenton County's sidewalk network, its
coverage, and its missing links to gauge the community's
walkability. The county has over 770 miles of sidewalks and
walkability focuses on points of interest that are within 50
feet of a sidewalk. Factors influencing walkability include
footpaths, sidewalks, traffic and road conditions, land-use
patterns, building accessibility, and safety.

Northern Kentucky mapLAB (NKYmapLAB), a product of the
Planning and Development Services of Kenton County, aims
to analyze a wide variety of data and present it in a more
visual format that facilitates a better understanding by the
public and its elected leaders. Through traditional maps and
story maps, NKYmapLAB has addressed a wide variety of
topics such as the walkability analysis shown here.

Courtesy of Planning and Development Services of Kenton County.

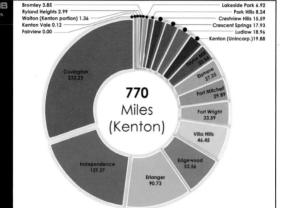

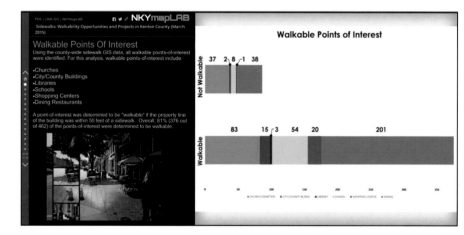

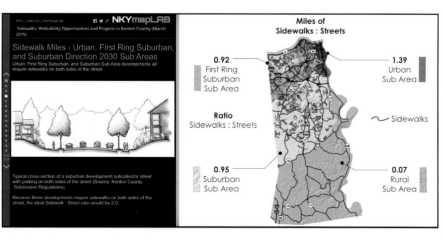

URBAN
Sidewalk Network
(all areas within the boundary are connected)

CINCINNATI

Ohio River

LUDLOW

BROMLEY

⑧

VILLA HILLS

PARK HILLS

I-75
I-71

②⑤

COVINGTON

KENTON VALE

CRESCENT SPRINGS

Dixie Hwy
785 foot gap

FORT MITCHELL

FORT WRIGHT

⑰

I-275

LAKESIDE PARK

I-71 I-75

Turkeyfoot
300 foot gap

⑯

I-275

ERLANGER

CRESTVIEW HILLS

EDGEWOOD

②⑤

⑰

TAYLOR MILL ⑯

⑰

①⑦⑦

ELSMERE

FIRST RING SUBURBAN
Sidewalk Network
(all areas within the boundary are connected)

Transit Ridership by Corridor

Valley Metro Regional Public Transportation Agency
Phoenix, Arizona, USA
By Cory Whittaker and Joe Gregory

Contact

Cory Whittaker
cwhittaker@valleymetro.org

Software

ArcGIS 10.3.1 for Desktop, Adobe Illustrator

Data Source

Valley Metro Regional Transportation Agency

Public transit ridership is constantly changing, with many factors influencing the number of people using transit. While the magnitude of riders may change, one aspect that seems to remain constant is certain corridors have a higher propensity of transit ridership. These maps illustrate the changes in the number of public transit riders in the Phoenix area over three years. In addition, analyzing the trends in 3D shows the magnitude of the ridership within the individual transit corridors.

October 2012: With an average gas price in Phoenix of $3.68, average daily temperature of 88 degrees, and schools in session, transit ridership was increasing.

October 2014: Fuel prices fell to an average in Phoenix of $3.04. But with the cooler temperatures and schools in session, modest increases are shown.

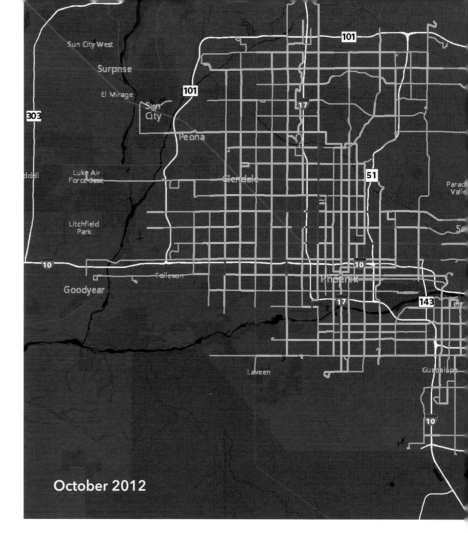

October 2012

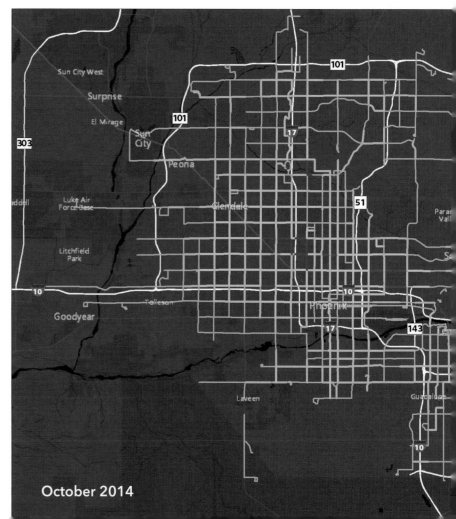

October 2014

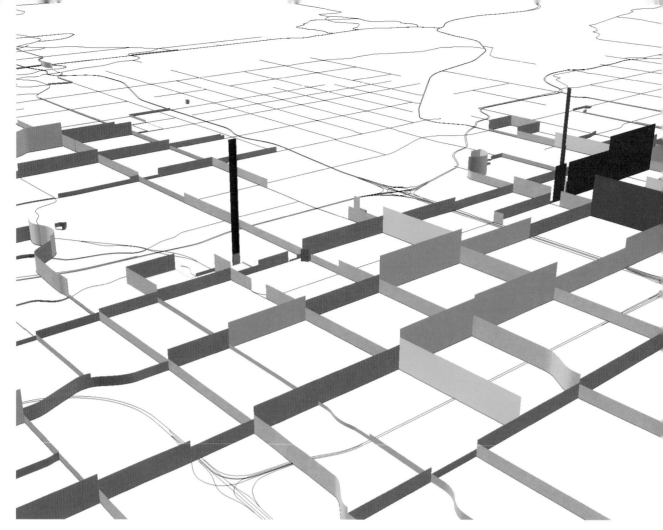

Using GIS to Support In-Flight Operations in the Event of an Airport Outage

PennDesign, University of Pennsylvania
Philadelphia, Pennsylvania, USA
By Susan Burtner

Contact

Susan Burtner
subu@design.upenn.edu

Software

ArcGIS 10.2 for Desktop

Data Source

flightstats.org for October 29, 2011

Airport diversions are typically handled on a plane-by-plane basis, which requires a lot of collaboration and can become dangerous if several aircraft begin running out of fuel trying to find a diversion airport. Airports that are inadequately equipped to receive several diverted aircraft at once can mean great discomfort for passengers that may have to sit for hours on a tarmac at a diversion airport.

This tool was created to optimize the diversion process systemically. It maps out each aircraft's location to a predetermined diversion airport using Great Circles. An OD-Matrix tool contains the distance from each diversion point to a diversion airport. The tool can then use these values in the mathematical programming software LINDO to find the solution that minimizes the total distance that is traveled for all of these aircraft. Constraints on certain aircraft unable to land at certain airports or an airport not being able to accept more than a certain number of aircraft can also be defined.

Courtesy of PennDesign and the Penn Institute for Urban Research.

Figure 1. *All diverted fligh*

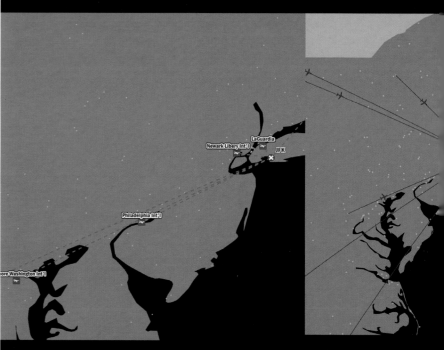

Figure 2. *The six candidate diversion airports*   **Figure 3.** *All scheduled*

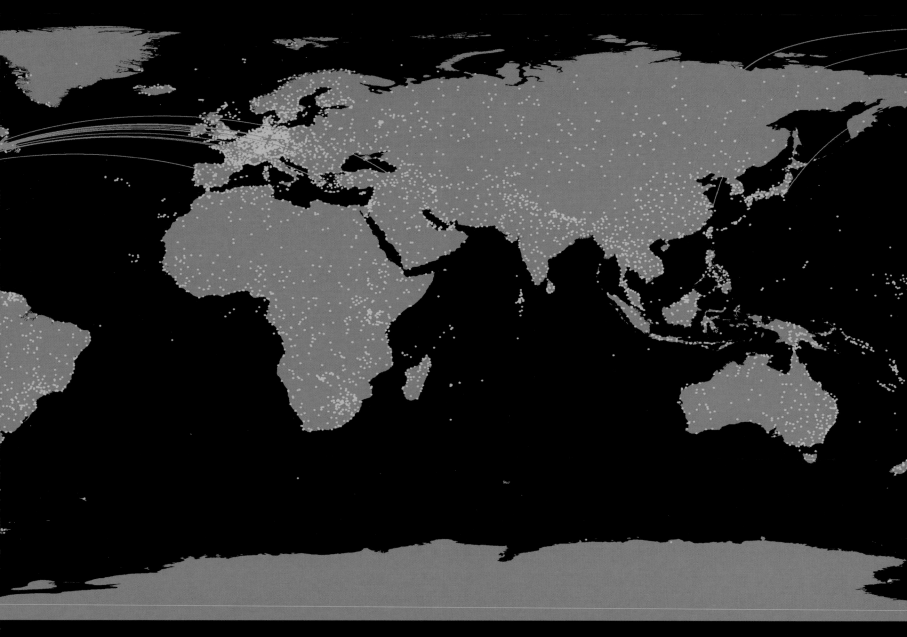

en route to JFK on October 29th, 2011. Flight data from **flightstats.org**

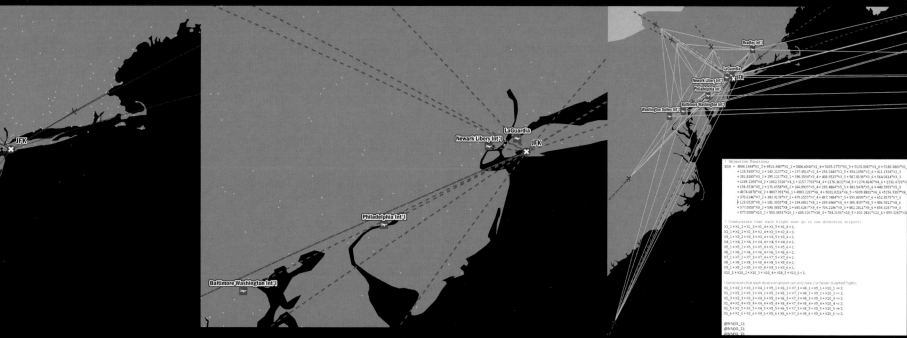

s on October 29th, 2011, from 12-1pm

Figure 4. *The scheduled and diverted flight paths that make up the network*

Figure 5. *The lines that make up the OD-Matrix and wwdesignate the path from each flight at the point of diversion and each diversion airport*

Vermont Route Logs: Python-Driven Map Automation with Straight-Line Diagrams

Vermont Agency of Transportation
Montpelier, Vermont, USA
By Kerry Alley and Michael Trunzo

Contact

Kerry Alley
Kerry.Alley@vermont.gov

Software

ArcGIS 10.3.1 for Desktop

Data Sources

Vermont Agency of Transportation, Vermont Center for Geographic Information (surface water data)

Straight-line diagrams, also known as route logs, are a key engineering tool used within the Vermont Agency of Transportation to provide a coherent, one-dimensional view of each section of federal aid highway and its associated data. The layout of the route logs allows a wealth of coincident data to be shown simultaneously and easily correlated by milepost.

Routes are represented as straight lines with a built-in linear referencing system (LRS). Highway data is rendered along those routes using dynamic segmentation, that is, located by route and mile marker values as opposed to x- and y-coordinates. The current tool for generating the logs consists of a single map document template and a suite of Python scripts that process data and automate map production. Noteworthy challenges addressed by the preprocessing scripts include managing colocated routes; displaying gaps in the route system; synchronizing data frame extents; summarizing highway statistics by page; identifying and adjusting overlapping labels; and integrating data from SDE databases, geodatabases, shapefiles, and Excel documents. Produced annually, the current series of route logs covers over 5,000 miles of Vermont's highways.

Courtesy of the Vermont Agency of Transportation.

DRAFT

Please Note: Errors and Omissions May Exist.
Contact the VTrans Mapping Section with questions or concerns.

DISTRICT	TOWN	ROUTE
7	ST. JOHNSBURY	US-2

US 2

KIRBY

ST. JOHNSBURY

CONCORD

LUNENBURG

ST. JOHNSBURY
URBAN COMPACT

WATERFORD

East Saint Johnsbury

STRUCTURE DESCRIPTIONS

Culvert 100:
Culvert - 1986
Structure No. 300028010003111
Length: 10'
Under Clearance: 10.0'
Facility Carried: US2
Bridge Type: CGMPP
Features Intersected: ACCESS ROAD
Maintenance: State

Culvert 102:
Culvert - 1975
Structure No. 200028010203112
Length: 56'
Facility Carried: US 00002 ML
Bridge Type: TWIN CELL RC BOX
Features Intersected: SLEEPER RI /ER
Maintenance/Ownership: State

Bridge 103E:
Stringer/multi-beam or girder - 1975
Structure No. 200028103E03112
Length: 327'
Width: 42.6'
Under Clearance: 21.0'
Facility Carried: US 00002 E ML
Bridge Type: 2 SP CONT WLD PL GIR
Features Intersected: I 91 UNDER US 2
Surface: Bituminous
Maintenance/Ownership: State

Bridge 104:
Girder and floorbeam system - 1943
Structure No. 200028010403112
Length: 890'
Width: 38.6'
Under Clearance: 13.25'
Facility Carried: US 00002 ML
Bridge Type: 8 SPN RIVET 2 GIRDER
Features Intersected: US 2 OVER PSR/MC/CRL RR
Surface: Bituminous
Maintenance/Ownership: Town

Bridge 105:
Stringer/multi-beam or girder - 1931
Structure No. 200028010503112
Length: 64'
Width: 41.5'
Facility Carried: US 00002 ML
Bridge Type: ROLLED BEAM
Features Intersected: MOOSE RIVER
Surface: Bituminous
Maintenance/Ownership: City/Municipal

Bridge 107:
Stringer/multi-beam or girder - 1929
Structure No. 200028010703112
Length: 64'
Width: 42.0'
Facility Carried: US 00002 ML
Bridge Type: ROLLED BEAM
Features Intersected: MOOSE RIVER
Surface: Bituminous
Maintenance/Ownership: State

Bridge 108:
Tee Beam - 1929
Structure No. 200028010803112
Length: 103'
Width: 30.0'
Facility Carried: US 00002 ML
Bridge Type: CONC. T-BEAM/SLAB
Features Intersected: MOOSE RIVER
Surface: Bituminous
Maintenance/Ownership: State

Bridge 109:
Slab - 1929
Structure No. 300028010903111
Length: 18'
Width: 25.0'
Under Clearance: 8.0'
Facility Carried: US2
Bridge Type: CONCRETE SLAB
Features Intersected: BROOK
Surface: Bituminous
Maintenance: State

District 7 - Lunenburg Garage

(Not NHS)

AADT (count)									
4900	8100	8300	6200	6100	6000	4400	4300	4000
4900	8100	8300	6200	6100	6000	4400	4300	4000
4900	8100	8300	6200	6100	6000	4400	4300	4000
5100	7600	7700	6700	6100	6000	5000	4300	4400
5200	7000	7100	7100	6100	6000	5500	4300	4700

Crash Locations
☐ Property Damage Only
☐ Unknown Crash Type

phone: 802-828-2600.

Mileage by Functional Class By Sheet			Mileage by Town By Sheet		DISTRICT	TOWN	Date: 10/27/15	ROUTE
028-4	2 - Other Freeways and Expressways	3.619	ST. JOHNSBURY - U002-0311	8.659 of 8.659				US-2
028-4	3 - Other Principal Arterial	5.040	Ghost Section - (US-5, MM 1.714 to 1.828)		7	ST. JOHNSBURY	1 of 1 TWN mileage: 0.0 to 8.659	ETE mileage: 110.311 to 118.97
	Total Mileage: 8.659 mi		Total Mileage: 8.659 mi					

Spatiotemporal Analysis of Traffic Collisions in Lakewood, California

City of Lakewood
Lakewood, California, USA
By Shannon Julius

Contact

Michael Jenkins Jr.
mjenkins@lakewoodcity.org

Software

ArcGIS 10.2 for Desktop, Microsoft Excel 2007

Data Sources

City of Lakewood, Los Angeles County Sheriff's Department

The City of Lakewood has managed GIS layers of traffic collisions since 1997. This project was an attempt to create a spatial and temporal visualization of general traffic collision patterns in Lakewood using data from 2005 to 2014.

The visualization uses a method called comapping to display traffic collision distribution over space and time. Each frame in the comap displays a density surface based on the locations of collisions that occurred during that frame's time period and days of the week.

Traffic collision data is used by the city to help track property damage and to aid decisions regarding traffic safety improvements. Using GIS to store this data ensures that a collision record can be easily recalled based on location as well as attributes. The comap visualization is an experimental statistical analysis method that may be used in the future to explore particular traffic phenomena such as speed-related incidents or driving-under-the-influence cases.

Courtesy of the City of Lakewood, California.

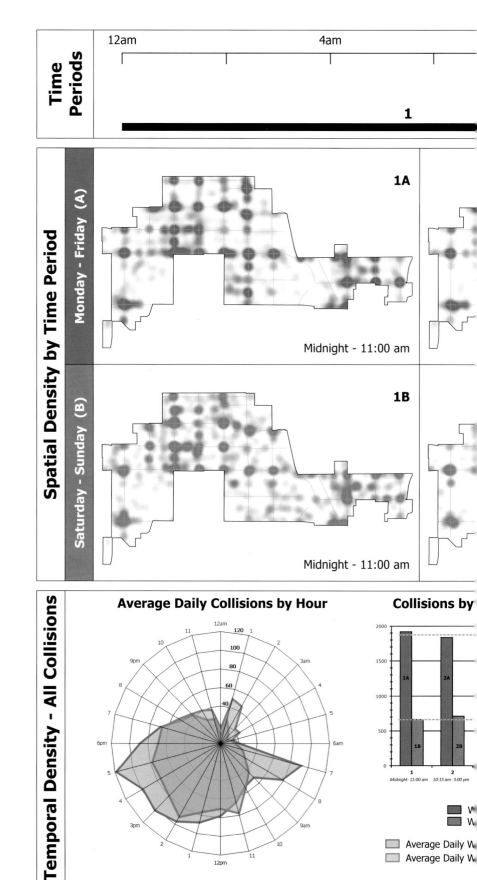

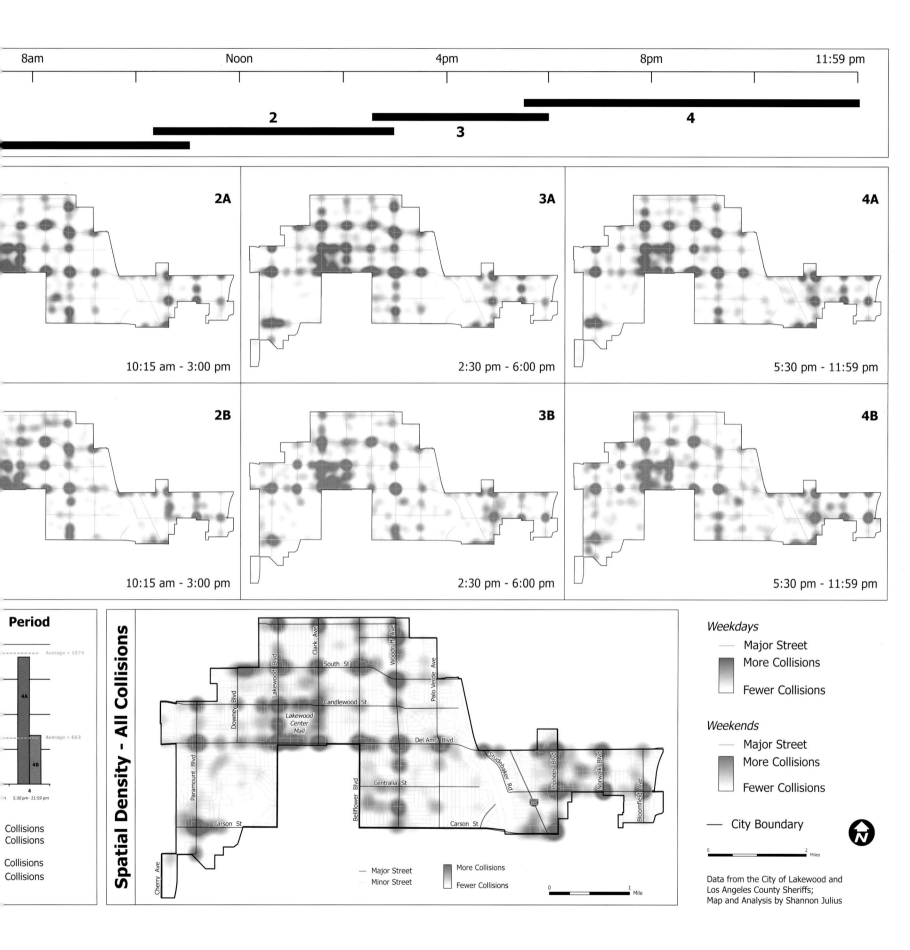

8am   Noon   4pm   8pm   11:59 pm

2

3

4

2A

10:15 am - 3:00 pm

3A

2:30 pm - 6:00 pm

4A

5:30 pm - 11:59 pm

2B

10:15 am - 3:00 pm

3B

2:30 pm - 6:00 pm

4B

5:30 pm - 11:59 pm

Period

Average = 1874

4A

Average = 663

4B

4

5:30 pm- 11:59 pm

Collisions
Collisions

Collisions
Collisions

Spatial Density - All Collisions

Clark Ave

Woodruff Ave

Lakewood Blvd

South St

Palo Verde Ave

Downey Blvd

Candlewood St

Lakewood Center Mall

Del Amo Blvd

Studebaker Rd

Pioneer Blvd

Norwalk Blvd

Bloomfield Ave

Paramount Blvd

Bellflower Blvd

Centralia St

605

Carson St

Carson St

Cherry Ave

Major Street
Minor Street

More Collisions
Fewer Collisions

0   1 Mile

Weekdays
— Major Street
  More Collisions
  Fewer Collisions

Weekends
— Major Street
  More Collisions
  Fewer Collisions

— City Boundary

0   2 Miles

Data from the City of Lakewood and
Los Angeles County Sheriffs;
Map and Analysis by Shannon Julius

IEC Electric Distribution ArcFM Map

Israeli Electric Company (IEC) and
Systematics Technologies
Tel Aviv, Tel Aviv, Israel
By Mor Yaffe

Contact
Mor Yaffe
mory@systematics.co.il

Software
ArcGIS 10.2.1 for Desktop, ArcFM 10.2.1

Data Source
IEC production geodatabase

The GIS system built for the Israeli Electric Company (IEC) by Systematics Technologies is unique in terms of size and complexity of its functionality and migration process. Apart from implementing a full-scale ArcFM system, the new system developed a complex migration process that incrementally added the data from over ten legacy information systems into a fully functional ArcFM geodatabase. This automatically built geodatabase is serving the company's design and maintenance workflows and will soon become the base for the operations (outage management) workflows of the IEC as well.

Courtesy of the IEC and Systematics Technologies.

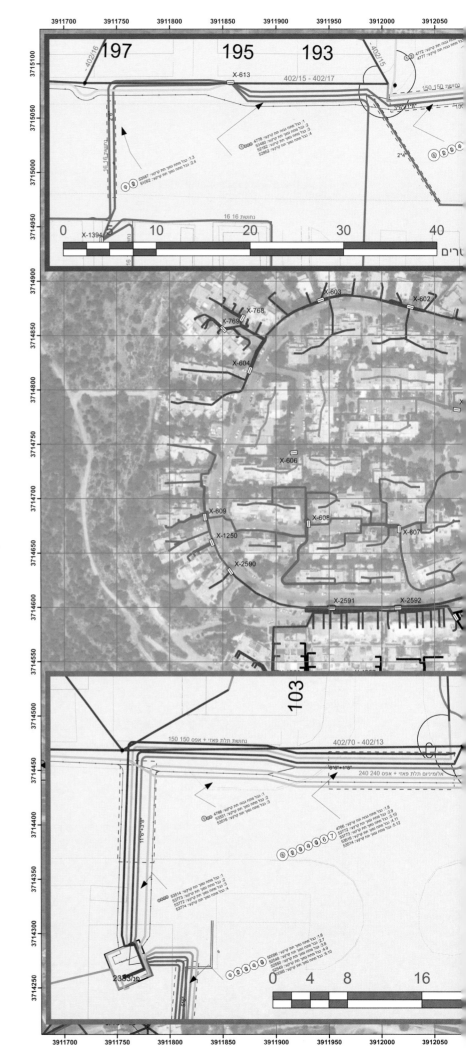

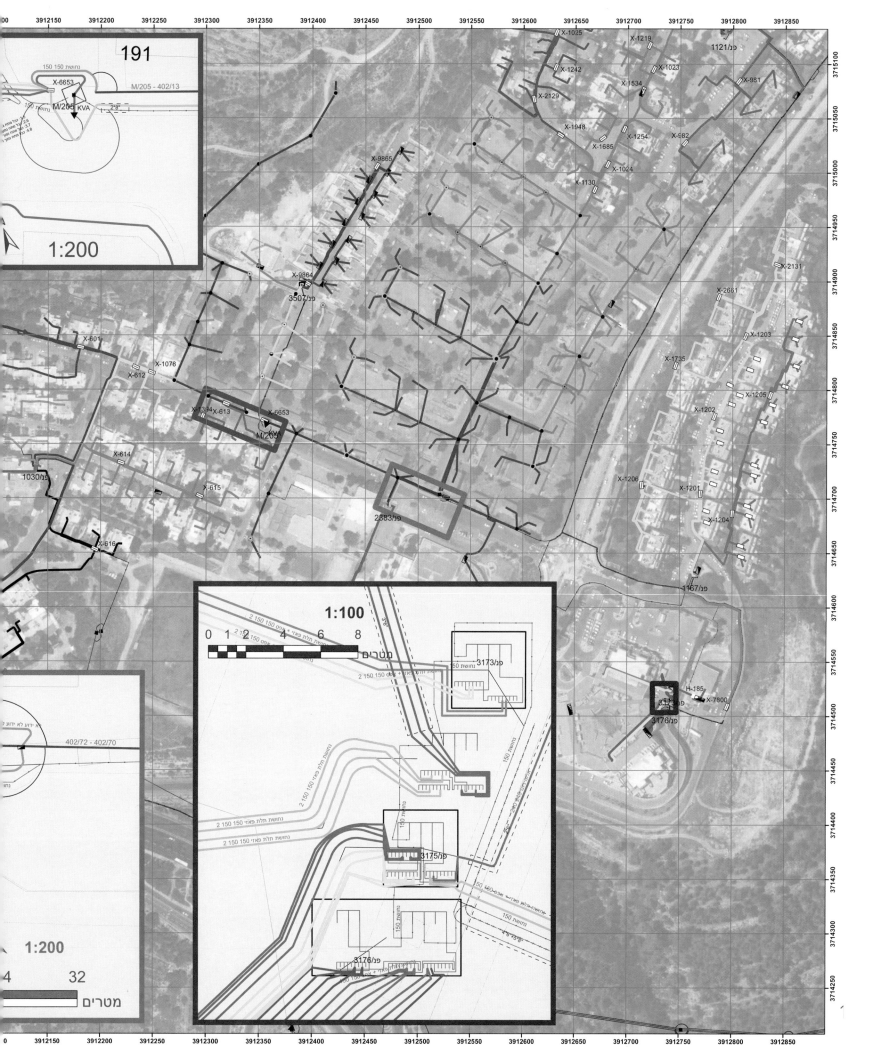

Addison Natural Gas Project Natural Resource Map

VHB

South Burlington, Vermont, USA

By Joshua Sky, Scott Manley, and Jesse Therrien

Contact

Joshua Sky

jsky@vhb.com

Software

ArcGIS 10.3 for Desktop

Data Source

Vermont Center for Geographic Information

This map is a part of a series that provides detailed information about the natural resources in the vicinity of a 42-mile natural gas pipeline expansion project through northern and central Vermont. The $70 million Addison Natural Gas Project will extend the Vermont Gas transmission network south to Middlebury and is scheduled to be completed by the 2016–2017 winter heating season. The project will provide natural gas to more than three thousand residential and business customers.

Courtesy of Vermont Gas Systems, Inc.

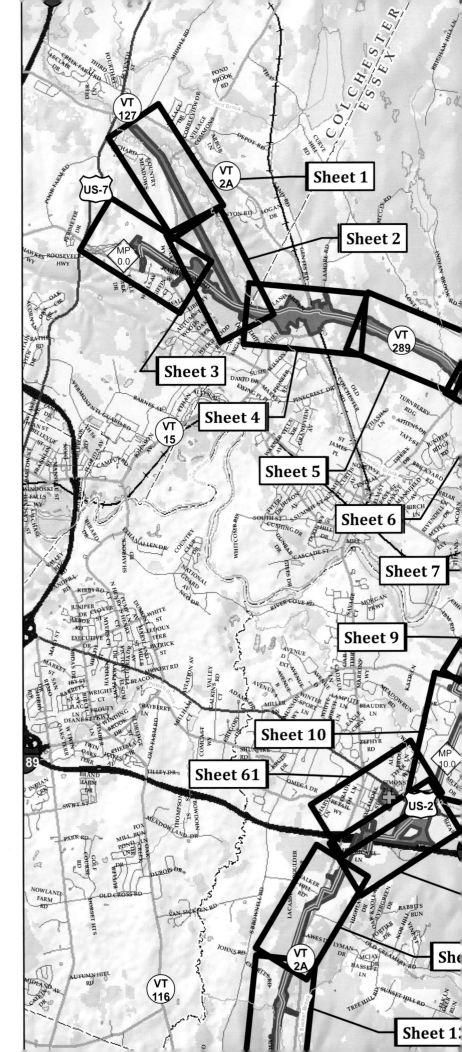

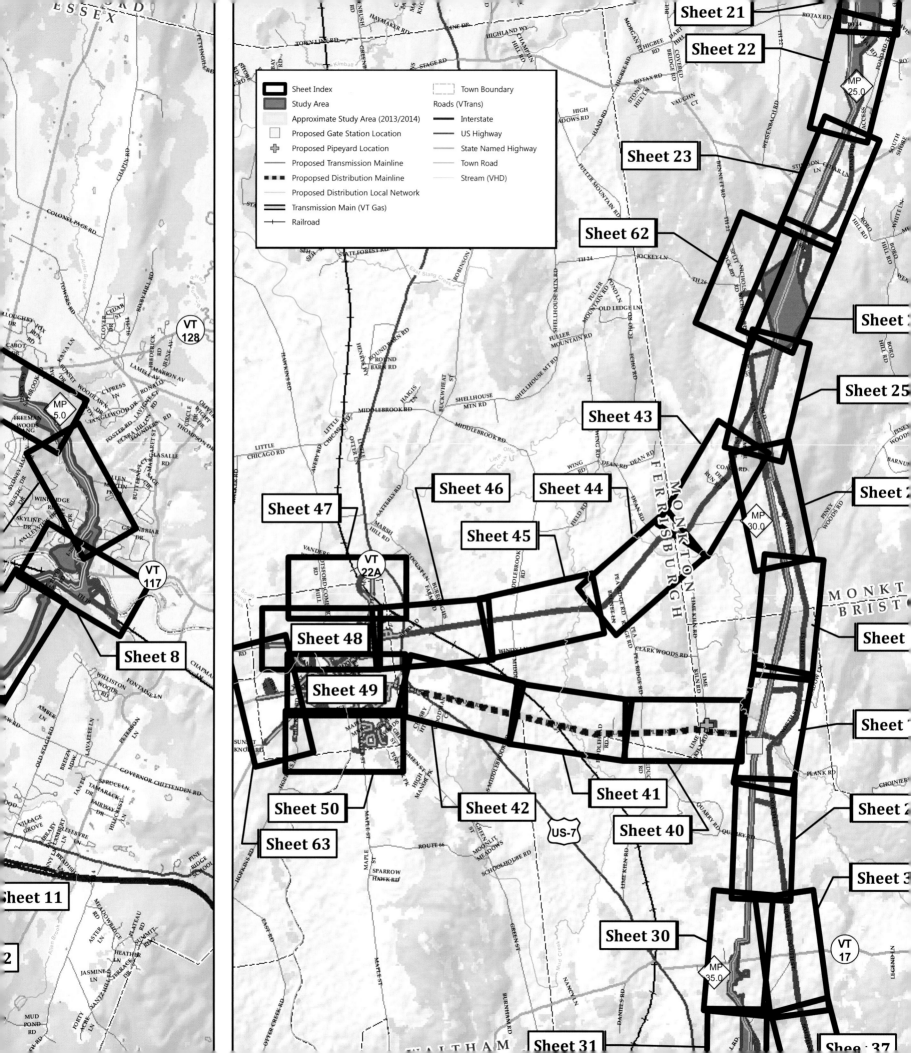

Fourteen-Year Groundwater Level Change

City of Tucson
Tucson, Arizona, USA
By Michael F. Liberti

Contact

Michael F. Liberti
michael.liberti@tucsonaz.gov

Software

ArcGIS 10.3.1 for Desktop

Data Sources

Pima County, City of Tucson, Tucson Water

Up until 2000, the City of Tucson relied entirely on mining groundwater for its potable water supply. In 2000, Tucson Water began delivering a blend of recharged Colorado River water and groundwater from its Colorado River recharge and recovery facility in central Avra Valley, the Central Avra Valley Storage and Recovery Project. Recovering recharged Colorado River water for the potable water supply decreased the need to mine groundwater from wells in central Tucson, an area of historic groundwater overdraft and decline.

In 2008, Tucson Water began recharging Colorado River water at a second facility in southern Avra Valley, the Southern Avra Valley Storage and Recovery Project. This second facility further decreased the need to mine groundwater from wells in central Tucson. The result of fourteen years of recharge and recovery of renewable water has been the recovery of groundwater levels in central Tucson of almost 60 feet and in southwestern Tucson of over 40 feet. Tucson Water currently recharges more Colorado River water annually than the current annual customer potable water demand.

Courtesy of the City of Tucson.

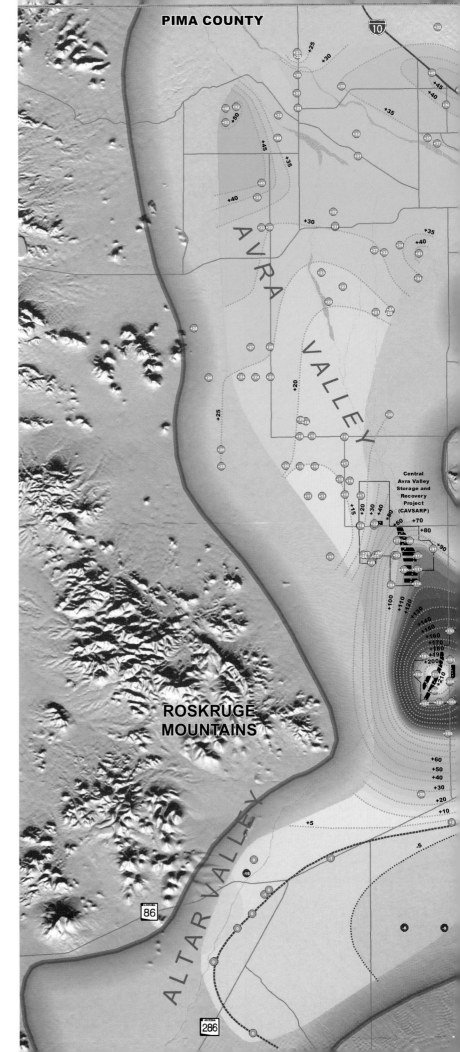

TORTOLITA MOUNTAINS

TUCSON MOUNTAINS

RINC MOUNT

Southern
ra Valley
rage and
covery
Project
AVSARP)

Pima
Mine
Road
Recharge

2014 Groundwater Elevation

City of Tucson
Tucson, Arizona, USA
By Michael F. Liberti

Contact

Michael F. Liberti
michael.liberti@tucsonaz.gov

Software

ArcGIS 10.3.1 for Desktop

Data Sources

Pima County, City of Tucson, Tucson Water

This map is based on Tucson Water's annual groundwater level monitoring program in the Tucson basin and Avra Valley. Water Resources Management staff annually measures groundwater levels from about 700 active and retired production wells to maintain long-term records to assist in management of local groundwater resources.

This map shows discrete groundwater elevation measurements and locations as well as hand-drawn contours depicting groundwater elevation in the Tucson basin and in Avra Valley from 565 Tucson Water wells and 135 wells from other water providers in the region. This map has been made available online from the Tucson Water website and is useful for determining flow direction and gradient. The resulting groundwater surface raster is also used for cross-section maps, 3D analysis and display, and temporal animations.

Courtesy of the City of Tucson.

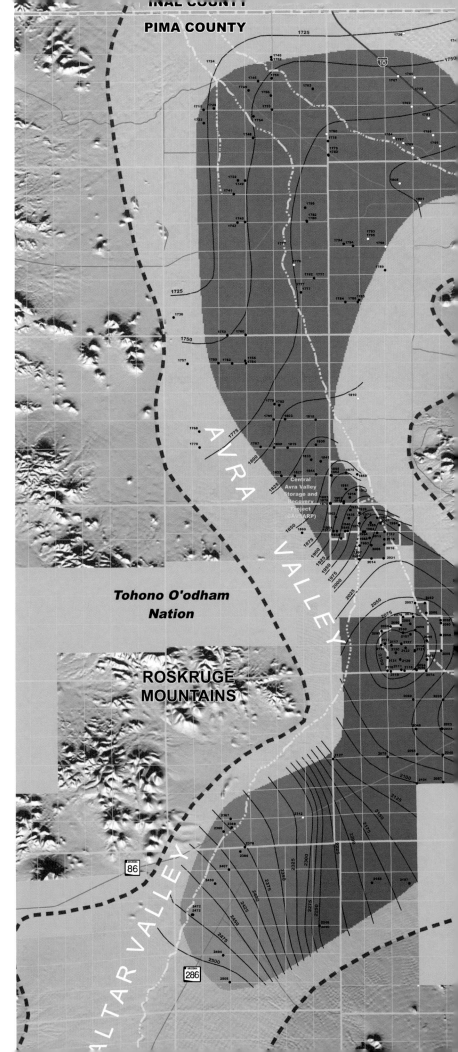

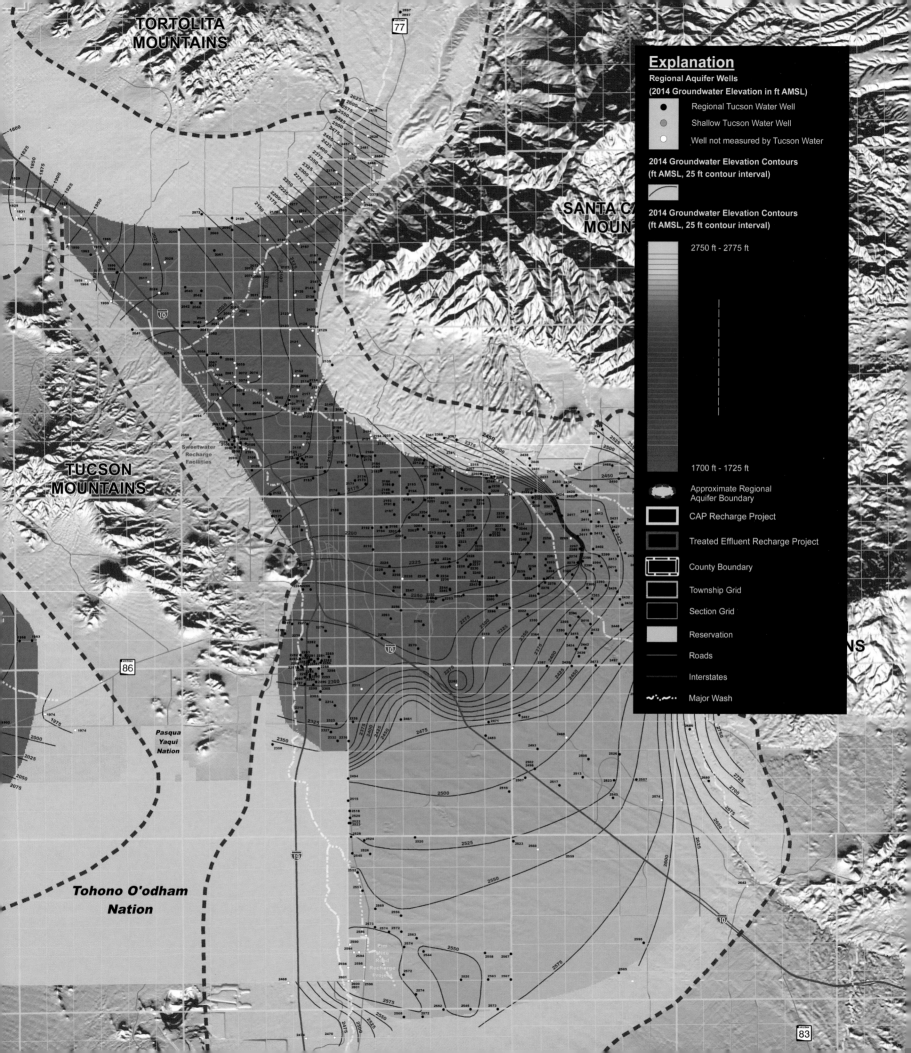

TORTOLITA
MOUNTAINS

77

SANTA CA
MOUN

TUCSON
MOUNTAINS

Sweetwater
Recharge
Facilities

86

Pasqua
Yaqui
Nation

19

Tohono O'odham
Nation

83

Explanation

Regional Aquifer Wells
(2014 Groundwater Elevation in ft AMSL)

- ● Regional Tucson Water Well
- ● Shallow Tucson Water Well
- ○ Well not measured by Tucson Water

2014 Groundwater Elevation Contours
(ft AMSL, 25 ft contour interval)

2014 Groundwater Elevation Contours
(ft AMSL, 25 ft contour interval)

2750 ft - 2775 ft

1700 ft - 1725 ft

Approximate Regional
Aquifer Boundary

CAP Recharge Project

Treated Effluent Recharge Project

County Boundary

Township Grid

Section Grid

Reservation

Roads

Interstates

Major Wash

2014 Depth to Groundwater

City of Tucson
Tucson, Arizona, USA
By Michael F. Liberti

Contact
Michael F. Liberti
michael.liberti@tucsonaz.gov

Software
ArcGIS 10.3.1 for Desktop

Data Sources
Pima County, City of Tucson, Tucson Water

This map is based on Tucson Water's annual groundwater level monitoring program in the Tucson basin and Avra Valley. Water Resources Management staff annually measure groundwater levels from about 700 active and retired production wells to maintain long-term records to assist in management of local groundwater resources.

This map shows discrete groundwater depth measurements and locations as well as contours depicting groundwater depth in the Tucson basin and in Avra Valley from 565 Tucson Water wells and 135 wells from other water providers in the region. Groundwater depth contours were generated by subtracting the groundwater elevation contour surface from a land elevation model surface. This map has been made available online from the Tucson Water website and is useful to consultants and regulators for permitting, environmental projects and well drilling.

Courtesy of the City of Tucson.

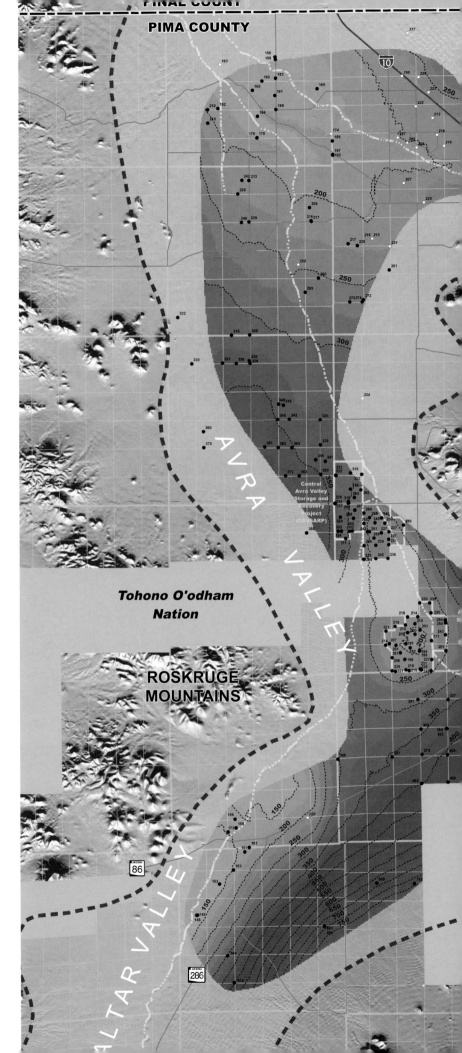

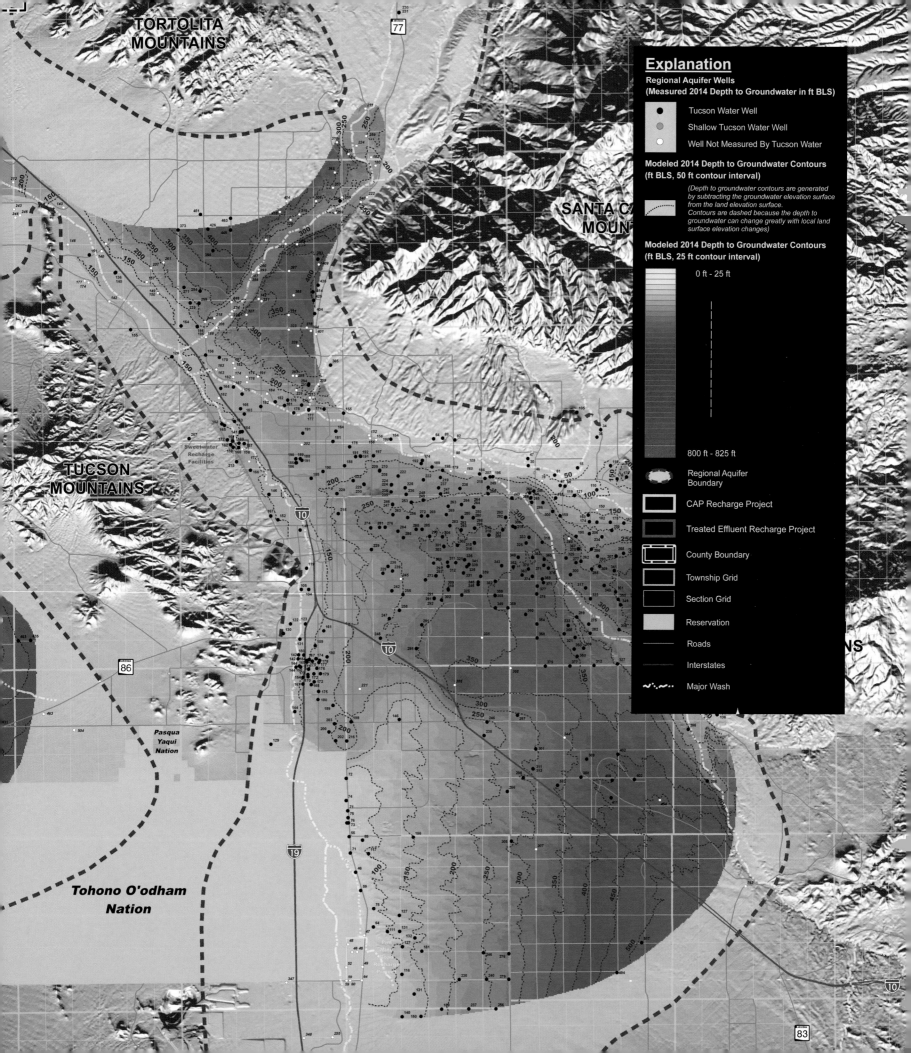

TORTOLITA
MOUNTAINS

SANTA C
MOUN

TUCSON
MOUNTAINS

Sweetwater
Recharge
Facilities

Pasqua
Yaqui
Nation

Tohono O'odham
Nation

City of Novato Storm Drainage Master Plan and Drainage Facility Database

Wood Rodgers
Oakland, California, USA
By Cheng Soo, P.E., and Satish Kumar, P.E.

Contact
Cheng Soo
csoo@woodrodgers.com

Software
ArcGIS 10.2.2 for Desktop

Data Sources
City of Novato, US Geological Survey and San Francisco State University Golden Gate Lidar Project, California Department of Conservation, Division of Land Resource Protection

Novato is located in the northeast corner of Marin County north of San Francisco. The city's drainage facilities collect storm runoff from three main watersheds and the runoff is conveyed through the enclosed conduit systems into San Francisco Bay.

In preparation for Novato's Storm Drainage Master Plan, engineering consultants Wood Rodgers and WRECO assessed the capacity of existing drainage systems, identified system deficiencies, and recommended improvements. Wood Rodgers used GIS to support the hydrologic and hydraulic modeling efforts and developed a storm drainage facility geodatabase using Esri's Local Government Information Model supplemented with hydrologic and hydraulic features. The geodatabase includes georeferenced as-built drawings, pipe and manhole data, channel features, watershed data, and hydrologic and hydraulic model results. The team also built an ArcGIS Online website for asset management, project coordination, and quality control checks. The website displayed daily progress of the project and provided a platform for the city to review and provide comments.

Courtesy of the City of Novato.

Water Main Failure Analysis– Erie, Pennsylvania

Erie Water Works
Erie, Pennsylvania, USA
By Amanda Donegan and Justin Stangl

Contact

Justin Stangl
jstangl@eriewaterworks.org

Software

ArcGIS for Desktop, Adobe Illustrator, Microsoft Excel

Data Source

Erie Water Works

To reduce the cost of water main breaks and limit water outages to its customers, the Erie Water Works uses ArcGIS to analyze spatial and tabular main break data on a yearly basis. Mobile GIS users capture the location of each water main break event and record all pertinent information directly into the enterprise GIS using versioned geodatabase replication.

The attribute data collected includes the type of main break, the water main material/age/diameter, air and water temperature, pipe depth, and the original soil type. This data is dissected and compared with historical main break records, underlying physical factors, and the actual condition of the underground water assets. The analyses are compiled into a map which ultimately influences capital improvement planning and future proactive prevention initiatives while increasing potential for continued GIS return on investment.

Courtesy of Erie Water Works GIS.

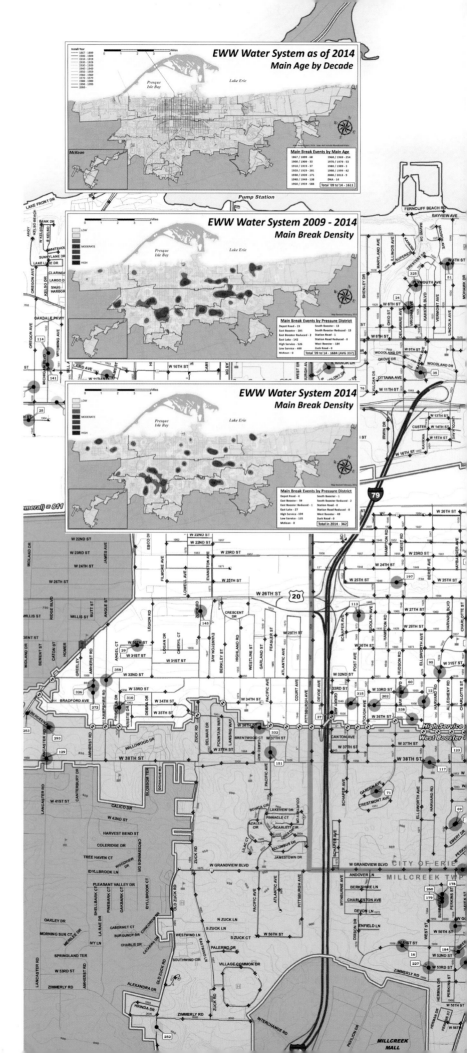

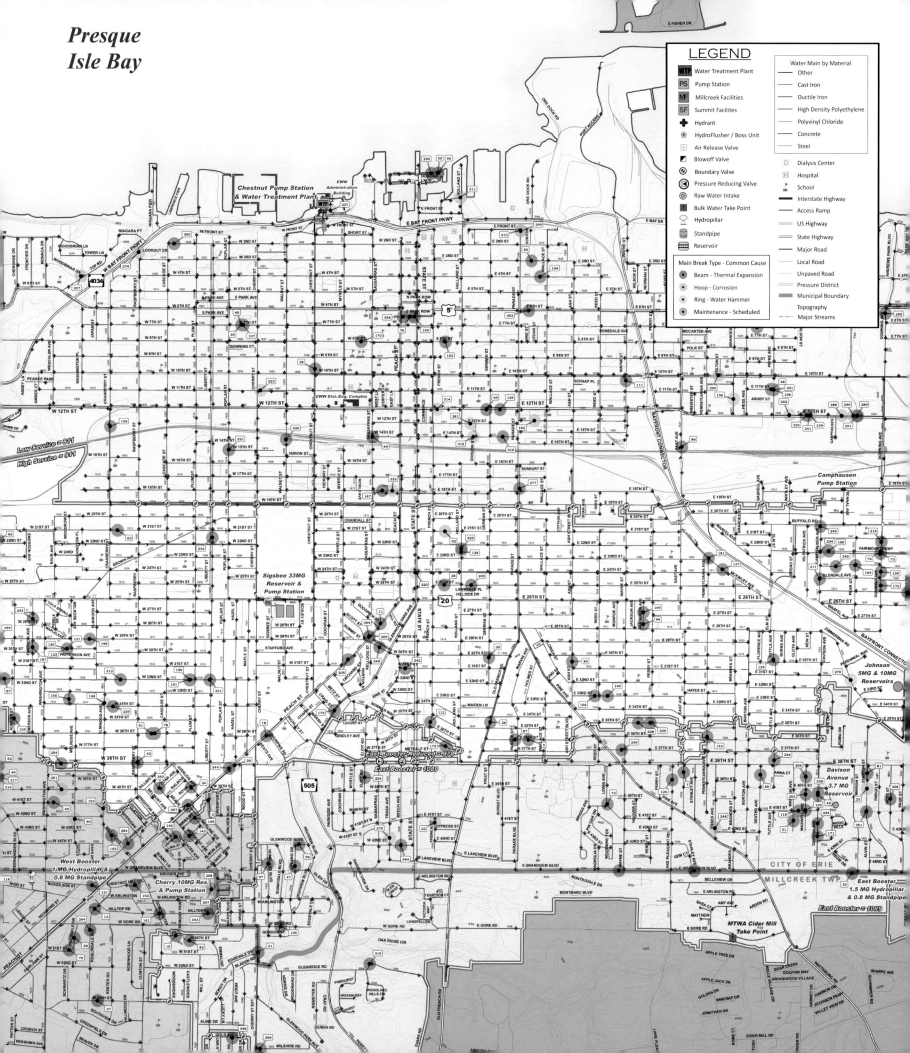

Water Replenishment District Map with Water Independence Now (WIN) Projects

Water Replenishment District of Southern
California (WRD)
Lakewood, California, USA
By Josi Jenneskens and Jason Weeks

Contact
Josi Jenneskens
jjenneskens@wrd.org

Software
ArcGIS10.2 for Desktop

Data Sources
The Water Replenishment District of Southern
California, Los Angeles County, Orange County,
US Geological Survey

The Water Replenishment District of Southern California (WRD) replenishes and protects the groundwater resources of southern Los Angeles County, serving nearly 4 million people. WRD is involved in groundwater monitoring, safe drinking water programs, combating seawater intrusion, and groundwater replenishment operations throughout its service area.

This map highlights the efforts of the WRD, working with other local and regional agencies, to manage and maximize groundwater replenishment efforts as a part of the Water Independence Now (WIN) program. The WIN program is a series of projects using locally available storm water and recycled water to replenish groundwater resources. In the past, a large percentage of replenishment water came from sources in Northern California and the Colorado River. WIN seeks to completely eliminate this dependence on imported water to ensure the future security of the region by developing local resources to create a locally sustainable groundwater supply.

Courtesy of the Water Replenishment District of Southern California.

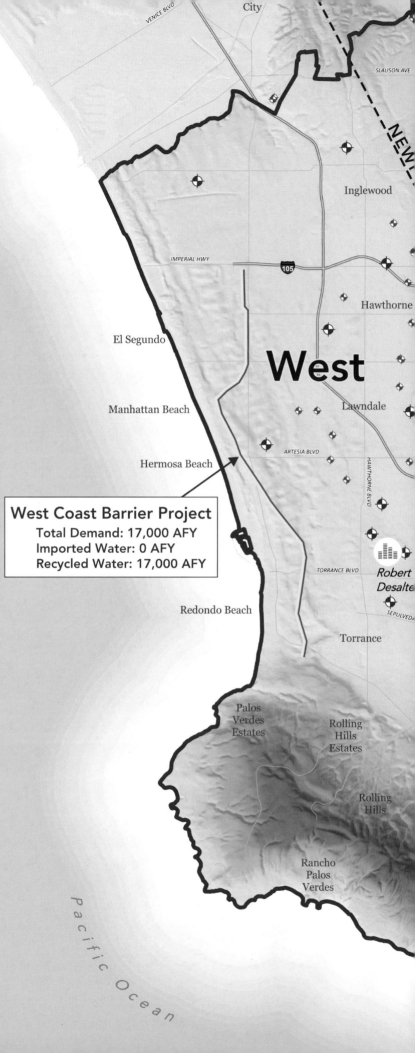

West Coast Barrier Project
Total Demand: 17,000 AFY
Imported Water: 0 AFY
Recycled Water: 17,000 AFY

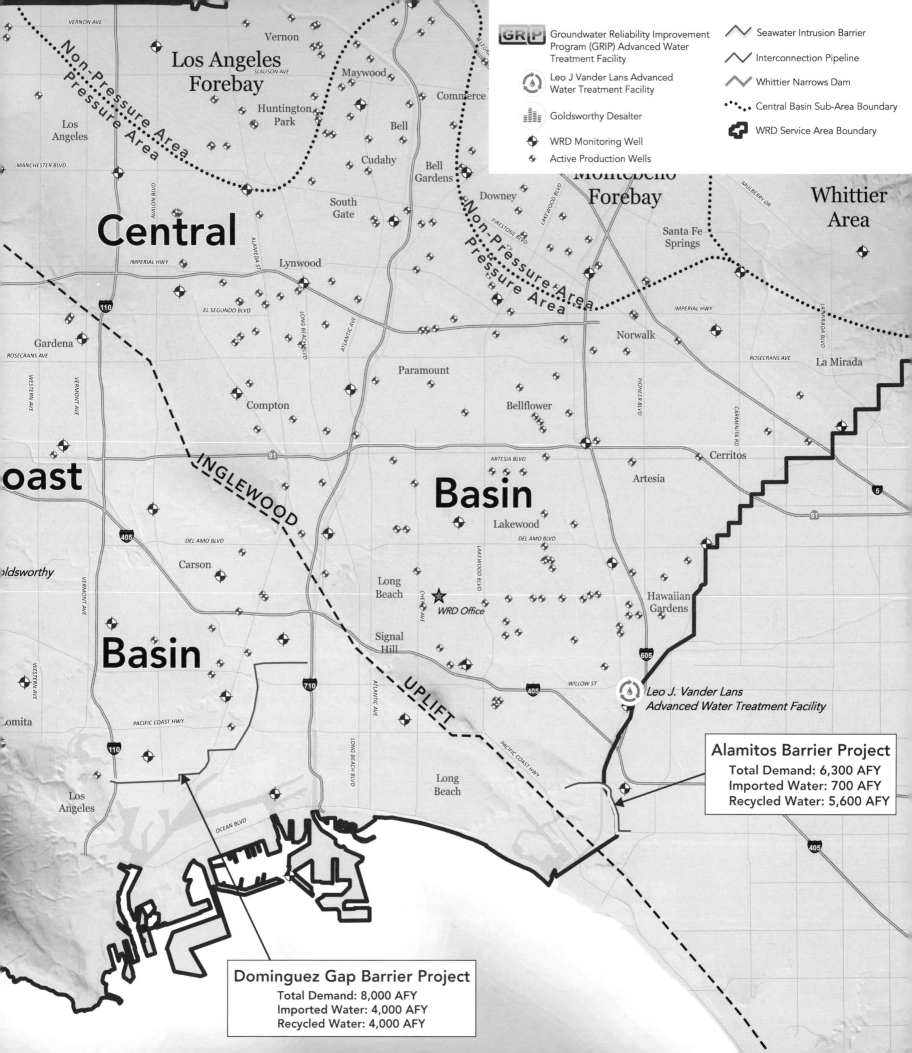

Measuring Sandy Impact and Recovery through Water Consumption

New Jersey American Water

Voorhees, New Jersey, USA

By Christopher Kahn

Contact

Christopher Kahn

christopher.kahn@amwater.com

Software

ArcGIS for Desktop

Data Source

New Jersey American Water

The recovery from Superstorm Sandy in late October 2012 has been slow and uneven in the Northern Barrier Island communities of New Jersey (Bay Head to Ortley Beach). The initial impact of Sandy is clearly evident in the precipitous drop in water use from the 2012 to 2013 summer seasons. As many sections of the island wait for funding, huge areas remain vacant and, as a result, do not use water. In fact, the "Reduction Delta" pattern of water use nearly perfectly aligns with storm surge, breach, and over wash patterns the islands suffered. Bay Head, however, experienced a reduction in water use unrelated to damage in 2015. (Pelican Island is not shown on the map.) New Jersey American Water is tracking the pace and patterns of recovery through water use statistics each summer.

Courtesy of New Jersey American Water.

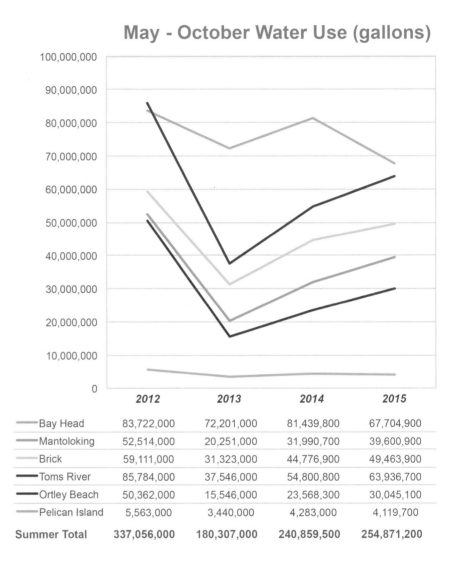

May - October Water Use (gallons)

	2012	2013	2014	2015
Bay Head	83,722,000	72,201,000	81,439,800	67,704,900
Mantoloking	52,514,000	20,251,000	31,990,700	39,600,900
Brick	59,111,000	31,323,000	44,776,900	49,463,900
Toms River	85,784,000	37,546,000	54,800,800	63,936,700
Ortley Beach	50,362,000	15,546,000	23,568,300	30,045,100
Pelican Island	5,563,000	3,440,000	4,283,000	4,119,700
Summer Total	**337,056,000**	**180,307,000**	**240,859,500**	**254,871,200**

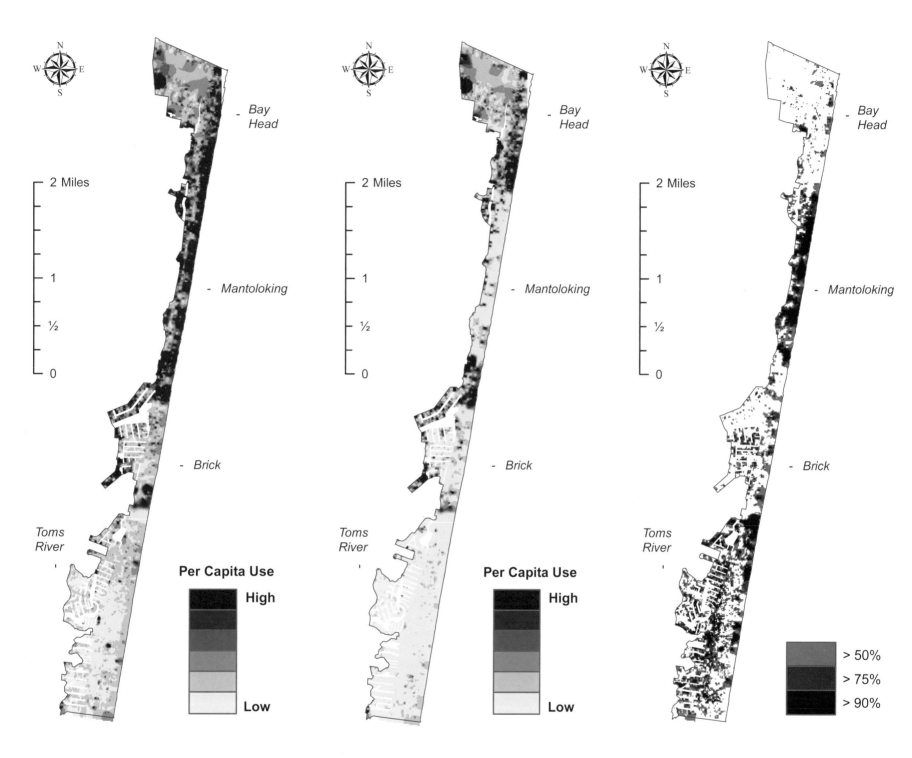

2012 Consumption (~ 337 MG)
May - October
~ 10,000 Active Customers

2013 Consumption (~ 180 MG)
May - October
~ 4,600 Active Customers

Reduction Delta
2012 - 2013 Summer

INDEX BY ORGANIZATION